LOST GODS

OF ALBION

The Chalk Hill-Figures of Britain

PAUL NEWMAN

In Memoriam:
Geoffrey La Fargue Newman & Doris Elizabeth Mary Newman

To gaze at the river made of time and water
And recall that time itself is another river,
To know that we cease to be, just like the river,
And our faces pass away, just like the water.

Jorge Luis Borges

First published in 1987
This edition first published in 2009

The History Press
The Mill, Brimscombe Port
Stroud, Gloucestershire, GL5 2QG
www.thehistorypress.co.uk

British Library Cataloguing in Publication Data.
A catalogue record for this book is available from the British Library.

ISBN 978 0 7524 4939 5

Typesetting and origination by The History Press
Printed in Great Britain

CONTENTS

FOREWORD

A s a uniquely British phenomenon, the thirty or so hill-figures cut into the turf of southern England have excited antiquarians, archaeologists, historians and the public at large for generations. Some, such as the regimental badges at Fovant, Wiltshire, are easily explained, relatively recent in date, and identifiable with historical events and particular individuals. Others, such as the Cerne Giant, Dorset, and the Uffington White Horse, Oxfordshire, are much older, far less explicable, and understanding them depends on detailed scientific, archaeological and art-historical research.

This new updated edition proves a comprehensive and scholarly account of all the recorded hill-figures in England, with abundant plans and illustrations to accompany the text. Building on the strengths of the first edition it includes not only description but analysis, discussion and interpretation too. For hill-figures have been the subject of many treatments, some grounded on fact, others drawn from fantasy.

Much has changed in the world of hill-figure studies in the ten years since the first edition of this book was published. Perhaps most significant is the absolute dating by scientific means of early silts incorporated into the Uffington White Horse. This work shows that the horse was constructed way back in the later Bronze Age, perhaps around 1000 BC. Such revelations change our perspectives on other hill-figures, open up new possibilities for interpretation, and re-define the research agenda that must now be pursued with renewed vigour.

However, it is not only these early dates that have changed thinking. It is now clear that the more ancient hill-figures did not stand alone in the landscape; they were intimately linked with burial monuments, boundaries, settlements, and enclosures. What they represent is only part of the story. How they worked in the everyday lives of the people who built them and used them is equally important. Hill-figures were active players in shaping people's minds to the way they regarded their landscape, moved about within it, and remembered it.

Hill-figures old and new still communicate important meanings today. The outline of the Uffington Horse has become a familiar symbol of the modern county of Berkshire, the Cerne Giant adorns everything from tea-towels to baseball caps and is one of the few pornographic images regularly sent through the post without censorship, while the Long Man of Wilmington keeps a watchful eye on everyone travelling the A27 in East Sussex.

Strangely, hill-figures probably represent the longest-lived tradition of landscape art known in Britain. Examples are still being created. In 1980 Devon artist Kenneth Evans-Loude suggested etching an image of Marilyn Monroe on the hill-slope opposite the Cerne Giant to provide a companion and partner. It was never done, although the outline of a naked giantess was set out next to the Cerne Giant in the summer of 1997 as part of an experiment to see how such images were surveyed and laid-out using only primitive technologies. And back in July 1994 cartoonist Steve Bell created a white hill-figure in Sussex which, for a few weeks, showed then Prime Minister John Major wearing a traffic cone on his head and dressed only in underpants. It has recently been suggested that a flock of hill-figure sheep be cut into the pastures of north Wiltshire to celebrate the turning of the millennia.

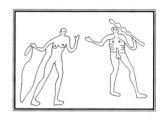

Hill-figures remain wonderful things to gaze at, well worth making a detour or a stop to appreciate. As this book shows, they are potent symbols in the landscape which can be read, engaged with, and understood at many levels, from the intellectual to the aesthetic. Some were no doubt gods in their time, all are graven images whose renaissance is probably only just beginning.

Timothy Darvill
Professor of Archaeology, School of Conservation Sciences,
Bournemouth University

ACKNOWLEDGEMENTS

By their nature, books such as these are collaborations rather than individual creations and it is always a pleasure to thank those many people who have helped during the assembly. They include Dr Richard Jones and the Sussex Archaeological Society for (among other things) drawing my attention to John Farrant's meticulous documentary research on the Long Man; Emma Jones and the staff of Warwickshire Museum Sites and Monuments Record for material on the Red Horse of Tysoe; David Miles of the Oxford Archaeological Research Unit, for outlining the theory and practice of OSL; Julia Wise, the Archaeological Records Officer of Buckinghamshire for making available her paper on the monuments of Whiteleaf Hill; Christine Whipp for sending me her own novel theory about hill-figures; Neil Mortimer, editor of the stimulating and eclectic *3rd Stone*; Jo Ann Wilder, for awakening my interest in the current state of antiquarian research; Nicola Pitman, of Trowbridge Library, for making available the 1773 map of Wiltshire by Andrews and Drury; Rodney Castleden, whose books on the Long Man and Cerne Giant form the bedrock of current knowledge; Kate Pym for lending me *Sun Horse, Moon Horse* by Rosemary Sutcliff; those numberless, unsung librarians and officials who have patiently responded to my enquiries; and finally the distinguished archaeologist and author, Tim Darvill, for gallantly stepping in at a moment's notice and contributing a foreword.

The author and publisher would like to thank the following for permission to reproduce illustrations: Alison Gouedard for her wash drawings; Rodney Legg (Dorset magazine); Martin Brown (Long Man photographs and slides); the British Museum (Aylesford Bucket); Routledge and Kegan Paul (*Gogmagog* by T.C. Lethbridge); Sussex Archaeological Society; Rodney Castleden (*The Wilmington Giant/The Cerne Giant*); HarperCollins (*Stonehenge, Neolithic Man and the Cosmos* by John North); Wiltshire Folk Life Museum; Country Life Books. Mr Graham Miller for the use of information and illustrations (Red Horse of Tysoe); Brian Edwards for his study of the Uffington Horse and Rodney Castleden for his scholarship and providing the latest Long Man findings. Every effort has been made to trace all copyright holders, and in any instance where we have not been successful, we offer our apologies.

View of the Cerne Giant from the National Trust car park.

INTRODUCTION

That the most ancient people, before the invention of books, and before the use of sculpture upon stones, and other smaller fragments, were wont to represent things, great and noble, upon entire rocks and mountains seems so natural that it is easily imagined and assented to by all. . . . Semiramis to perpetuate her memory is reported to have cut a whole rock in the form of herself. Hannibal, long after the invention of books, engraved characters upon the Alpine rocks, as a testimony of his passage over them. . . . But what is most to our purpose, it appears to have been particularly the custom of the Northern nations. . . .

(Revd Francis Wise 1742)

There is a story by Ray Bradbury which tells of an American tourist, George, walking along a beach in the south of France. He comes across an old sunburnt man carving out fantastic shapes on the sand with a discarded lollipop stick, a mural composed of palm trees, temples, mermaids, musicians and a troupe of dancing satyrs and maidens. Instinctively it dawns on him: the man is his hero, Picasso, amusing himself by doodling an effaceable masterpiece in old age. George wants to preserve the amazing work. Hearing the whisper of the incoming tide, he races back to his wife to get a camera, so at least a record will survive, but he is too late. The waves are already washing it away . . .

This type of thing happened to hundreds of hill-figures and ground carvings. Probably many were seasonal gestures, ritual inscriptions, not intended to survive. For there is a difference between the artist who chooses the 'eternal' medium of stone and the one who works in friable soil and sand. Hill-figures are not statements of permanence; that a number of them *have* survived demonstrates the triumph of tradition over social upheaval and soil erosion. Furthermore, they are not person-centred artefacts, memorializing an individual, but stand as the collective expression of a tribe or community and, in order to survive, require regular, coordinated attention.

Generally speaking, if a community falls apart, so does the god, hero or beast emblematic of its unity. When the Romans left Britain, their temples, gods and idols were left to crumble. The desires which gravitated around them had departed; only the shells of their significance remained, and little happens to shells save that they are broken down into smaller and smaller units until not a trace remains. Thus the continued existence of the Uffington Horse, the Cerne Giant and the Long Man testifies to an impulse both meaningful and tenacious.

So many layers of meaning have been imposed upon hill-figures down the centuries that the problem they pose is as much phenomenological as historical. The images are defined by the varying responses they provoke. The present endlessly rewrites the past, either because new knowledge has come to light, or because a shift in historical perspective has inspired a reappraisal, seeing an event or series of events from a different angle.

Unlike historians of ideas, archaeologists hold that the meaning of a religious object is the source meaning or what the original makers had in mind. If that fully matured insight could be recovered, then the problem might be solved once and for all. However, that assumes what the early creators felt is translatable, that language can wrap itself round the primal experience of long-vanquished peoples. How much can we understand? Is it possible to recapture the essence of past ages? Or do we merely trade language for experience, thicken the barrier of separation with more words, more theories?

The mystic P.D. Ouspensky described one of his conversations with Gurdjieff. The latter described coming across a statue in Central Asia, at the foot of the Hindu Kush:

At first it produced upon us simply the impression of being a curiosity. But after a while we began to feel that this figure contained many things, a big, complete and complex system of cosmology. And slowly, step by step, we began to decipher this system. It was in the body of this figure, in its legs, in its arms, in its head, in its eyes, in its ears, everywhere. In the whole statue there was nothing accidental, nothing without meaning. And gradually we understood the aim of the people who built this statue. We began to feel their thoughts, their feelings. Some of us thought that we saw their faces, heard their voices. At all events we grasped the meaning of what they wanted to convey across thousands of years, and not only the meaning, but all the feelings and the emotions connected with it as well. That indeed was art!

This, surely, is the aim of archaeologists and historians: to inhabit and occupy the breathing past. Unfortunately such instants of insight – when, in a single visionary flash, one embraces contexts and cultures – are elusive, and no reliable work of history has been founded solely on mystic intuition. However, Gurdjieff's approach touches the poetry of yearning that shrines of past civilizations inspire. It leads to the question concerning our common humanity which Housman expressed when he heard the wind blowing through the wood on Wenlock Edge:

> Then, 'twas before my time, the Roman
>   At yonder heaving hill would stare:
> The blood that warms the English yeoman,
>   The thoughts that hurt him, they were there.

Whatever the trappings of the period, the poet affirms that all humans are united by the same mystery and grow old under the same sky. Their feelings and responses are essentially timeless. Furthermore, if, as the physicists say, an atemporal view should be cultivated, then the distinction between past and present dissolves and all is active and recoverable.

The Long Man of Wilmington and the Cerne Giant as reproduced in Plenderleath's *The White Horses of the West of England*, 1885.

Despite these musings at the fringe, it has to be acknowledged that antiquarian speculation on hill-figures has been more conspicuous for weird erudition than common sense. The latter, unfortunately, cannot get one much beyond the prosaic, 'This figure, of unknown origin, was cut in the chalk in the distant past.' If we abandon common sense, however, and allow a surge of Delphic inspiration to take hold, the result can be more exciting. Puffing out his chest, flourishing his pen like a sabre, a writer like Francis Wise can produce lines of rolling Gothic prose, rounding it off with a noble quote from Greek or Latin. This is a natural temptation to which one might succumb, on the supposition that prose should be as noble-sounding as the monument under consideration.

Since their earliest notices, the Cerne Giant, Long Man and the Uffington Horse have attracted interpretations that might strike one as faintly outrageous in view of the lack of evidence. One of the most charmingly surreal of recent theories pertaining to Britain's trio of hill-figures is that of Christine Whipp (1996) who dates the carvings from the time of the Plantagenets. She starts by relating the Cerne Giant to Dick Whittington marching off to London to make his fortune. Where is his companion cat, she asks? Study the ribs, nipples and belly button – see how the face of a cat assembles itself. Next, picking up a reference to the Giant's missing lionskin cloak, she transforms it into a bigger, fiercer cat. The Giant is none other than a portrait of Richard the Lionheart. His challenging stance celebrates his courage and skill as a fighter; the mighty penis stands as a possibly satiric allusion to his inverted sexuality. As for the Long Man of Wilmington, he is none other than Richard's chancellor, William Longchamps, the son of a Norman serf, who raised the ransom for Richard's release and also shared homosexual inclinations. To complete the trilogy, the Uffington Horse might portray an Arab mare brought back from the Crusades.

To justify the inclusion of such material, I wrote in an earlier version of this book that part of the appeal of hill-figures lies in the varying responses they have evoked down the ages. There is much to be said for such a view, and some academics, such as Barbara Bender, glory in the romantic confusion – the stark refusal of these artefacts to sit up and be identified. It is a view with which I have some sympathy and yet, after ploughing my way through fifty-odd summaries and possibilities connected with a single figure, I found myself rubbing my eyes and thinking that a little narrowing and fixing might be no bad thing.

Before the recent development of silt-dating, no method existed for dating hill-figures. Evidence had to be adduced from artistic evidence, usually appended by oddments of folklore and hearsay. This left the field open, for art does not evolve like weapons or technology. It is not measured by its practical qualities or refinement of a single form. On the contrary, it often combines tradition with innovation, simultaneously harking back and looking forward, creating an entirely new synthesis, and it is this mobile, suggestive quality that – quite apart from the skill of the original designer – eludes easy categorization. After all, in a sense, what modern artist has produced a more accurate impression of a deer in flight than the Stone Age 'amateurs' of Lascaux? Or a more potently suggestive spirit-horse than the carving at Uffington? And for that matter, what ancient artist has produced works as vigorously 'primitive' as Pablo Picasso?

To characterize and identify the people who carved a hill-figure is a further problem. The ambiguous nature of the evidence allows few archaeologists to produce unequivocal statements about the nature of the racial or cultural differences between successive occupants of the British Isles. Did the Bronze Age seamlessly merge into the Iron Age as a culture adapted to changing conditions? Were the Celtic-speaking peoples strongly established in Britain during the Bronze Age? Or was an older order, or orders, displaced by influx and invasion?

If there were, quite naturally, physical and cultural divides, there was also trading, intermarriage, diffusion of customs and artefacts, such as the distinctive 'Beaker' or drinking vessel. The latter was once seen as the symbol of a dynamic, round-headed, warrior culture, which swept over Europe with bronze swords and battleaxes and subjugated the Neolithic peoples. The current interpretation tends to be less dramatic, emphasizing continuity, adaptation and the spread of metal-making skills by itinerant smithies.

Stripped of names, dates, invasions and ethnic clashes, how does one make a story? One is left pondering a heterogeneous bundle of urns, graves, henges, skulls, tools and weapons? Each artefact provokes a network of transcontinental links and archaeologists find themselves deciphering patterns of settlement, trade and burial rather than chronicling the achievements of individuals. In this sense alone, archaeology conforms to Tolstoy's view of history, in which great leaders like Napoleon feature as puffed-out, deluded bubbles of self-importance, while the action proper lies in the intimate workings of men and women as they move through time and changing environments.

The process is dense and probably unchartable. To unravel one tiny causal strand is an accomplishment; to weave together a broader scene an overpowering challenge. And making it readable and gripping is a further dilemma. Would Edward Gibbon have shown the same narrative flair if he had to rely on the dating and placement of voiceless bones and artefacts?

A further vexing issue is the need for specific identification – for saying who exactly the Cerne Giant or the Long Man represent. A glance at the history of the giants of London, Gogmagog and Corineus, show them changing names and qualities down the centuries. On the matter of Celtic gods, we rely on testimonies and icons after the deity had become 'Romanized', so to speak, and bartered part of its identity, like Mercury borrowing attributes from Mars or Nodons from Sylvanus. Add to this the shape-shifting with which the Celts privilege their immortals, and it becomes questionable how interested parties, some two thousand years later, can comment on psychic constructs never possessed of a 'written' or stable significance. A thorough and microscopic scholarship tends to convert a weird amorphous being into something even more alien – namely, a fixed pocket of meaning.

Against such mistily defined contexts, it is rash to draw conclusions about those who carved the horses or the giants on British hillsides, or about whom they are intended to depict. But books, by definition, are expected to provide answers or at least clear expositions and, for this new version of an earlier work, I have included some theories which are improbable but have become part of the integral history of the figure, such as Alfred the Great ordering the cutting of the Uffington Horse. I have trimmed back some flocculent meandering on Celtic gods, added new material on the Uffington Horse, the Long Man, Gogmagog and the Cerne Giant and updated the chapter on Earth Mysteries.

There are sections about which I am less than complacent, especially those folkloristic excursions which mix disparate sources and draw parallels from different cultures and epochs, instead of sticking rigorously to a context; there is the additional problem that so many traditional festivals disappeared and resurfaced after the Interregnum, so that one cannot be dogmatic about what is 'original' as opposed to innovative. No doubt readers, scholars and critics will echo my doubts. However, when primary sources are no longer extant, it is necessary to cast one's net wide, either to illuminate parallels or hint at possibilities.

CHAPTER ONE

THE UFFINGTON HORSE

Beneath my hands the planes
Of his bleached shoulders move,
And the bow of his neck bends to the flint-shaped head.
I ride the chalk-white horse
That moves over bone-bare hills,
And from his streaming mane time falls away.

Between the thighs of kings
Who are now chalk-bare bones
His ancestors, the stallion-herds once strode,
Who, bending their bird-beaked heads,
Are now a shrinking scar
Across the downs from which time ebbs away.

(Margaret Stanley-Wrench 1958)

Introduction

The White Horse of Uffington dominates the vale that bears its name. Artistically it is a triumph of imaginative omission – for it is the mind's eye that completes the design. Carved by human hands, it does not seem of this world, on account of its eerie whiteness, and a form that brings together aspects of dragon, bird and rodent. The lines that define it are landscape lines; they curve and melt into the greens and browns of scarp, dip and glacial terrace. Little more than a collusion of wind-thin streaks, it is close to something half-glimpsed or apprehended in the dark of a dream – a long, lancing backbone merging into a beak-head and streaming tail. The legs are minimalist addenda, the hooves non-existent, the mouth a splayed beak. As for the eye, that is a prominent feature, ringed, spectral and alarmed, like a jewel at the bottom of a well.

Uffington Horse seen from the flanking hillside.

The White Horse is older than England, predating the invasion of the Angles and Saxons and vying with Stonehenge, the Tower of London and the Houses of Parliament as one of the country's most recognized monuments. Countless travellers have noted it and passed by — almost reluctant to be drawn into the enigma. Antiquarians have picked and puzzled over it. Archaeologists have probed and measured its layers and textures. Folklorists have brooded on it, drawing in tales of gods, heroes and sun-chariots. Poets have encased it in blank verse and rhymed stanza:

> Age beyond age on British land,
> Aeons on aeons gone,
> Was peace and war in western hills
> And the White Horse looked on.

> For the White Horse knew England
> When there was none to know;
> He saw the first oar break or bend,
> He saw heaven fall and the world end,
> O God, how long ago.
>
> (G.K. Chesterton 1911)

Few gaze upon it without becoming aware of its sad, timeless quality. This is not intrinsic to the carving but something it confers upon observers who sense that the Horse has outlasted generations and will be there when their children's children have passed on. It stirs them to reflect upon mysterious past ages from which they were excluded, and future worlds from which they will be absent, but in which that strange creature will continue to canter and evoke curiosity, like the familiar, undying spirit of history.

The Horse lies in an area of intense prehistoric activity. Along the top of the Downs runs the Ridgway (known to locals as the Rudgway) and at Uffington this Neolithic track converges with the Icknield Way, another ancient branch-line used by the Romans. About one mile distant lies Wayland's Smithy, a chambered long barrow with Norse associations and an almost savage atmosphere. At Ashdown House, in the vicinity, sarsens crouch in the fields, and to the south lies the Bronze Age cemetery of Lambourn barrows.

PRESERVATION

Preserving the Horse has always been a problem. It is a landmark to which people are magnetically drawn, yet it is highly vulnerable. Sheep congregate and graze on top of the hill, dropping down into the Manger if there is a strong southerly and sheltering in the hillfort at night. They keep the grass cropped, maintaining the downland habitat, but also contribute to the wear and tear. How does one protect such an exposed site without ruining the atmosphere?

There was a dramatic change in the pattern of upkeep when the Right Hon. David Astor donated the hill and surrounding land to the National Trust in 1979. Previously the horse had been 'hobbled within a green paddock' and protected by rusting barbed wire. With the advent of Trust ownership, constraining fences were removed, the surrounding ploughland was put to pasture, scars in the chalk were infilled and a new car park established in a disused quarry. The site acquired its windswept, open approachability, making it attractive to tourists and locals. However, new problems were introduced, such as increased erosion and soil loss which had to be countered by re-seeding, the filling of deep scars with sandbags and the laying of well-defined footpaths. It is estimated that White Horse Hill currently receives around 200,000 visitors per year, drawn along the major 'desire lines' of the trig point, the castle ramparts and the head of the White Horse. In the light of such numbers, the only feasible strategy is to concentrate visitors' attention on specific points, relieving pressure elsewhere.

Site and Appearance

The Horse lies two miles south of the prosperous agricultural village of Uffington, a favourite resort of John Betjeman, the name derived prosaically from a Saxon landowner, Uffa. The B4507 runs by White Horse Hill from which an approach lane branches off and leads past Dragon Hill and up to a car park above the Horse. From there it is a brief stroll to the monument.

Examining the Horse at close quarters may be a disappointment. Like many magical objects it fades upon close scrutiny, seeming merely an affair of curved scars and tapering stripes in the dull yellowish chalk. The animal is discreetly consolidated with concrete edging and is well-maintained by the National Trust, who acquired it from the Department of the Environment in 1979.

To see it to best advantage, an aircraft should be hired, but failing that the Swindon–Reading railway line, four miles distant, is a useful vantage point, and so is the car park of the Seven Stars on the Shrivenham to Faringdon road.

It has been assumed that the Horse has undergone the least tampering of all English hill-figures. This seems to be true, yet points need clarifying. Gough (1806) refers to the long white line delineating the upper half of the body, but there is a letter from Dr Richard Pococke (1757) stating, 'The green sod remains to fill the body'. This remark caused Morris Marples some puzzlement: was the body once green turf outlined by trenches? This is a possibility if one interprets the numerous sweeping curves discernible below the Horse as originally forming the belly and lower neckline. The accepted explanation is that they are the evidence of the Horse climbing uphill with each fresh scouring.

Looking down the beaked head
of the Uffington Horse.

Several engravings, notably in Lyson's *Britannia* (1813), show
a creature with a thicker back, a corrugated spine (presumably
representing the saddlepiece) and a lumpy, eyeless head. Divergence
of illustration and description has given rise to debate over the beast's
original appearance – whether it was naturalistic or impressionistic.
Those who favour a Celtic dating uphold the skinniness of the beast;
those who prefer a Saxon origin argue for a round-bodied version.

The Horse is carved out of solid chalk rather than being merely
entrenched. Its flying curves and abrupt arcs form terraces in
the escarpment. The steepness of the slope, approximately 30°,
makes it prone to soil-slip and erosion, and the end of the tail and
hindlegs are banked up to maintain stability. Up close, the eye is a
levelled dome of chalk, over 1 m in diameter, the head an irregular
rectangle and the ears a deeply incised V, contrasting with the thin,
bent jaws.

Impression of Uffington Horse
from Lyson's *Britannia*

Dragon Hill.

Overlooking the fertile vale bearing its name – a patchwork of cultivated fields and random coppices – the creature faces north-west and is 110 m (360 ft) long and 40 m (130 ft) tall. Below it, there falls away a deep combe called the Manger, while to the west are a series of spectacular ice-cut terraces known as the Giant's Stair. Standing on the tail and looking northwards, one gazes down on the dramatic stump of Dragon Hill, a spur of the Down which has been artifically shaped for a reason unknown. The flattened summit, streaked with gashes of exposed chalk, seems a fittingly grandiose backcloth for the slaying of a serpent.

UFFINGTON CASTLE AND THE PILLOW MOUND

White Horse Hill is crowned by Uffington Castle, some 152 m above sea level. It lies south of the Horse and dates from 700 BC. This double-walled hillfort began as a timber box-rampart and was later revetted by a sarsen wall or breastwork. Identified by an older generation of antiquaries as the Danish encampment routed by Alfred the Great, it seems to have been disturbed or besieged in the Roman period, when the sarsens 'collapsed' or were pushed into the ditch, and coins and debris were scattered over the interior.

Coins of the Dobunni have been recovered in the vicinity, a tribe which may have manned the encampment. They occupied the Upper Thames Valley, spreading into Gloucestershire and the Lower Severn Valley and, according to Dio, they surrendered to Rome in the early stages of the conquest. Their coins bore the motif of a horned, triple-tailed and chisel-nosed horse, stouter than the hill-figure, but possessed of a similar strangeness.

Between the Horse and Uffington Castle is a 'pillow mound', 23 m long by 12 m wide and about 1 m high. Excavated in 1857 by Martin Atkins, an industrious if hardly meticulous investigator, it contained some forty-six Roman burials. Four of the bodies were headless and five of the skeletons had small bronze coins placed in their mouths – the traditional payment to Charon for ferrying souls across the Styx? In the centre of the mound was a coarse urn with two 'handle-like bosses' packed with cremated remains. The vessel may well have been the core of an original Neolithic cist burial that was added to down the centuries.

During the 1993 explorations, an oddly 'occult' discovery was made in the centre of a ring ditch above the mound, most likely the remains of a round barrow excavated in 1862. In a shallow pit in the centre was found a buckram-bound copy of Sir Walter Scott's *Demonology and Witchcraft* (second edition, dated 1831); the inside pages were inscribed with a pentacle and a 'pseudo-antique' dedication rendered in red paint – *Demon De Uffing*. Is this a coda to the Victorian excavations? From the reference to the demon or pagan image, exorcism might have been the motive and the pentacle suggests ritual cleansing, but surely a Bible might have been more fitting than Sir Walter's blood-curdling tome. One would not have expected Squire Atkins to indulge in such Crowleyesque pranks and the matter must remain open.

History and Interpretation

Thomas Baskerville Esq., of Bayworth in the parish of Sunningwell, was the son of Hannibal Baskerville, formerly of Brasenose College. A gentleman of curiosity and learning, his wayfaring tendencies prompted the students of Oxford to nickname him 'The King of Jerusalem'. Thomas composed a journal (1677–8) of his travels over the greater part of England in which allusion is made to the Uffington Horse:

> Here I may take occasion to speake of that Ancient Landmarke or remarkable work of Antiquity, which gives name to our Country the Vale of the White Horse; for in the way betwixt Faringdon and Hyworth, some 5 or 6 miles distant, you have the best prospect of the White Horse, cut in the side of white chalky hill, a mile above Uffington. The Manger, as they caleth it, or sides and bottome, where this Horse is cut, is now in possession of my loving friend and neigbor, Mr Wiseman of Sparswell's Court: and some that dwell hereabout have an obligacion upon their Lands, to repair and cleanse this Landmarke, or else in time it may turn green, like the rest of the hill, and be forgotten.

The Horse, then, was being regularly maintained in the seventeenth century. However, it was an established landmark long before that period and is noted in a cartulary of the abbey of Abingdon dating from the reign of Henry II. The document mentions two monks, Leofric and Godric Cild, who inherited manors, and Godric became 'possessed of Spersholt, near the place commonly known as White Horse Hill'. This took place in the second half of the eleventh century when Aldhelm was abbot (1072–84) and thus dating is no problem. A century later the Horse features in Ralf de Deceto's 'Tract of Wonders' (c. 1180) as one of Britain's foremost marvels:

> Fifth is the White Horse with his foal.[1] It is wonderful that it was so made in the figure of a horse that over the whole place where

---

[1]   The Red Horse of Tysoe has been mentioned as having a 'foal' but no further reference to Uffington Junior has been traced.

that image of a horse is, no grass may grow. Grass never grows over the shape of the horse but always there the earth is bare to the full extent of the horse.

The first wonder, apparently, was the Peak Cavern, the second Stonehenge, the third Cheddar Hole and fourth the Rollright Stones. By the fourteenth century, the Horse had been promoted to the second wonder after Stonehenge – a claim set out in a manuscript entitled *Tractacus de Mirabilibus Brittannniae* (Treatise on the Wonders of Britain) which is held at Corpus Christi College, Cambridge.

The earliest reference to the Horse by Camden (1586) is brief and dismissive. He refers to the 'Vale of the White Horse after some shape or other of a white horse pictured on a whitish hill'. At a later date the topographer Richard Gough translated and expanded Camden's compilation, including additional noteworthy features and illustrations. In his edition of *Britannia* (1806) he describes the county of Berkshire with its 'sweet and healthy air' and plentiful stores of timber, especially oak and beech; also its flourishing wool and malt production – barley being among its chief crops – centred in the Vale of the White Horse:

> The figure which gives its name to this vale is cut on a high steep hill facing the north-west, in a galloping posture, and covers near an acre of ground. His head, neck, body, tail and legs consist of one white line or trench cut in the chalk about two or three feet deep and ten broad; the rays of the afternoon sun darting on it make it visible for twelve miles round at least. The neighbouring inhabitants of several villages have a custom of *scouring the horse*, as they call it, at certain times, about which they hold a festival, and perform certain manly games for prizes. This horse is with great probability supposed to be a memorial of Alfred's victory over the Danes at Ashdown, half a mile from Ashbury Park, Lord Craven's seat in the neighbourhood, AD 871.

Earlier John Aubrey, the eccentric Wiltshire antiquarian (d. 1700) stated that the Horse was cut by Hengist, who carried one on his standard. The two Jutish princes, Hengist and Horsa, after the Saxons had sued for their aid, helped defeat the Picts and Scots at Stamford (AD 450). Subsequently, being reinforced from home, they changed their allegiance and united with the Picts and Scots against the Britons, whom they ultimately dispossessed. Hengist, who lost his brother in a battle near Ailsford (AD 445), founded the kingdom of Kent, established his seat at Canterbury and died in AD 488.

Modern scholarship doubts the historicity of these brothers whose titles have been considered purely emblematic. 'Hengist' signifies 'stallion' in German and 'Horsa' means just plain 'horse'. The horse was the badge of the Saxon leader and implied his power and authority. Parallels can be drawn here with the German emperor being styled 'the eagle', the King of France 'the lily' and the Emperor of China bearing the title of 'True Dragon'. One imagines the rather tenous link between the Uffington Horse and Hengist is by an alternative translation of the name as 'Stone Horse', placing emphasis on the first syllable, 'Heng', or 'arrangement of stones', as in Stonehenge.

ALFRED AND THE DANES

The first extended appreciation of the Horse was a treatise by the Revd Francis Wise, Fellow of Trinity College, Oxford, Keeper of the Radcliffe Library. He wrote two booklets *Letter to Dr. Mead concerning some antiquities in Berkshire* (1738) and *Further Observations upon the White Horse and other antiquities in Berkshire* (1742) which constitute primary source material for anyone disposed to study these monuments.

When Wise was writing, the owner of the Horse was the Right Hon. William, Lord Craven who encouraged the clergyman in his investigations and made available information relating to that part of his estate.

Wise toiled up the steep hillside and scrutinized the Horse. Although the head needed repairing, the tail was well shaped and appeared longer than the legs. However, the wind and rain had taken their toll, filling the trench with turf specks and blearing over the original whiteness. There was no danger, however, of the figure being obliterated, for 'the neighbouring inhabitants have a custom of *Scouring the Horse*, as they call it; at which time a solemn festival is celebrated, and manlike games with prizes exhibited, which no doubt had their original in the Saxon time, in memory of the victory'.

The Horse made a powerful impression on Wise. His evocation of it tingles with patriotic pride, inclining to rhapsodic exaggeration when he states that the animal is 'enough to raise the admiration of

every curious spectator being designed in so masterlike a manner'
that it would defy the painter's art to provide a more exact rendering.
No small skill in 'Opticks' had gone into its execution and the whole
speaks eloquently of an illustrious sovereign:

> If ever the genius of King Alfred exerted itself, (and it never
> failed him in his greatest exigencies) it did remarkably so,
> upon the account of this great trophy . . . Though he had not
> the opportunity, like other conquerors, of raising a stupendous
> monument of Brass or Marble, yet he has hewn an admirable
> contrivance, in erecting one, magnificent enough, tho' simple in
> its design, executed too with little labour and no expense, that
> may thereafter vye with the Pyramids for duration, and perhaps
> exist, when those shall be no more.

So Wise, possibly influenced by tradition, credits King Alfred, who
was born locally at Wantage (AD 848), as the creative genius behind
the figure. The Horse commemorates the defeat of a whole army
of Danes at Ashdown (AD 871). According to John Asser, Alfred's
chronicler, 'The flower of pagan youths were slain, so that never
before or since was ever such destruction known since the Saxons first
gained Britain by their arms.' Allegedly Alfred ordered his men, the
day after the battle, to cut out the White Horse, standard of Hengist,
on the hillside beneath the castle.

Battle of Ashdown, AD 871.
From T. Hughes' *Scouring of the White Horse*.

This argument, always forcibly expressed, although fragilely
supported by factual data, gained wide currency and was adopted
by such local worthies as Thomas Hughes, social critic and author of
Tom Brown's Schooldays, who later modified his opinion. In a letter to
The Times (1871), he expressed doubt over the site of the battle and
the veracity of local tradition:

> I cannot, therefore, aver positively that the Danes occupied
> Uffington Castle and the Saxons Barwell and Alfred Camps on
> the night before the great struggle. Nor am I sure (and this is,
> perhaps, greater heresy) that our White Horse was cut out on the
> hill after the battle. Indeed, I incline to the belief that it was there
> long before, and that Etheldred and Alfred could not have spent
> an hour on the work in the crisis of AD 871.

This view is pertinent and caught the more scholarly temper of the
times. Serious research was beginning to part ways with folklore and

hearsay. The idea that hill-figures may have originated in prehistory, and could not be confidently attributed to datable events, caused antiquarians to ponder more deeply on these relics and produce vaguer, if no less imaginative, solutions to the problems they posed.

RIPOSTE TO THE ANTIQUARIAN

The fact that the Revd Francis Wise had praised the Horse for its precision and naturalness provoked a lengthy rebuke some two years later. Admittedly Wise's choice of phrase had not been judicious. He had not adequately acknowledged that the hill-figure was a skeletal impression rather than a faithful reproduction after the manner of Stubbs. The broadside, entitled *The Impertinence and Imposture of Modern Antiquaries Displayed by Philalethes Rusticus* (1740), epitomizes the exuberant facetiousness that masqueraded as wit in the eighteenth century – a style that would have made Dean Swift's flesh creep in revulsion:

> Though he has Resemblance enough to be called a Horse as properly as any other quadruped [Philalethes argues], yet I cannot say he is a Perfect Picture of a Horse. As to his Head, it wants a little Repairing. The rest of His forehead is not so much amiss, especially not at all too short, being from his ears to his withers about fifty of my Paces, i.e., 150 feet. But then he is quite a *light bodied* one: I may say for a Horse that has lain so long at grass, carries *no body at all*, insomuch that he should take up the hill, were I upon the Back of Him, I should be under the terrible apprehension he would slip through his girth.

Not content with belabouring the Horse in prose, Philalethes Rusticus turns his hand to poetry by printing an effusion that, so he informs us, was the work of an Oxford scholar led to the spot:

> See here the pad of Good King Alfry,
> Sure never was so rare a Palfrey!
> Tho' Earth his Dam, his Sire a Spade,
> No Painter e're a finer made.
> Not Wotton on his hunting pieces
> Can show one such a Tit as this is.

William Asplin, alias Philalethes Rusticus, the author of *Impertinence*, was vicar of Banbury and rival contender for the post of Radcliffe's

librarian. There is malice lurking beneath the effusive jollity. Wise
is even accused of being sympathetic to the Pretender to the throne,
who was known as the Chevalier de St George – Asplin connects
the Horse with the galloping creature on the arms of the House of
Hanover. 'Under pretence of Scouring the Horse,' he mischievously
hints, 'you may find a posse got together would scour the Country
with a vengeance.' Furthermore, he ridicules Wise for comparing
the Horse to the creature on the Saxon standard and invokes the Red
Horse of Tysoe:

> It was one of the wise sayings of our ancestors, that 'a good horse
> was never of a bad Colour', and might I be worthy to impose my
> private opinion, the horse we are now upon happens to be *White
> One* only because the native soil abounds with Chalk or a sort of
> Limestone. Just as that other Nag of Renown, from whom the
> Vale of the Red Horse is denominated, happens to be red only
> because he is cut in ruddy soil.

A CELTIC ARTEFACT?

Although the unremitting levity of Asplin's style becomes tedious,
he does have some insight, for he draws attention to similarities
between the Horse and the stylized steeds on old British coins. Wise
himself was a numismatist, so this may be a little additional baiting,
yet the suggestion was taken up seriously by later commentators and
effected a reappraisal of the Horse.

The Revd W.C. Plenderleath (1885) includes illustrations of
Belgic coins derived from the gold stater of Philip of Macedonia
(d. 336 BC) which passed into Britain *c.* 100 BC. The artistry varies
from a recognizable horse to an amazing assemblage of sunwheels,
half moons and dumb-bell-shaped limbs. These coins by no means
reproduce the Horse, but they do show some marked likenesses,
particularly in such details as the rounded eye, beaky jaws and
residual legs.

In an important article in *Antiquity* (1931), Stuart Piggot
developed this approach by citing other artefacts of the Iron Age
to which the hill-figure might relate: two buckets from Aylesford
and Marlborough and a Romano-British horse from Silchester.
The *repoussé* horses on the Aylesford bucket are more birdlike or
serpentine than equine: snaky Ss form intensely mobile bodies that
sprout looping tails and pouting, leaflike mouths. The Marlborough

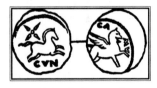

Coin of Cunobeline struck at
Colchester.

Coin of Buduo or Boadicea,
Queen of the Iceni.

19

The Aylesford bucket with its design of sinuous horses.

beasts are less assured in execution, yet again the design is curvilinear and the mane represented by a flying pennant of hair. In many ways the small bronze Silchester Horse bears the greatest resemblance to the Uffington carving, with its primitive ring-and-dot eye and stark minimalist outline. Drawing mainly on artistic evidence, coupled with the fact that the Horse was unlikely to be cut during the Roman occupation, Piggott concluded 'that the horse is a monument constructed at the end of the Early Iron Age, probably in the first century BC'.

What of the purpose of the Horse? The archaeologist O.G.S. Crawford (*Antiquity*, 1929) suggested that it was a tribal emblem of those who erected or occupied Uffington Castle, while the Department of the Environment stated in its official list that it was probably cut by the Belgae. At Uffington Castle a coin of the Dobunni was discovered; they were a partly Belgic tribe, more culturally advanced than the Coritani or Iceni, having absorbed the manners and customs of Rome. Their immigration into Britain was thought to have started about 100 BC.

Silchester Horse.

Anne Ross (1967) compared the Horse and castle with the great mound of Emain Macha in Ireland which celebrates the Amazonian horsewoman Macha, who raced against the swiftest steeds in the land while giving birth to twins. She also invoked Epona, the most important Gallic horse deity, who embodied woman-as-divine-mare and was worshipped by the Roman cavalry. Epona, some of whose qualities are shared by the Celtic goddess, Rhiannon, is commonly depicted astride a horse together with the crescent moon and holding the key to the stables.

SYMBOL OF ODIN

The Celtic interpretation of the Horse settled into general acceptance. The figure of Alfred the Great dimmed to legendary association. Articles on the subject cited Piggott as the authority, until a spirited counterblast appeared in *Folklore* (1967) wherein Diana Woolner pointed out that 'the present form of the Horse is vestigial, that in common with all other hill-figures it is unstable, and that no deductions as to its age and origin can be made from its present appearance'.

This argument was based on a paper published by the Newbury and District Field Club (*Transactions*, Vol. XI, No. 3) which, after studying the Horse in detail, found traces of many legs and necks in different positions, together with the shadowy outline of what they interpreted as a larger horse.

This was not a radical observation; in 1738 Francise Wise had observed how the turf on the upper verge tended 'to crumble . . . which is the reason why the country people erroneously imagine that the Horse, since his first fabrication, has shifted his quarters, and is got higher upon the hill than formerly'.

Relying mainly on folkloristic evidence, Diana Woolner reinstated the Saxon case. The present Horse amounts to no more than preliminary sketchwork. Weathering has destroyed the original full-bodied creature leaving only the initial pencil strokes, so to speak, and it is this natural deformation that has encouraged comparisons with Gallic coins and other Celtic artefacts.

The identity proper of the creature is supplied by the surrounding landscape and fragments of local tradition:

> If it is true as I heard zay,
> King George did here the dragon slay,
> And down below on yonder hill
> They buried him as I heard tell.
>
> If you along the Rudgway go,
> About a mile for ought I know,
> There Wayland's Cave you may see
> Surrounded by a group of trees.
>
> They say that in this cave did dwell
> A smith that was invisible;
> At last he was found out, they say,
> He blew up the place and vlod away.

WAYLAND'S SMITHY

The above verses, lifted from Thomas Hughes' novel *The Scouring of the White Horse* (1857), were composed by Job Cork, a rhyming shepherd of the district. King George replaces St George, in deference to the Hanoverian accession, and Wayland's Cave is Wayland's Smithy, a Neolithic chambered long barrow linked to the Horse by the Ridgeway.

Set in a grove of whispering beeches, with its façade of four immense sarsens, the Smithy is an almost sinisterly atmospheric place, once believed to be the tomb of Baegsaeg the Dane, slain at Ashdown. In a charter of Edred's (AD 955), it is referred to as Wayland's Smithy after the Norse hero, master of metalcraft, who was imprisoned in a cave by King Niduth and kept working at his trade. To prevent his escaping, the King had him maimed. Wayland

Wayland's Smithy in its grove of beeches.

avenged this by decapitating the King's two sons and having their skulls made into goblets which he presented as gifts to their father. The King had a daughter, Beadohild, who took Wayland a ring, asking him to mend it, but Wayland took the opportunity to rape her, producing an illegitimate son called Wittich. Finally he escaped the palace, flying away on wings he had forged.

The Wayland legend, naturally, took root in Saxon territories, including the Vale of the White Horse, where allegedly the smith settled, spending his time making armour for heroes and providing shoes for horses – including, of course, the White Horse carved on the hill. After his death, it was said that any traveller desiring his horse to be shod had only to place a groat on the flat, horizontal stone and the repairs would be effected by an invisible agency. Walter Scott used the legend in *Kenilworth*, a tale of a Berkshire farrier.

In 1919 two currency bars of the Early Iron Age were found beneath one of the collapsed sarsens at the entrance. Leslie Grinsell (1939) speculated whether they were left as payment for an Early

Iron Age metal-worker. The long bars have also been translated as 'unfinished swords' – again accentuating the Wayland connection – but such casting about is wishful rather than warranted.

The most important thing about Wayland, in Diana Woolner's view, is that he is a localized manifestation of Odin, the Norse god of prophecy, inspiration and battle. Places like nearby Ashdown, where his sacred trees once flourished, testify to his cult. Hardwell Camp, between the Horse and the Smithy, was called in the ninth century Tilsburh or Til's Castle – Til being the brother of Wayland – and other names mentioned in Saxon charters, such as Beahild's (Beadohild?) burial place and Hwittuc (a corruption of Wittich?) can be related to Wayland–Odin.

What of George or St George? He was merely the dashing Christian hero–saint imposed upon local Norse tradition, replacing Wayland, yet retaining many of his notable qualities. Not only did George slay a dragon – the attribute of so many Norse heroes – he, like Odin, was also the focus of a horse cult. Thus, to a great extent his personality is coloured by his pagan predecessor.

This argument emphasizes the potent Norse heritage of the region and the plenitude of Saxon lore, but many of the structures invoked predate the period by thousands of years: Wayland's Smithy is not Saxon, and neither are the numerous earthworks. Not that the general drift is audacious or far-fetched, for if the Tysoe Horse honours Tiw – and many think that it does – it is perfectly feasible that the Uffington beast pays homage to Odin.

The most exciting feature of Diana Woolner's article is the account of the wonderful fourteenth-century bell in the church at Dorchester-on-Thames. Dedicated to St Birinus, an apostle who landed in Wessex (AD 634) and converted the West Saxons, its sides show mouldings of a galloping horse and a dragon. The horse is full-bodied and fluidly rendered, with the neck arched forward. Is this, then, a portrait of the Saxon Horse of Uffington? Does the accompanying dragon refer to the legend of St George? Furthermore, a local rhyme states:

Uffington Horse? Dragon and horse cast in relief on the bell at Dorchester-on-Thames.

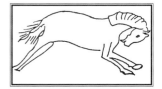

> Within the sound of the great bell
> No snake nor adder ere shall dwell

Is this an allusion to the suppression of a pagan cult? Was the dragon–horse of Uffington, or Wayland's steed, impaled by the knightly Christian saint?

Abetting Diana Woolner's theory is the prominent flat-topped knoll below the Horse called Dragon Hill? The summit has been artifically flattened – for ceremonial or strategic purposes? – and is streaked by a bald patch of chalk, marking the spillage of dragon's blood after St George had dispatched it. Wise (1738) mentioned the tradition, thinking the hill might be a barrow, and earlier Aubrey in *Monumenta Britannica* (*c.* 1670) wondered whether it might not be the tumulus of Uther Pendragon: 'That Uter Pendragon fought against the Saxons is certayne: perhaps was here slayne, from whence Dragon-hill may take its denomination.'

THE SMITHY EXCAVATED

After the First World War, the Smithy was excavated scientifically for the first time by Mr C. Peers and Mr R.A. Smith of the British Museum. The burial chambers beneath the stones were exposed and the remains of eight skeletons found. The barrow was measured and found to be 26 m long by 14 m wide, the original height being about 2.5 m. The passage was estimated to be about 2 m high by the capstone.

Built by Neolithic people who lived on the hill some five thousand years ago, the first mound was an ovoid enclosing a wooden mortuary structure with a stone floor. About fifty years later, the enormous sarsen-kerbed wedge-shaped mound was superimposed on it. This became apparent during the second excavation by Professors Piggott and Atkinson (1962) who supervised the restoration of the Smithy to its Neolithic state. During the final stages, they uncovered the wooden mortuary and explored it the following year, finding fourteen bodies – one skeleton was crouched and in a complete state while the rest were lying loose. Tree trunks had been split in two and set up 'like great totem poles' and further search disclosed pottery, leaf-shaped arrowheads and stone hand-mills. Radiocarbon tests on the charcoal from the trees that had been felled and burnt to make room for the tombs provided the date, *c.* 2800 BC. The smooth finish of certain of the larger stones suggested that they might have been pounded with mauls – a technique used at Stonehenge – but Atkinson and Piggott concluded the effect was natural.

SCOURING

That the Horse was maintained down the centuries points to the tenacity of local tradition. In his edition of *Britannia* (1720), Thomas Cox stated that 'the neighbouring parish have a custom, once a year, at or near Midsummer, to go and weed it in order to keep the Horse in shape and colour; and after the work is over they end the day in feasting and merriment.' Twenty years later, William Asplin noted that the scourers' reward after cleansing the Horse was 'a good belly-full of ale' but made no mention of an organized festival.

Presumably those who cultivated the open fields around the Horse in Saxon times performed the cleansing – a practice legated down the centuries to the neighbouring villages and manors. Baskerville refers to the 'obligacion . . . to repair and cleanse this landmark', but it seems to have been more of a festival than a duty, for it was accompanied by merrymaking and games which, according to Wise, had by 1738 lost much of their 'ancient splendour'.

This custom lapsed but was revived during Victorian times when it became the subject of Thomas Hughes' novel *The Scouring of the White Horse*. The literary interest of the story is limited, though it offers stable fare for Berkshire patriots and cullers of White Horse lore. Lightly narrated, the content is intensely moral; the final chapter consists of a thunderingly righteous sermon from the parson, approving such 'feasts' so long as God is taken into account. The story is told through the eyes of Richard Easy, a London clerk. He takes a holiday in Berkshire and meets the squire, young Miss Lucy, a host of merry milkmaids and his ex-schoolmate, a ruddy-cheeked young farmer called Joe, who introduces him to the characters and customs of the Uffington region. There are immortal lines of dialogue:

Squire: Good Morning, Thomas. How about the weather? Did the White Horse smoke his pipe this morning?
Thos: Mornin' Sir. I didn't zee as 'a did. I allus notice he doos it when the wind blaws moor to th' east'ard.

Richard arrives at the time of the scouring. Hughes' description well evokes a large country fair with its groupings of booths and stalls 'all decked out with nuts and apples and gingerbread, and all sorts of sucks and food, and children's toys, and cheap ribbons, knives, braces, straps and all manner of gaudy-looking articles'. In addition, there were musicians and performing acrobats, publicans' booths bedecked with flowers, skittle-grounds and a greasy pole to frustrate the supplest shins, all presided over by 'a great white tent' occupied by the County Police.

Competitions for the men included sack-racing, cheese-rolling and cudgel-playing for a gold-laced hat and pair of pumps, while more

Scouring the Horse.

ingenious activities included burrowing one's mouth in a tubful of flour in order to locate a hidden silver bullet and a competition, introduced in 1808, inviting ladies ('only two gipsy women entered,' noted Hughes, 'and it seems to have been a very abominable business') to indulge in a pipe-smoking marathon, for which the prize was half a guinea or a gallon of gin.

From the perspective of the present, the events listed seem very quaint and rustic, yet essentially they were part of a large, lucrative revel. Like many festivities, the Scouring started out with a religious intent, but the ritualistic element steadily diminished, until all semblance of ceremony was swamped by clamour and merrymaking; and, by the end of the eighteenth century, it had become a profit-making enterprise with regular stalls and competitions.

The traditional time-scale for repairing the Horse was every seven years. Whether this was kept to in earlier times is not known, but the eighteenth- and nineteenth-century documents show intervals varying considerably. So did the time of the year: Whitsun (a traditional time for feasts and sports) seems to have been popular, as was Michaelmas, in mid-September. A note in the 1857 programme confirms the latter as the older date: 'That a pastime be held on the White Horse Hill, on Thursday and Friday, the 17th and 18th of

September, in accordance with the old custom at the time of *The Scouring of the White Horse*.'

A fire festival may have been the precursor of the various manly games on White Horse Hill. Earlier references pick up a Midsummer date, around the solstice, 21 June, associated with burning bonfires and fumigating cattle. If this *was* the original date, it may be reflected by customs of an older lineage described by Hughes, such as rolling a wheel down the Manger (the deep combe below the Horse) for men to chase after, harking back to Midsummer rites when flaming bales, tar barrels and straw-packed sunwheels were launched down steep slopes – magically sympathetic devices to boost the sun around the bend of the year.

In Jackson's *Oxford Journal* (1780), along with a list of traditional scouring sports, there is mentioned 'Riding down the hill upon a horse's jawbone for 2/6' – a diversion bringing to mind Obby Oss ceremonies and the equine rites of St John's Eve noted by Charlotte Elizabeth and others.

Scouring sports – downhill race. From T. Hughes' *Scouring of the White Horse.*

THE BLOWING-STONE

The physical toil of the Scouring was lightened by singing a ballad which, although of no great age, draws in several points of local folklore.

> The Old White Horse wants setting to rights
> And the Squire has promised good cheer;
> So we'll give him a scrape to keep him in shape,
> And he'll last for many a year.
>
> He was made a long, long time ago
> With a great deal of labour and pains,
> By King Alfred the Great, when he spoiled their conceit,
> And caddled those worsbirds the Danes.
>
> The Blowing-Stone, in days gone by,
> Was King Alfred's bugle horn,
> And the Thorning-Tree you may plainly see,
> Which is called King Alfred's Thorn.
>
> They'll be backsword play, and climbing the pole,
> And a race for pig and cheese;
> And we think as he's a dumble soul
> Who don't care for such sports as these.

The Blowing-Stone at
Kingston Lisle.

Berkshire dialect words are employed: 'caddled' means harassed,
while 'worsbird' is a corruption of whore's bird and 'dumble' signifies
dull.

The Blowing-Stone is a large stone about 3 ft tall, pierced with
several holes, one of which has a Y-shaped channel. By blowing
through this, practised lungs can reproduce a sound akin to the
bellowing of a calf – allegedly it can be heard at Faringdon church,
six miles distant. Cooper King (1887) maintained that the 'higher
art and skill of Saxon times' required no such primitive instrument
for summoning warriors into battle: 'But the ancient Celtic tribes
lived on the open area of the downs, and here therefore would this
rude trumpet of stone be of value for collecting the bands of pastoral
nomads with their herd and treasures, their wives and children
within the stout rampart of Uffington.'

The Stone is at Kingston Lisle, a thatched village about three
miles from the Horse. It is marked on Rocque's map of Berkshire

(1761), apparently in its present position, where it is pluralized as 'Blowingstones'. Today it stands within a fenced enclosure beside a cottage which was once a smithy. During the last century, the smith was said to have taken the stone from the Downs and placed it in his workshop, but this is contradicted by Mr Sowerby (1809) who placed the Blowing-Stone 'near the front of a little public-house, to which it gives its name. It is an unwrought Sandstone, about three feet high, and nearly eighteen inches in thickness, having natural perforations . . .'

Appearing in *Tom Brown's Schooldays* (1857) and *Scouring of the White Horse* (1857), Blowingstone Inn was well established during Victorian times. Thinking the sarsen a useful novelty, the landlord entertained customers by blowing through it. (In my experience, ladies seem to be prim about using the stone, but I have watched gentlemen fearlessly tromboning away, producing noises guaranteed to exclude them from polite society for at least a month.) In *Tom Brown's Schooldays* the noise is described as 'a gruesome sound between a moan and a roar, sounding over the valley, up the hillside, and into the woods – a ghost-like awful voice'.

That the tradition of Alfred using the stone is not mentioned by Francis Wise, who was zealous in his pursuit of any Saxon attachment, may suggest that it does not predate his own theories; but memory of the 'Thorning Tree' is retained by the nearby 'Roughthorn Farm', said to occupy the site of the Battle of Ashdown (AD 871).

NEGLECT

After the First World War the White Horse suffered a brief period of neglect, and the *Daily Mail*, 26 August 1922, ran the following headline: 'Famous Landmark Which Requires Cleaning'.

The famous White Horse on the Berkshire Down near Uffington, to which reference is made in *Tom Brown's Schooldays*, is but a shadow of its former glory. It can scarce be seen for want of scouring. It has become so dirty of late that travellers on the Great Western Railway line who still remember it as it was many years ago, standing out clear and active on the long range of chalk hills, complain that something ought to be done to renovate it.

Current Opinion and Evidence

During the Second World War, the Horse was concealed in order that it should not help enemy bombers to fix their whereabouts. At the end of conflict, it had to be uncovered and cleaned by agricultural workers, superintended by W.F. 'Peter' Grimes. The latter, having more than average curiosity, seized this opportunity to dig a test-pit in the Horse's beak. He found that it was not simply etched on the green but entrenched into the bedrock and then built up with hard white chalk. Grimes' report and cross-section were relegated to the Ministry of Works' files where they gathered dust. No technology existed to take the evidence further.

NEW LIGHT ON A WHITE HORSE

The status of the Horse as a mysterious dateless artefact, hovering over many epochs but belonging to none, has been challenged by a new method of dating called Optical Stimulated Luminescence or OSL. Sounding like a device that enables ghosts to glimmer more brightly, silt-dating – or measuring when buried soils were last exposed to sunlight – is the ideal method to examine a deeply incised earth etching, or graffito, that has become infilled and overgrown.

The method relies very much on those periods of neglect when outlines of hill-figures become overgrown and fill with soil. It is essential to locate an early cut or infilled trench, so that layers of 'original' soil can be analysed.

It seemed to archaeologists David Miles and Simon Palmer that Grimes' report was evidence 'that the White Horse had an anatomy which could, potentially, be dissected'. The obvious place to start was by re-opening the cut through the Horse's beak. This was sunk a metre deep in the brownish hillwash, showing that the Horse had been 'built up' or dug out, then backfilled with clean hard chalk. Successive layers of 'beaks' – some over a metre longer than the present projection – were traced and, at the base of the cutting, was found a halfpenny that Grimes had deposited in 1952. A trench through the body indicated that it had once been a metre or so wider, but never strikingly different from its present design. However, the angle of the etching *had* changed, climbing the hill over the centuries, so it now took up the flatter upper slope and was less visible from a distance.

Samples taken from colluvium found between two of the lower layers of the Horse's body, and from another cut near the base, produced three dates of approximately 1400–600 BC, the earliest of the samples being 1240±360 BC and the latest 900±340 BC, indicating an Early Iron Age or Late Bronze Age origin.

When published, the figures raised a few eyebrows. Like the Hercules theory of the Cerne Giant, the Iron Age origins of the Horse had become 'officialized' on the basis of artistic evidence, coupled with a resistance to the idea that the regular repair of the Horse could have been persistently maintained long before the Roman occupation. To some, the Horse seems so typical of La Tène art that a Bronze Age dating further destabilizes the cultural assumptions.

Earlier writers had anticipated this. Flinders Petrie thought the horse belonged to the Bronze Age and Morris Marples (1949) favoured a Bronze Age origin, illustrating his point with comparable rock-carvings of horses from Kivik, Sweden, and a Libyan–Berber rock-carving from Taghit. With admirable prescience, he noted that 'this way of drawing a horse was characteristic of the Bronze Age in widely separated regions. Alike in Scandinavia and North Africa, we find the same graphic technique employing a minimum of lines and in particular carrying through one long sweeping curve from the head to the tip of tail.'

SYSTEMS COLLAPSE

Renewed speculations on the Horse's origins may seem opportunistic or premature, but the Late Bronze Age was a time of large-scale resettlement. The earth of the heavily populated regions had been overfarmed and leached of nutrients. Evidence drawn from soil analysis indicates a 'systems collapse' in which the climate deteriorated, and the population shrank as grazing land gave way to bog and heath. Whether the decrease in numbers was owing to the onslaught of disease, slaughter or lack of nourishment, is not known, for the evidence is scattered and ambiguous. There is a tendency during such intervals for society to break into component parts, into smaller and smaller tribal units or even single families.

No henge monuments were raised after 1200 BC. The difference in the way of life must have been as dramatic as when the Egyptians ceased pyramid-building. An emergent sense of individual value may have created new networks and undermined the authority of the warrior-priest hierarchy. As cohesion loosened and weather deteriorated, the tribes took stock of their shrinking resources and priorities switched to the basics of survival.

Was this reaction founded on environmental factors? Or had a religious impulse, after attaining a kind of ritual decadence, exhausted itself? It is often necessary to live to a great age in order to obtain a dramatically altered world. Yet one disillusioned or renascent generation can break down a tradition shaped over a thousand years. Archaeologists have come to recognize that change is not always the result of invasion or exotic implant. There may never have come a point of recognition among priests or elders that age-old rituals – the beating out of sun-discs, the aligning of celestial markers, the raising of henges and stone rows – had not secured a golden future in which the crops thrived under clear skies, but rather an epoch of rainy autumns and flooding fields. If they *did* believe the gods had abandoned them, all they had to look to was themselves, and it was now the task of the warrior, the god-man or super-hero, to take possession of his destiny.

As the climate became wetter and the land less utilizable, tribes abandoned old hunting and fishing grounds – the moors of the West Country, the downlands of Wessex and the Upper Thames Valley – and began to occupy the hitherto neglected regions of the Fens, the Lower Thames estuary and the coastal strips. They took up their new positions, safeguarding what they had brought with them in palisades of earth and timber. The hillfort replaced the ceremonial enclosure, a gated rampart instead of an open one, underlining the need to re-establish the protocol of possession, to achieve mastery and continuity over new territory.

It was a period of upheaval – but none of this could have been entirely new. Stonehenge had inaugurated no 'golden age' of peace and plenty. Instead it marked the long despotism of priest and warrior, a society anchored by rote and ritual. When resentment articulates into rebellion, an underclass may break the mould that has encased it. Following that, it must struggle to gain self-definition beyond what it has abandoned. From 1200 BC onwards, there were such signs of an order grinding to a standstill, triggering chaos and warfare:

It was an age of violence. Rapiers of bronze were manufactured for roving bands of young warriors eager for plunder. In turn, these weapons were supplanted by leaf-shaped swords, round shields and studded leather helmets. Ditched-and-banked fortifications were built around the tops of hills where people could retreat with the flocks and herds when their lands were threatened by marauders. Buried caches of metal axes, broken daggers and ingots for resmelting gold bracelets and torcs, tell of tinkers and merchants concealing the bulk of their wares before taking a few objects to trade locally. The unrecovered hoards show grimly that their owners never came back.

(Aubrey Burl 1987)

Along with the movement of skills and communities, another figure entered British prehistory: the mounted horseman, of use in both war and herding, although it was long before the solid stock breeds, capable of drawing a plough, came on the scene. Eloquent testimony of this increasingly important accomplishment has been gathered from many sites, especially the bleak, peaty, crag-shadowed lake of Lyn Fawr in Glamorganshire where an amazing hoard was recovered. Placed at the juncture between the Bronze and Iron ages (*c.* 600 BC), it included two bronze pony cheek-pieces, three bronze discs or 'phallerae' from harness decorations, an open-work harness mount and a belt hook. Along with sickles, knives, sword chapes and cauldrons, these objects had been cast in the water, a tribute to the aquatic deities who were becoming increasingly important.

We find at this period, too, plentiful traces of Bronze Age ranching. The flat-bottomed ditch and low rubble bank at Ram's Hill, Berkshire (*c.* 1100 BC) were shaped as a cattle corral, to stop animals from straying and to deter rustlers. Intensive trading took place here, judging from the variety of pottery styles excavated, suggesting that it flourished as a market centre.

In the same region, the ramparts of Uffington Castle were built, first around a timber box-rampart, and then later, as hostilities and jostling for territory deepened, the sarsen buttressing. If the Horse was carved during this period, such a coordinated venture was more likely to have taken place during a settled interval, a time when a gesture of cohesion, a statement of unity, arises like an exhalation of the spirit.

Days went by, and days went by, and the men with their mattocks and broad deer horns were digging down into the chalk itself, cutting away the dull earth-stained top layers for the women to carry away and stack in spoil-heaps; then into the clean white chalk thigh-deep beneath the grass. And that, too, was stacked nearby, ready to go back on top when all the duller surfaces had been shovelled in again.

(Rosemary Sutcliff 1977)

Just as tattoos individualize their wearer, so the massive hill-figure was a gesture of solidarity, a badge of identity aside from the ritual or religious function it fulfilled. It was also a splendid appendage to the hillfort, a landmark that could be picked up at a great distance.

Conclusion

Evidence of more or less continuous settlement up and around White Horse Hill has led to varied interpretations, pointing to the White Horse originating in Bronze Age, Celtic and Saxon times. Its curvilinear style suggested La Tène influence; therefore, an Iron Age dating seemed likely to Stuart Piggott, Leslie Grinsell and others. With the advent of OSL, the Horse was found to be an earlier artefact, probably coeval with Uffington Castle, stretching back to the Late Bronze Age.

In view of this new information, time-scales will have to be adjusted, but the interpretation of the hill-figure is not radically altered, simply because it is is now thought that the Celtic peoples were present in Britain long before the advent of the Iron Age, and their icons and beliefs are no longer attributed to sudden invasion or immigration from the Continent.

In the 1930s a third-century water jar was found by Chrisopher Hawkes near Ringwood in Hampshire. Scratched on its lid was a schematic outline of a horse, suggesting the Uffington beast, yet bearing not a rider but a phallus. A clay image of a four-horse chariot found at Wroxeter is also drawn from a phallic emblem which raises the question: did the Uffington Horse have a similar extension on its back? It suggests the possibility that similar principles were being revered at Uffington and Cerne, inviting the possibility of a common origin.

35

CHAPTER TWO

THE WESTBURY HORSE

And then, that evening
Later in the summer the strange horses came.
We heard a distant tapping on the road,
A deepening drumming; it stopped, went on again
And at the corner changed to hollow thunder.
We saw the heads
Like a wild wave charging and were afraid.
We had sold our horses in our father's time
To buy new tractors. Now they were strange to us
As a fabulous steed set on an ancient field
Or illustration in a book of knights.
We did not dare go near them.

(Edwin Muir 1965)

Introduction

The story of the Westbury or Bratton Horse is problematic and complicated by the fact that the original beast was enlarged and conventionalized in 1778. The old horse had a rude and forlorn appearance which provoked speculation among such antiquaries as Gough that it was coeval with the Uffington Horse. Counterbalancing this is the more cautious testimony of Francis Wise (1742) who for once abandoned his Saxon mania for a more temperate line.

Site and Appearance

The Westbury Horse is cut on the steep slope of Bratton Down, in Wiltshire, about one mile south-west of the village and below the Iron Age fortress of Bratton Camp. The situation is exciting and impressive – on a plunging escarpment which provides an excellent

Westbury Horse seen from the hillside.

launching pad for hang-gliders. A road leads up to the crest of a hill enclosed by the writhings of a double-walled hillfort. A permanent wind is usually blowing at this height and the turf makes for exhilarating walking. The Horse borders on an area enclosed by the Ministry of Defence and a vast quarry supplying the cement works in the valley. The animal is the whitest of all hill-figures, emitting a brilliant detergent glow, and its green backcloth has been described by an old Wiltshire man as 'the stables of the moon stallion'. No aerial antics are necessary to get a good photograph of the steed. If you traverse the hillside to the left, a perfect view of the beast in its entirety will be revealed. The valley is dominated in the near distance by the commercially necessary, if aesthetically irritating, cement works, usually trailing long squirrel tails of smoke from its flues. On clear days the Horse commands attention from a great distance and Charles Tennyson Turner (1808–79), brother of Alfred, celebrated it in one of his more effective sonnets. Like most literary men, he was content to dramatize the Saxon thesis:

As from the Dorset shore I travell'd home,
I saw the charger of the Wiltshire wold;
A far-seen figure, stately to behold,
Whose groom the shepherd is, the hoe his comb;
His wizard-spell even sober daylight own'd;
That night I dream'd him into living will;
He neigh'd – and, straight, the chalk pour'd down the hill;
He shook himself, and all beneath was stoned;
Hengist and Horsa shouted o'er my sleep,
Like fierce Achilles, while that storm-blanch'd horse
Sprang to the van of all the Saxon force,
And push'd the Britons to the Western deep;
Then, dream-wise, as it were a thing of course,
He floated upwards, and regain'd the steep.

Facing westwards on a 50° slope overlooking the Vale of Pewsey, it appears a sturdy, well-fed creature. It is maintained by English Heritage, which is also responsible for the camp. As a work of art, it is executed with considerable care, yet when compared with the Uffington steed, it seems rather stiff and mechanical, lacking the fluent mobility and grace of its ghostly colleague. Rather it puts one in mind of some handsome, docile creature staring idly over a farmer's fence. The B3098 road skirts the hill-figure and provides a good view – in clear weather the creature can be easily identified from Bradford-on-Avon and farther afield.

The Horse is some 55 m long and 33 m high. Its tail is not docked but hangs limp and flowing, and the eye is a cushioned dome of turf surrounded by chalk. The hocks and hooves are boldly carved and the head is lifted high. The outline is banked up with concrete blocks – a precaution against shrinkage and elongation – and seems destined to endure. This was not always so. Like the Cherhill Horse, not many miles distant, it formerly suffered from rainfall damage – crumbling verges and fraying feet. This tendency was corrected by the fitting of gratings in 1903.

History and Interpretation

King Alfred is as ubiquitous a figure on the Wiltshire Downs as King Arthur throughout the West Country. He is credited with being the author of the Westbury Horse, which is associated with yet

The embanked head of the Westbury Horse.

another glorious Dane-routing episode duly chronicled by his biographer.

> In the same year [John Asser writes, referring to AD 878] after Easter, King Alfred, with a few of his partisans, found a stronghold in a place which is called Ethelingey, and from that stronghold continued indefatigably to wage war against the Pagans, at the head of the noblemen, his vassals, of Somersetshire. And, again, the seventh week after Easter, he rode to the stone of Egbertha, which is in the eastern part of the forest which is called Selwood, but in Latin, *Silva magna*, in British Coitmaur; and there met him all the inhabitants of Somerset and Wiltshire, and all such inhabitants of Hampshire as had not sailed beyond sea for fear of the Pagans, and upon seeing the King received him as was proper, like one come to life again after so many troubles, and were filled with excessive joy, and there they encamped for one

night. At dawn of the following he came to a place that is called Ethandun, and fiercely warring against the whole army of the Pagans with serried masses, and courageously persevering for a long time, by Divine favour, at last gained the victory, overthrew the Pagans with very great slaughter, and put them to flight, and pursued them with deadly blows, even to their stronghold, and all he found outside of it, men, horses, and sheep, he seized, immediately killed the men, and boldly encamped before the entrance of the Pagan stronghold with all his army.

After the King had stationed his troops outside the fort, a fourteen-day siege ensued, and then the enemy surrendered, whereupon Alfred, to commemorate his victory, ordered that a white horse be cut on the hillside.

The legend is open to grave doubt. Aside from the employment of that rather tired equation, Alfred the Great + Battle with Danes = White Horse, the location of Ethandun is debatable. It has been variously claimed by Heddington, near Calne, by Yattondown, near Chippenham, and – likeliest of all – by Edington Hill above the Sedgemoor fenland. Nevertheless, Edington outside Westbury is a distinct possibility. Bratton Castle, the Iron Age earthwork above the white horse, is naturally identified as the Danish encampment; it is rounded by double ramparts and encloses some 23 acres of ground.

This Saxon origin of the Westbury Horse is an agreeable hotchpotch of history and hearsay. However, even the Revd Francis Wise, whose general theories may have assisted its popular promotion, confessed to meeting inhabitants of Westbury who asserted that the animal 'had been wrought within the memory of persons now living or but very lately dead'.

Richard Gough, the editor of Camden's *Brittania*, surveyed the Westbury Horse in 1772. He differed with Wise and forcefully re-argued the Saxon case. After discussing the views of Bishop Gibson on the significance of Cley Hill overlooking Warminster – did Alfred use it as a camp in AD 848? – he turned his attention to Bratton as the Danish fortress:

But in fact there is on Clay Hill a small circular camp double trenched, and its distance is not too great from Bratton Castle but that Alfred could march from one to the other in twenty-four hours. This last no doubt was the fortification to which the Danes fled, and held out a siege of fourteen days. It is situated on the

Statue of King Alfred at Wantage.

point of a high hill, commanding all the country, and is double ditched on the south and north sides with very deep trenches. It has two entrances from the south-east to the plain, and from the north-east to Edington, both guarded by a redoubt: on the west side is a spring. It is oval, 350 paces long by nearly 200 broad, and its area is 23 or 24 acres. Near the middle is a large oblong barrow 60 paces long, under which have been found many skulls and bones mixed with stag's horns, fragments of urns, and pieces of iron weapons, and millstones like the modern Scottish querns, fifteen and eighteen inches in diameter. Under the south side within the trenches is a circular mound of earth made in the last century called the *Table*, with a kind of horseshoe in the centre. The soil of the hill is chalk abounding with petrefactions, belemnites, spines of echini, &c. On the south-west face of the hill is a most curious monument unnoticed by Bishop Gibson: a white horse in a walking attitude cut out of the chalk, fifty-four feet high from his toe to his chest, and to the tip of his ear near one hundred feet high, and from ear to tail one hundred feet long: an undoubted memorial of this important victory, and like that by which Alfred commemorated his first great victory in Berkshire eight years before. The whole of this figure is hollowed out of the chalk, and not marked with outlines so hollowed as Mr Wise seems to insinuate the Berkshire horse is. I am surprised this very learned investigator of these kind of monuments among us should doubt the antiquity of this horse, which so exactly corresponds with the other both in execution and intention, and to represent it as of modern make within memory. As I could find no such tradition when I surveyed it in 1772, he must have been misled to confound the scouring as they call it with the original making.

Fortunately, Gough includes a sketch of the figure. It is wistful-looking with a large, round eye set just under the ear, a saddle, hoofless legs, elongated body (sometimes compared with a dachshund) and the mildest hint of a male sexual part. Gough implies an affinity with the Uffington Horse, but this is not obvious, for while the latter is fluid, mobile, arresting, this creature is homely, comical and clumsy, like a child's drawing. One notable feature is the tail, which resembles a bend in a piece of tubing and has a tuft on the end. Plenderleath (1885) identified this trifling appendage with the crescent and related it, somewhat rashly, to Ceridwen, a Welsh fertility goddess akin to the Greek Ceres, who is sometimes represented as a mare and to whom horses were considered sacred. In one of his poems Taliessin (*c.* 550 AD) refers to the 'strong horse of the crescent', an allusion to one of Ceridwen's sons by the sea-god Neptune.

Westbury Horse, after Gough, 1772.

Current Opinion and Evidence

So there are arguments, albeit frail, inconclusive ones, that the Westbury Horse, with its sickle tail and stunted appearance, may hark back to the old dark gods. However, this must remain pure conjecture because the old beast no longer exists – 'ruined by the same unenlightened spirit which has destroyed so many precious historical remains of medieval architecture.'

Plenderleath's hand-wringing lament on the passing of a noble stallion was provoked by a steward of Lord Abingdon going by the name of Mr Gee – a title, as it turned out, of uncanny appropriateness. Mr Gee, who has been branded as a wretch and an upstart, remodelled the Westbury Horse in 1778, doubling its size and strikingly altering its appearance. 'The old one', to quote Sir Richard Colt Hoare, was of the 'cart breed' and the new one 'of the blood kind'. Mr Gee produced a competent, literal portrayal of a horse, thoroughly lacking the strangeness of the original.

Plenderleath's own sketch of the two Westbury horses superimposed.

There is yet another unresolved problem concerning the Westbury Horse. The engraving in Gough's version shows it facing right but Mr Gee's handsome thoroughbred faces left. If, as has been alleged, Mr Gee completely resculpted the older figure, would he have imposed upon himself the trouble of turning it round? Plenderleath (1885) attributes this discrepancy to Gough's engraver reversing the plate, but Morris Marples (1949) demonstrates that the second horse could be contained within the body of the later animal whichever direction it faced. He includes a sketch of the old horse fitting snugly inside the belly of its successor.

T.C. Lethbridge, that spirited controversialist, expressed a different view. In *Gogmagog* (1957) he claimed that the old Westbury Horse had not been recut but merely allowed to become overgrown. 'If one looks at air photographs of the modern horse,' he wrote, 'the shadowy figure of the older animal is visible close behind it and appears very much if it had the beaked head of an Iron Age monster.' Just to emphasize this point, Lethbridge included a sketch of his own, based upon an aerial view in Marples' book, showing a most extraordinary beast, with sinister tusk-like extensions jutting from the mouth and a mysterious blanket (saddle?) draped over the body. Lethbridge at times had the almost magical gift of producing a pea-soup fog where formerly there had been a twinkling mist.

Finally there is yet another opinon – that expressed by Mary Delorme (1985). She believes that the true portrait of the original Westbury Horse is not to be found in Gough but in a map that came out a year later, in 1773, drawn by John Andrews and his partner, Drury, both surveyors and reliable recorders. Since there were two of them, they would tend to correct each other's inaccuracies or imaginative liberties.

Mary Delorme thought that Gough's steed looked 'like a dachshund of mallard ancestry', but one detail she thought accurate

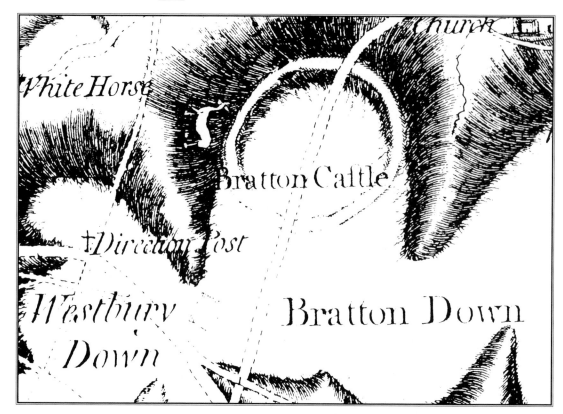

Westbury Horse on the 1773
map by Andrews and Drury.

— 'he had caught the perky lift of the ears' which Andrews and Drury
also reproduced.

> They both saw the hillside during the surveying process. The horse
> faced towards Edington, as might be expected. It had a sturdy body
> but slender legs, and it seemed to be moving forward, flicking its
> tail. The overall effect was graceful. Its accuracy may be assumed,
> for the map was intended for the nobility and gentry of the county
> of Wiltshire, of whom eighty, as subscribers, paid for its production.

Why did Gough's sketch go unchallenged if it did so little justice to
the carving? Mary Delorme does not tackle this question head-on,
but she believes that what unusual features the horse possessed were
fitting. The moon-tail was a comical grace-note rather than a tribute
to Ceridwen or any other goddess.

Intrigued by this lively counter-argument, I obtained the map of
Andrews and Drury and studied the drawing of the horse. It was very

small and did not possess quite the élan I expected from Delorme's fetching description. Its long ears were mulish, its belly saggy and pantomimic; no sign of a tail (a slightly broader hachure stroke may have been misinterpreted) and it had strange mallet-like feet.

I did not feel convinced that this was the 'definitive' portrait, being too much a quick sketch, though it stands as a sharp corrective to Gough whose drawing does not accord with his description.

Conclusion

Although the heart-rendingly pathetic appearance of the old Westbury Horse suggests the work of a highly primitive draughtsman of prehistoric times, or a highly sophisticated artist of the present day, the documentary evidence is not sufficiently convincing to adduce an early date for the carving. It probably belongs to the eighteenth century, the heyday of structural larks, when follies and grottoes were commissioned so lavishly that almost every major landowner's estate was temporarily transformed. The cult of the picturesque ruin produced a rich crop of oddities and Morris Marples in his 1949 book argues: 'In this age of false antiquities, when landowners vied with one another in the creation of fake altars, bogus tombs and sham temples, it would have been a triumphantly original idea to produce a pseudo-primitive white horse to rival the one at Uffington.' This, admittedly, is a sensible and cautious conclusion, excluding the glamour of Alfred and the grim-visaged Danes and muffling the symbolic resonance of the moon-shaped tail. These fragments are too slight to build an argument, particularly when such a normally steadfast devotee of the distant past as Francis Wise delicately hints at a fairly late date. Mary Delorme's evidence concerning the map of 1773 by Andrews and Drury would seem to support this.

Finally, Lethbridge's argument that the old horse can still be traced lurking behind the outline of the new is not to be trusted. Ardent seekers of lost hill-figures become almost preternaturally aware of faded forms, shadowy hints and half-obliterated patterns. The upshot of all this is that innocent slopes and meadows are seen as grassed-over art galleries.

CHAPTER THREE

THE RED HORSE OF TYSOE

All this evidence suggests that the enormous solid figure of the
Horse, nearly an acre in extent, was scoured by the Saxon farmers
as a Spring jollification, and as a magic ritual to ensure a good
summer and a fine crop. If one goes beyond this sober hypothesis,
one lands in a bog of folkloristic nonsense with the Corn-Spirit as
a Horse, the goddess Epona as a divine mare, the ritual slaughter
of horses and blood-broth ceremonies. It is not impious to say that
we hope our forefathers were not so silly.

(Miller and Carrdus 1965)

Introduction

Michael Drayton, a contemporary of Shakespeare, composed an
immense poetic topography called *Poly-Olbion* in which he equated
the Red Horse with his standing as a poet:

> White Horse . . . is exalted to the skies,
> My Red-Horse of you all contemned lies,
> The fault is not in me, but in the wretched time,
> On whom, upon good cause, I may well lay the crime,
> Which as all noble things, so mee it does neglect.

Self-appreciation is better than no appreciation whatsoever, and
Drayton, who composed those lines in 1612, was probably indulging
in a bout of restorative self-pity. He became Poet Laureate in 1626,
so he triumphed over his obscurity, and neither was the Red Horse
neglected. It was famous and acclaimed, and the map in *Polyolbion*
shows it grazing peacefully on a leash held by an Elizabethan lady.
Around it are the hills, streams and the standing stones known as
the Rollrights. Only in more recent times has it faded from the

race memory and been demoted to scattered entries in topographical tomes.

One difficulty is that the Red Horse, so eloquently championed by Drayton and later the Revd Mr Jago, has such a muddled history. Various figures of contrasting dimensions were cut, became overgrown and were recut. Therefore, it is necessary to resort for reliable information to its most recent chroniclers, W.G. Miller and K.A. Carrdus. Together they did much to disperse the fumes of unwarranted assumption, slipshod guesswork and garbled recollection that reduced an important hill-figure to a mere evocative name, recalling something vaguely spendid but essentially obscure.

Site and Appearance

The Red Horse was cut where the Banbury–Stratford road descends the Edgehill escarpment, about eight miles from Banbury, near the village of Lower Tysoe. Dugdale, in *Antiquities of Warwickshire* (1656, 422), described it as 'in the Red Horse ground, opposite the east window of Tysoe church', and the Enclosure Award (1798), alluded to 'certain houses and gardens under Red Horse Hill'. This latter reference enabled the site to be pinpointed just below the slope called 'The Hangings' above Old Lodge Farm, and slightly west of the Ratley–Chipping Norton road. In 1959 the hill was afforested by Lord Bearsted, and although this did not deter the pioneer work of

The Red Horse of Tysoe

Miller and Carrdus (1964), the trees have now attained maturity and mask the site.

A contemporary engraving of the Red Horse can be seen among the Aylesford Collection of Warwickshire Drawings in the Birmingham Reference Library. It shows a classically proportioned beast, conventionally handsome, with one raised foreleg and backleg, a hanging tail and details including a saddle and a longish stirrup. Also, there is a wash drawing of recent date, attempting to portray how the beast must have appeared to former generations, superimposed on a landscape of coppices and hedges.

Red Horse, from the Aylesford print.

History and Interpretation

The last Horse of Tysoe was ploughed over in 1800, but this does not appear to have been the creature of renown which attracted the notice of the early antiquaries. An allusion to Red Horse Vale is made by the cartographer John Speed in 1606, but the earliest mention of the hill-figure occurs in Camden (1607): 'Of the redy soil here comes the name of Rodway and Rodley; yea, and a great part of the very vale is thereupon termed the Vale of Red Horse, of the shape of the horse cut out in a red hill by the country people hard by Pillerton.'

Sir William Dugdale was an English antiquary born in 1605 of a good Warwickshire family. In 1644 he was made Chester Herald, and he accompanied Charles I through the Civil War. He may have viewed the Red Horse at the Battle of Edgehill (1642), for he includes an account of it in his tome devoted to Warwickshire antiquities:

> Within the precincts of that Manour of Tishoe now belonging to the Earl of Northampton (but antiently to the family of Stafford as I have showed), there is cut upon the side of Edgehill the proportion of a horse in a very large forme; which by reason of the ruddy colour of the earth is called the Red Horse, and giveth denomination to that fruitful and pleasant country thereabouts called the Vale of the Red Horse: the trenches of which ground where the shape of the said horse is so cut out, being yearly scoured by a Free-holder in this lordship who holds certain lands there by that service.

A widespread explanation for the presence of the Red Horse, fostered by the ingenious Revd Francis Wise, attributes it to a somewhat callous act of bravado by Richard, Earl of Warwick, during the Wars of the Roses. The incident took place at Towton, Yorkshire, on Palm Sunday 1461. Warwick had a force of 40,000 men opposing Queen Margaret's 60,000, and the battle was going against him. In a fit of inspired recklessness, he leapt off his horse, plunged his sword up to the hilt in the animal's side and cried aloud that he would henceforth fight shoulder-to-shoulder with his men. This combination of panache and brutality served its purpose. The earl's force revived to such an extent that 28,000 Lancastrians were said to have fallen that day.

This commemorative explanation, neat and unexceptional, typifies the bland patriotism which past scholars like Francis Wise tended to impose upon prehistoric relics. The idea that hill-figures are the upshot of bloody battles, great men and valorous incidents assumes that the unlettered peasantry expended excessive energy raising monuments to their betters. A more modern, possibly better-informed approach to such artefacts prefers to visualize them as totem objects which express the collective concerns of a tribe or community.

DIMENSIONS AND DILEMMAS

The size of the Red Horse of Tysoe is not easy to establish. Dugdale (1656) states it was of 'a very large forme' but the Revd Francis Wise (1742) dismisses it with uncharacteristic brevity and severity. Adopting the tone of a hardline Berkshire patriot, he describes it as 'vastly inferior to the Uffington Horse' and as the work of a later age and clumsier craftsmen.

Another perplexing reference occurs in Richard Gough's additions to Camden (1806). This compilation lists the dimensions of the Red Horse: from croup to chest it was 34 ft, from shoulder to ground 16 ft, while its tail 'more like a lion's' reached a full 18 ft. These humble statistics are not easy to reconcile with the marvellous beast of legend:

The Red Horse according to Gough's measurements.

> And Tysoe's wondrous theme, the martial Horse,
> Carved on the yielding turf, amorial sign
> Of Hengist, Saxon Chief! Studious to preserve
> The fav'rite form, the treach'rous conquerors,
> Their vassal tribes compel with festive rites
> Its fading figure yearly to renew
> And to the neighb'ring vale impart its name.
>
> ('Edgehill' by the Revd Mr Jago)

The map of Warwickshire made by Beighton (1727) indicates that a Red Horse lay east of Tysoe church and faced right. As the original Red Horse faced left, one presumes that this was the 'inferior' figure observed by Wise and Gough and not the majestic Saxon mare and her colt.

Convinced that the horse observed by Francis Wise and Richard Gough was not the original landmark but a later substitute, K.A. Carrdus and W.G. Miller studied all the available guidebooks before 1800, pored over the Enclosure Award of 1796 and checked and rechecked every possible reference in an attempt to establish where the original horse was cut. After a false start on a site undergoing afforestation, they concluded that the most likely location lay on a slope called the Hangings above Old Lodge Farm. This site was subjected to detailed examination. Miller photographed sections of the hillside during different times of the day; tinted filters were used so that any irregular vegetation pattern would be highlighted. After the negatives had been printed, the results clearly showed patches of light-shaded green, suggesting the shape of a large, galloping horse, which, when measured, appeared to be nearly 91 m (300 ft) long and 64 m (210 ft) high. Accompanying it was another large figure, 'two thirds the size of the original', and this may have been the foal galloping ahead of its mother.

North of the second horse the turf intimated the outline of a third beast, small, undistinguished and about 16 m (54 ft) long. It was possibly this animal, not the magnificent galloping beast and its foal, which called forth the contempt of Francis Wise (1742) and the modest statistics of Richard Gough (1806). When the highly impressive figures became grassed over, this third horse was cut to replace them and was itself ploughed over in 1800 when the proprietor of Sunrising Inn, Simon Nicholls, acquired Sunrising Farm from the Marquess of Northampton. One must assume that, after acquiring independence and full ownership, he felt no obligation to maintain the toilsome task of scouring. However, his reluctance to observe the custom cost him the patronage of the Palm Sunday scourers and his takings diminished. Dismayed, he cut yet another horse as an inn sign. This lacklustre creature resembled 'a happily inebriated pantomime horse with human feet'.

Current Opinion and Evidence

Unlike the Gogmagog hill-figures of Cambridgeshire which, upon rediscovery, were generally greeted with comments somewhat less enthusiastic than T.C. Lethbridge's bubbling prose, the Red Horse of Tysoe has been investigated and verified.

Following the discovery of a vegetation pattern on the Hangings in September 1964, a soil resistivity survey was conducted over two weekends, in September and November 1967, by Dr J.S. Stanley. Parts of the head and body were traced, and these corresponded with the cropmark disclosed by aerial survey. The readings were high in the disturbed areas and the report noted: 'Prolonged exposure of the soil would occur if a hill-figure was scoured regularly over a period, resulting in compaction of the soil and reduction of humus content which would reduce the water-holding capacity of the soil. Both these factors would tend to increase resistivity on the scoured areas.'

Impression of the Red Horse from aerial photographs.

This survey was followed by an excavation in the spring and summer of 1969. Two trenches were cut, across the ear and neck. In the region of the ear, a depression of the clay line 0.5–0.71 m (20–28 in) was recorded. The soil at the bottom was found to be different from the general subsoil, 'a rather brighter red silt' contrasting with the underlying yellow clay. This red silt – rich in iron oxide – was used to pick out the original horse. In the neck trench, the clay line was 'depressed' at both ends, indicating the edges, and an 'area of red infill' was found at the north end.

Further confirmation of the site's significance was found in the geophysical survey of 1980 conducted by C. Heathcote. It drew attention to the effect a long-standing hill-figure might have on the soil.

Variations in the resistivity of the soil occur naturally but also can be produced by the activities of men. Structures of stone (walls, floors, etc.) of high resistivity and infilled ditches, which tend to have lower resistivities than the subsoil, are the usual features sought by the earth resistance method. It is thought that changes in the soil profile could be brought about by the continued exposure associated with hill figures. The surface layers of soil could have been exposed to the effects of wind and rain due to the removal of all forms of vegetation and root systems for perhaps hundreds of years – any changes would be expected to be limited in depth. The correlation between the resistivity results of Dr Stanley and the aerial photographs is very good, the high resistivity areas corresponding to the poorer areas of plant development.

The results of this test were presented in a form of a shaded contour plot which acknowledged the presence 'of two recognisably horse-like figures', one possibly overlapping the other, together with a third 'linear feature' of high resistivity running diagonally across the hillside. To an untrained eye, the patterns seem complex, dislocated and smudgy, but if one allows for non-surveyed areas and attempts to piece together the isolated shapes, there can be little doubt that the old Red Horse and its attendants occupied this site.

Such disclosures led to the idea of recutting the old Saxon Horse and restoring the Stour Valley to the status it possessed when Celia Fiennes, the indomitable rider, described it in the late seventeenth century: 'We went by Eshum [Evesham] and the Vale of the Red Horse, being a Vale of great extent, the earth is all red, it's a very rich Country for corn and fruites and woodes; it's called the Vale of Eshum or of the Red Horse from a red horse cut on some of the hills about it, and the earth all looking red the horse lookes so as that of White Horse Vale.'

However, as Miller and Carrdus observed, the task is a hopeless one. The Edgehill escarpment south of Sunrising Farm has been afforested, and the Red Horse lies buried beneath roots, brambles and furze and is now part of England's ancient, irrecoverable heritage.

Nevertheless, despite the fact that the beast is erased from living memory, local place-names enable more emphatic conclusions to be drawn than is usual with most English hill-figures. The name Tysoe signifies 'spur of land dedicated to Tiw', the Germanic Mars, who, like other warrior-deities, was multi-functional and in times of peace served as a patron of agriculture. Tacitus informs us that the Germans sacrificed for victory (usually prisoners of invading armies) to Mars and Mercury – that is, to Tiw and Woden. The early title of the god was Tiwaz, related to the Greek Zeus; this sky-god possessed only one hand, the other having been bitten off by the Fenris wolf. In England the third day of the week, Tuesday or Tiwaz-day, bears his title.

The Angles who colonized the Stour Valley *c*. AD 600 probably cut the large Red Horse, accompanied by its foal, to emphasize fecundity and fruitfulness, and Palm Sunday, the Sunday preceding Easter when Christ entered Jerusalem, was the traditional time of scouring.

The Red Horse from Michael Drayton's *Poly-Olbion*

Reconstructed image of Red Horse on Old Lodge Hill (*Carrdus & Miller*).

RITUAL AND RELIGION

Spring unfolds in March, the month of Martius or Mars, the Roman god of war and agriculture, who can be fairly equated with Tiw, for the horse was sacred to both. In the Roman religion, on 14

March a racing festival was held in honour of the god. This was called 'Equirria' and took place on the Campus Martius, or Field of Mars. Other races and celebrations to placate this important deity punctuated the year. On 15 October, there were chariot-races, wherein the horse of the winning team was sacrificed to the divinity. The blood of its tail was dripped onto the hearth of the king's former residence, the Regia. Also, more barbarically, horses were sometimes driven over precipices as offerings to the oceanic deities.

Heroic nineteenth-century image of Tyr or Tiwaz

The Salian (from the Latin *salire* 'to leap or dance') priests, who practised the cult of Mars, held rituals in March to promote crop growth and fertility. Chanting old hymns to the god, they would process along a fixed route carrying outmoded spears and shields, stopping to beat the ground and summon the earth's fruitfulness. A ritual three-step governed their progress, and their ceremony was deemed to cleanse the community and its utensils.

Although it is an unwarranted assumption that such rites reflect the Tysoe scouring ceremony, there exist striking points of resemblance in all primitive horse rites. This likeness is further strengthened by the similarities between Tiw and Mars, both being patrons of war and agriculture, and the vernal nature of the festivities.

Lying north of Tysoe are the Spring and Sunrising Hills. This tends to confirm that the Red Horse bears reference to the first equinox of the year, approximately 22 March, and featured as a focus for the Angles' 'spring jollification'. Assuming that the more eloquent records preserved by the Romans do apply to the Warwickshire carving, it may be inferred that the Angles indulged in horse-racing and martial rites, together with the sacrificing of horses and the eating of their flesh.

How Tiw's festival became entangled with Palm Sunday is none too clear. Perhaps, at a loss to correlate the scouring ceremony with anything in their calendar, the church decided to imply that the huge Saxon emblem portrayed the ass on which Christ rode into Jerusalem.

Conclusion

Although there are legends associating the Red Horse with figures like the Saxon Hengist and with the Wars of the Roses, the soundest theory, which has gained broad acceptance, relates it to the Angles

who settled in the Stour Valley *c*. AD 600. The investigations of
Miller and Carrdus (1965) shed useful light on the sheer multiplicity
of horses carved around the original site. Odds and ends of data are
tidily resolved and dovetailed in their admirable booklet. Predictably
some of their findings and assertions have been challenged, but their
research forms the bedrock of current knowledge of the Red Horse.
The Warwickshire Museum Sites and Monuments Record has little
to say about the Red Horse on the Hangings, calling it a 'ceremonial
hill-figure' to which Saxon, medieval and post-medieval dates have
been ascribed, adding that it was probably obliterated when the
common field was enclosed in 1798. The smaller horse at Sunrising
Covert is listed on another sheet.

A FIFTH HORSE?

Once the idea of cutting horses in turf seizes the mind, a strange
process may take hold, akin to a kind of psychic equine impregnation.
This seems to have occurred at Tysoe, for, apart from the four horses
already chronicled, there appears to have been a fifth creature cut on
Spring Hill, to the south of the trees in Sunrising Covert. This was
attested by Mr J. Smith, who was employed at Sunrising House, and
a local teacher, Mrs Wright. No one seems to know who cut it, and
there is a faint element of doubt about its existence. Yet some memory
of it lingers, like the Cheshire Cat's grin.

MORE LOST GODS AT TYSOE

> I tried to recover the lost Red Horse; I failed to do so . . . What I
> did find was something which I think is even more interesting: a
> collection of four great hill-figures representing the legend of the
> Saxon god Tiw (or Tiu or Tig).
>
> (S.G. Wildman 1971)

The problem of deciphering hill-figures is even more dramatically
highlighted in the escapade of S.G. Wildman who, in a charmingly
unorthodox book, argued that the well-known inn sign of the Black
Horse bears reference to King Arthur. The British chieftain, in his
view, utilized large black Fresian horses well suited to hard riding
and down the years his highly mobile cavalrymen, moving from
engagement to engagement, made a nick in folk memory and finally
were enshrined in pub lore.

While engaged upon Arthurian fieldwork, Wildman found himself in Tysoe and became curious about the possibility of recovering the old Red Horse. He contacted another interested party, Mr Graham Miller, who took him to a site south of Sunrising Hill, where Spring Hill curved back into a bowl-shaped inlet in the escarpment. The site had been planted with small trees, mostly larches, and the hillside was reverting to wildness. This was a disappointment to Wildman – he had hoped to undertake an ecological survey – but then another idea occurred to him. All of the trees had been planted in a regular pattern and, if some of them had been actually seeded in the area of the Red Horse, might not they grow taller as a result of the deeper soil? So he suggested to Mr Miller that the tree rows be systematically measured and recorded on paper.

The business turned out to be tedious and arduous but after a few months, and aided by volunteers and friends, they had measured thirty-five vertical rows of trees. Next the statistics were transferred to a grid chart, all the tall trees being set down as isolated dots, so that they could be eventually joined to form a pattern. When this was complete, the outlines of two horses, oddly elongated, were identified by Wildman. However, Miller was more sceptical. To him the procedure seemed like arbritary picture-making. Besides, he had recently unearthed an old map clearly indicating that he had selected the wrong site and the true Red Horse lay elsewhere.

So Mr Miller amicably abandoned the exercise while Mr Wildman, becoming more resolute, doggedly pursued his discovery. He wrote to the *Birmingham Post* about his undertaking; the article was published and offers of help came his way, but weather and other adverse circumstances held up the project. Things only gained momentum when there came an unexpected offer of aerial photographs, taken on a clear day in December 1965.

Wildman was excited by the photographs but uncertain how to interpret them, so he contacted a friend, Dennis Jones, whose wartime services had made him familiar with such evidence. Upon scrutiny, the form of a horse with a huge mane of curls could be made out, together with the outline of a 48 m man brandishing a whip, a vaguely ornithological shape and a sprawling, indistinct mass beneath them.

In the same way that Lethbridge, intent on finding one giant figure, was rewarded with the discovery of a complex mural, Wildman found himself presented with the figure of a man with a whip, a dragon-like top horse, a bird which he thought was a goose, and a lumbering dead-looking animal beneath it all. 'If genuine,' he remarked, 'there was nothing like it in England, indeed in the world.' He concluded that it represented Tiw asserting his mastery over the horse with his whip; and the accompanying goose, a bird associated with solar myth, may have been an attribute or avatar arising from the cadaver of the slaughtered animal below.

Wildman's book attracted some scepticism, but it seems clear that his discovery was not wholly imaginary – indeed, his design may have been composed from traces of the two later horses cut on Spring Hill. He went to the trouble of analysing the soil and found long, friable strips indicating disturbance in the past. Furthermore, the forestry foreman, Mr Hopkins, confirmed the presence of soft, powdery soil running in continuous lines.

As for the elaborate pattern of the god and goose, that is a more difficult matter, the forms we observe being conditioned by a combination of physical makeup and cultural implant. In Kant's words, 'our representation of things, as they are given, does not conform to these things as they are in themselves, but that these objects as appearances conform to our modes of representation.' Everyone who has looked at a cloud, a dried leaf, the stump of a tree, the whorl pattern in a shell, tends to extend a familar metaphor. We translate from nature the morphologies closest to us – clouds are like wool, shells the human ear, daffodils trumpets. The imagination is always forcing a relationship between random pattern and established form, and it is this tendency that places a question-mark beside such discoveries of long-lost hill-figures.

CHAPTER FOUR

MIGHTY QUEENS AND SACRED STALLIONS

Horses, always horses! How the horse dominated the mind of the early races, especially of the Mediterranean. You were a lord if you had a horse. Far back, far back in our dark soul the horse prances. He is a dominant symbol: he gives us lordship: he links us, the first palpable and throbbing link with the ruddy-glowing Almighty of potence: he is the beginning even of our godhead in the flesh. And as a symbol he roams the dark underworld meadows of the soul. He stamps and threshes in the dark fields of your soul and mine. The sons of God who came down and knew the daughters of man and begot the great Titans, they had 'the members of horses' says Enoch.

(D.H. Lawrence 1930)

To recapture the primary meaning of the Uffington Horse, it is necessary to look at the religious practices of our prehistoric ancestors. Not that they were the first devotees of the horse, for the animal was an icon of the Scandinavian peoples. In the renowned Trundholm chariot, dating from the Middle Bronze Age, it was styled as the draught animal of the sun which it charioted across the blue fields of the sky. A trace of this solar significance is possibly retained in Uffington's association with St George, a Christian martyr who, like Perseus, slew a dragon and acquired the characteristics of a sun-god. Further traces of a British horse-cult may be traced from Scotland to Wales, from Warwickshire to Dorset where, on the hills above Portesham, there are the remains of a long barrow called Old Grey Mare and her Colts, in front of which used to be a crudely carved head of a horse.

However, the union of horse and man extends beyond any local cult. Six thousand years ago, on the bleak steppes of the Ukraine, a stallion was elaborately buried in a ritual grave. This animal had not only been hunted and killed for food, but it had also been domesticated and ridden by its owner. It was one of the thousands whose bleached bones decorate the inhospitable wastes and whose incredible speed transmitted that euphoric surge of energy and control to the rider. The wild horse conferred kingship upon the horseman who must have felt for the first time in his life that he was possessed of a strength far beyond his normal power of summoning. It is perhaps ironic that this shy and most sensitive of creatures was utilized as an agent of war and intimidation. The pounding of hooves heralded the sacking of camps and villages and, as the prestige of the mounted warrior grew, the horse became an iconic object, worthy of prayer and praise.

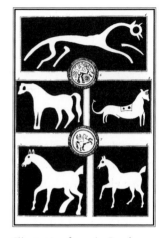

Illustration from the Revd W.C. Plenderleath's 'White Horses of Wiltshire', *Wiltshire Archaeological Magazine*, 1874:
1. Uffington White Horse;
2. Westbury White Horse;
3. Westbury White Horse according to Gough;
4. Pewsey White Horse;
5. Cherhill White Horse;
6 & 7. Ancient British Coins.

What is incontrovertible is that the veneration of horses was diffused centuries before the Christian era and appears to have continued in an unbroken tradition down through the early Greeks, Romans, Celts and Saxons. This hints at a uniformity of belief and brings into question the value of the many racial and cultural distinctions. The Uffington Horse was regularly repaired and scoured despite the onslaught of several waves of invaders – so how marked were the differences between these peoples? Although wave after wave of migrations are conceded to have taken place, with successive factions dispossessing one another's property and lands, miraculously the Horse was dug out and built up with hunks of fresh chalk as if its primacy as a religious symbol was immediately acknowledged.

The high value placed on horses is underlined in the writings of the Classical authors and their successors. Herodotus relates how, when Cyrus, King of Persia, arrived at the River Gyndes, one of his sacred horses plunged 'through wantonness' into the stream and drowned. The King deferred the invasion of Babylon and punished the river by ordering his troops to dig up the channel. For a whole summer, they toiled at the arduous project, until the broad-flowing current had been divided into 180 separate rivulets, so harmless that a woman was capable of fording them without wetting her knees.

This story, almost certainly apocryphal, has a laughable quality similar to that of Caligua promoting his steed, Incitatus, to the rank of priest and consul, but it is nevertheless related by Herodotus with gravity, as if the avenging of one's grievances on natural phenomena was a permissible act. In later chapters, the same historian tells us that sacred horses preceded Xerxes himself during the crossing of the Hellespont.

Five centuries later, Tacitus relates how the Teutonic tribes kept horses in their sacred groves and observed their neighings and whinnyings as auguries. Believing the horses to be favourites of the gods, privy to vital information, they naturally kept an alert ear to what insights might be relayed. Such rites appear to have been passed down to the Anglo-Saxons who, when seeking counsel on important issues, listened closely to equine responses, as presaging the outcome of battles. They also resorted to harupiscation – the inspection of beasts' entrails – as a method of foretelling the future.

An eleventh-century historian, the Bishop of Merseburg, described how the Danes assembled at their capital 'called Lethra' and there sacrificed to their gods 'ninety-nine men, and as many horses, together with dogs and cocks'. A feast followed the sacrifice which required the king or leader to ingest the uncooked flesh.

Hengist and Horsa landing in Kent. Their horse banner is being borne up behind.

Perhaps the most disconcerting account of this type of ceremony is set down by Giraldus Cambrensis in his *Topography of Ireland* (*c.* 1185). He graphically evokes 'a most barbarous and abominable rite' whereby the people of northern Ulster create their 'king'. The tribes of that country gather together and a white mare is led into their midst. The man elected to be king debases himself before them, confessing that he is no better than a beast, after which the mare is killed, cut in pieces and boiled, and then a bath is prepared for the king. Sitting upright in this gory, intestinal stew, he laps the broth with his mouth, and in this manner 'his royal authority and dominion are ratified'.

The meaning is reasonably straightforward. Before being elected leader, a man is obliged to act out, or mimic, the role of stallion to mare, after which the real horse is killed, and he is required to bathe in its blood and ingest its body-substance. By swallowing and immersion, the man partakes of the most enviable qualities of the horse: sexual potency and fecundity. This was vital to a king: his virility mirrored the health of the tribe, and any deficiency in this area might be reflected back on them.

Despite their unappetizing ceremonies, the Celts are known to have valued their horses. The destinies of their warrior-heroes are sometimes portrayed as being bound up with their steeds. They are shown being born at the same time as their mounts, sharing exploits and adventures, and in certain instances exhibiting their prominent sexual features. Fergus mac Roich, a renowned Irish hero, was 'Fergus, son of Great Horse' and, like a well-reared stallion, possessed large genitals, requiring seven women to appease him.

A FINE LADY

Female Deities also shared equine characteristics. Rhiannon, a Celtic queen, did penance after murdering her son by emulating a horse and carrying strangers astride her back to court. The Roman Epona, often compared with Rhiannon, was a protectress of horses and also connected with fertility: a bronze from Wiltshire shows her with ears of corn in her lap, accompanied by horses with protruding tongues. Birds also number among her attributes, and on a tile from Roussas, Drôme, in France, Epona rides on the back of a kind of antlered goose.

Horse-Goddess Epona.

So the horse-goddess cannot be narrowed and fixed to a mere patron of cavalrymen. Ears of wheat and geese establish a broader context of meaning, the first standing for richness and fertility, the second being a bird that is sometimes depicted drawing the sun-chariot. Conceivably an echo of such a confident horsewoman filtered down through the ages and surfaced in nursery rhyme:

> Ride a cock horse
> To Banbury Cross,
> See a fine lady upon a fine horse:
> Rings on her fingers, bells on her toes,
> And she shall have music wherever she goes.

The origins of these lines have been particularized as referring to Celia Fiennes, daughter of Colonel Nathaniel Fiennes, Governor of Bristol during the Civil War. In 1697 she undertook a grand tour of the north of England on horseback; her stately bearing and quality apparel so impressed the country folk that the traditional jingle became attached to her.

However, the closeness of Banbury to both Tysoe, the site of the Red Horse, and Southam and Coventry, where Godiva ceremonies were enacted, suggests the lady has a longer ancestry. The allusion to rings and bells, producing pleasant jingling sounds, may refer to the belief that evil spirits could be deterred by such sweet sounds: church bells were supposed to summon the good and repel the wicked.

The story of Lady Godiva of Coventry is best known as a Christian fable. Briefly it recounts how certain exactions were imposed upon the citizens of Coventry by Leofric, Earl of Mercia. When his wife, Lady Godiva, interceded, Leofric laughed at her and informed her, half jocularly, that he would grant her request if she would ride naked through the streets of Coventry. Taking her husband at his word, Godiva requested that all apertures and windows should be blocked, and that no one should look out till noon was past. Then she mounted her palfrey and rode naked through the town. She returned to Leofric who, in fulfilment of his promise, freed the citizens from the burden he had imposed.

Yet there is a further incident in the legend. One citizen, 'Peeping Tom', did briefly rest his eyes upon Godiva's body, for which transgression he was struck blind, recalling the punishment meted out to Actaeon who stumbled upon the moon-goddess Diana bathing with her sylph-like attendants.

Although the real Godiva was a known benefactress of Coventry who, together with her husband, restored the monastery of St Osburg, there is little fact in the legend, which may pick up on something older. In fact, it is feasible that the tyrannical earl and his tender-hearted wife are historical embroideries of ancient horse-ceremonies, uniting the male and female principles. The element of nudity was of prime importance, for the bare hide of the horse was thought capable of transmitting its aura to the flesh of its rider.

Lady Godiva by John Collier (1897), a tasteful Victorian eroticisation of the legend. The first recorded Godiva procession took place in Coventry in 1678. James Swinnerton's son stood in for Lady Godiva; a medal was struck in commemoration.

THE BLACK GODDESS

At the village of Southam, hard by Coventry, in the eighteenth century another Godiva festival took place at the end of May. In this event, however, the procession was headed by a man wearing a bull's mask and horns. He was dubbed 'Old Brazen Face', a title intimating radiance and solar power, bringing to mind Homer's 'Oxen of the Sun' and the horned Ooser of Dorset. Following after him were two Godivas, one dressed in white lace, the other stained entirely black, after the fashion of the early British tribes during their festivals (Pliny records that 'they resembled swarthy Ethiopians'). Coventry was in the area occupied by the Brigantes. These peoples worshipped a female deity later Christianized as St Brigit, referred to variously as Danu, Anu and Black Annis of Leicestershire, who appears to have been an important fertility figure.

So, tentatively, we may deduce that the bull-masked figure denotes a solar deity, the White Godiva and Black Godiva the two opposing aspects of the goddess, winter and summer, sterility and abundance. Black is associated with death or sacrifice, and black sheep and goats were traditionally offered to Demeter in Greece. Also, the women who got caught under the skirts of the Padstow

Obby Oss – another black-painted effigy – formerly had their legs marked with charcoal.

The Beltane rites of the village of Callander in western Perthshire featured a huge bonfire, lit to encourage the sun towards harvest, and a large cake known as the Beltane Cake. After it had been prepared, it was divided into several portions among the people. One piece was daubed all over with charcoal until perfectly black, and then all the bits of cake were put together in a bonnet. Each participant was then blindfolded and required to draw out a portion, the last piece being reserved for the person holding the bonnet:

> Whoever draws the black bit is the devoted person who is to be sacrificed to Baal. They now pass through the act of sacrificing, and only compel the devoted person to leap three times through the flames.

> (D.A. Mackenzie 1935)

Why Baal? Baal was the Phoenician and Semitic weather-god, sometimes depicted as a warrior with springing bull's horns, but one would hardly expect to find him at a traditional Scottish function. In this context, one presumes Baal to be a corruption of Belinus fostered by ardent Bible-reading. Belinus was a Celtic pastoral god, lord of Beltane, and a figure sometimes argued over by Celtic scholars. Did he have a solar character? Does his name imply bright or shining one? Is Belinus the original of 'Old Brazen Face' who accompanied the two Godivas at the Southam procession? Was it his duty to impregnate the waiting earth? The penance of leaping through the flames to mollify him sounds a little sinister, and we are told that the Druids drove cattle between fires during a similar ceremony. Sacrifices may have taken place too during the pagan period.

This is not to infer that, because Godiva was blacked over, she was, originally, a sacrificial victim. Rather, she deputized for the night-side of the goddess. The colour – or absence of colour – reflected darkness, winter, death, the negative aspect of growth, when light and warmth are withheld and offerings – perhaps blood offerings – were required for placation. The hag-like version of Brigantia, known as Black Annis, reappears in folklore as a taloned, child-eating witch.

In connection with Peeping Tom, the shrine of Brigiddu, or Brigantia, in Kildare, Ireland, was enclosed by a fence through which no man was allowed to pass or peep. Intimate communion with

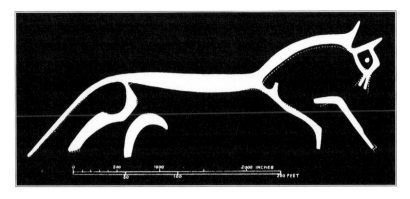

Uffington Horse.

the goddess appears to have been the prerogative of her virginal handmaidens, and the tradition of ritually blinding rule-breakers, like ritual decapitation, was not unknown to the pagan Celts.

Therefore, it is possible to see in such an ostensibly stark image as the Uffington Horse a corpus of associations, winter and springtime, death and growth, sacrifice and rebirth. For just as the Christian emblem of the lamb symbolizes an entire doctrine with its attendant rituals, so does the hill-figure embody a theology of its own.

St George and the Obby Oss

After the Christianization of the Celts and Anglo-Saxons, the sacrifice of live animals was discouraged. Even the eating of horseflesh was considered an unclean act. Pope Gregory III in his *Epistle to Boniface* (AD 737) alludes to it as an 'execrable habit' and exhorts the Apostle of Germany to 'impose a suitable penance upon the offenders'.

What did continue to flourish, however, was the adoption by men of animals' skins and horns – another diversion which offended the Early Church Fathers. 'If you ever hear anyone carrying out that most filthy practice of dressing up like a horse or stag,' St Augustine declared, 'chastise him most severely.' The latter custom, deriving from sympathetic magic and intimate communion with the natural world, appears to be one of the few legacies of Celtic life on which information can be freely drawn. Let us consider the classic surviving relic of horse magic.

The mask of the Padstow Obby Oss.

Every year, on May Day, at Padstow in Cornwall, an Obby Oss ceremony takes place wherein a monstrous effigy, made out of hoopwork, tarpaulin and sprays of horsehair, is paraded through the streets to the accompaniment of singing and a crashing Breton drum. The Oss is attended by a Teazer, a man holding a phallic club who, as his title implies, teases the Oss by thrusting his implement below and above its body. The songs which accompany this mime have altered over the years and many versions of the May Day song exist. Several of these variant texts, with their references to invading French soldiers and local residents, would appear to obscure the significance of the ceremony. The following may be cited:

Centaur – mythical creature arising from the impact of the early mounted warrior on the peoples of the eastern Mediterranean.

> O where is St George? O where is he O?
> He is in his longboat upon the salt sea O.
> And for to fetch the summer home, the summer and the May O!
> For summer is acome, and winter is ago.

What is the significance of St George in this context? A popular explanation alleged that the by-play of the Oss and Teazer, together with the symbolic death of the monster following the end of the Day Song, re-enacts the legendary battle with the dragon, but this is an accretion or late medieval assimilation.

Uffington too has draconian associations, for the White Horse has been identified with the crocodilean serpent slain by the saint near Beirut. Tradition attributes the grassless patch crowning Dragon Hill to the deleterious effects of the monster's blood. The nearby church honours the saint and Job Cork's rhyme extols his valour:

> If it is true, as I heerd zay,
> King Garge did here the dragon zlay,
> And down below on yonder hill
> They buried he, as I've heard tell.

Therefore both at Padstow, the scene of the May Day festivities, and at Uffington, the site of the chalk carving, St George features prominently, yet his presence remains enigmatic.

As we have seen, such ceremonies were once widespread and frowned upon by the Church, primarily because they were associated with sexual licence. Religious teachers took the view that man, being made in the image of God, should be duly satisfied with such a glorious resemblance and not yearn to frisk and prance in animal attire. Yet seeing that the banning of such ceremonies would be unacceptable, the Church decided to tone them down and effect a shift of significance by absorbing them into harmless pageants. Old religious tales, drawn from the *Golden Legend*, became garbled and mixed with earlier customs, and years later, after further additions, the resultant knot would be almost impossible to disentangle.

Conceivably many of the large municipal pageants, incorporating St George, St Margaret and the dragon, absorbed elements from the rumbustious Obby Osses caperings observed by Walter Scott, Harrison Ainsworth and others. Rather than suppressing them, the Church imposed its own meaning: hence the duel between summer and winter, death and rebirth, pregnancy and sterility, assumed the guise of a straight good-versus-evil confrontation. St George was a natural favourite, his feast-day falling on 4 May, the last day of the ceremonies. It is likely that he supplanted Michael as a hero-saint, being less august and more amenable to country-folk. Once George had been adopted as the Crusaders' patron, he became ubiquitous; similarly, Margaret of Antioch enjoyed an equally strong cult, being associated with women in childbirth as well as dragons.

Assimilation of pagan rites affected the character of Christian heroes. St George absorbed the qualities of a horse-god, presumably Celtic, and at the well of Llan San Sior, near Abegele, horses were actually sacrificed to him. The female goddesses associated with horses and fertility were masked by personages like St Margaret and Lady Godiva, devout females who paraded through the streets of Coventry and Leicester on palfreys.

So the Christian saints became riders of white steeds. Although the early Church Fathers thought the horse haughty and lascivious (it was said to neigh longingly when it saw a woman pass), its working usefulness was indisputable; the colour, or absence of it, implied purity. They adopted the White Horse in the manner they had adopted the image of the cross, the Madonna and Child, the brazen sun-disc, the festival of Christmas and other icons of faiths they had superseded. Albert Crantz (d. 1515), author of works on the ecclesiastical and political history of Europe, provides an example of such a switchback: 'Witichund, upon his conversion from the darkness of paganism was the first who took the white colt for his device, in allusion to the brightness of Christianity, having till that time used a black one.' Similarly Mr W.J. Thoms, in a letter to the Society of Antiquaries (1846), suggested that the Uffington Horse stood as a memorial to the conversion of the Saxons.

Hence the snowy mount, its pagan riders unseated, was mounted by St George, St Michael and St Margaret, and after them by Sir Gawain, whose steed was called Gryngolet, together with various

This famous 18,000 year old cave painting of the 'dancing shaman' is found in *Les Trois Frères* in the French Pyrenees and recalls the rulings of Archbishop Theodor (AD 668-90) in his *Penitentials*: 'If anyone at the kalends of January goes about as a stag or a bull, that is, making himself into a wild animal and dressing in the skin of a herd animal, and putting on the heads of beasts...penance for three years because this is devilish.'

other standard-bearers of Christ. Its spectral association with death and the underworld became forgotten.

ALL CATTLE

To grasp the significance of the white horse, in terms of recurring seasonal ceremony, it is useful to invoke the appearance on the Gower coast at midwinter of the Mar Llywyd, a beribboned skull-type head carried by a cloaked man, as well as these midsummer rites taken from Charlotte Elizabeth's *Personal Recollections* (1847):

> On that great festival of the Irish peasantry St John's Eve, it is the custom at sunset on that evening, to kindle immense fires throughout the country, built, like our bonfires, to a great height, the pile being composed of turf, bogwood, and other such combustible substances as they can gather. The turf yields a steady, substantial body of fire, the bogwood a most brilliant flame, and the effect of these great beacons blazing on every hill, sending up volumes of smoke from every point on the horizon, is very remarkable. Early in the evening the peasants began to assemble, all habited in their best array, glowing with health, every countenance full of that sparkling animation and excess of enjoyment that characterises the enthusiastic people of the land. I had never seen anything resembling it, and was exceedingly delighted with their handsome, intelligent, merry faces; the bold bearing of the men, and the playful but really modest deportment of the maidens; the vivacity of the aged people, and the wild glee of the children. The fire, being kindled, a splendid blaze shot up; and for a while they stood contemplating it with faces strangely disfigured by the peculiar light which was first emitted when the bogwood was thrown on it. After a short pause, the ground was cleared in front of an old blind piper, the very *beau ideal* of energy, drollery and shrewdness, who, seated on a low chair with a well-plenished jug within his reach, screwed his pipes to the liveliest tunes, and the endless jig began. When the fire burned low, an indispensable part of the ceremony commenced. Every one of the peasantry passed through it, and several children were thrown across the sparkling embers; while a wooden frame of some eight feet long, with a horse's head fixed to one end, and a large white sheet thrown over it, concealing the wood and the man on whose head it was carried, made its appearance. This was greeted with

loud shouts as the 'white horse', and having been safely, by the skill of its bearer, several times through the fire with a bold leap, it pursued the people, who ran screaming in every direction. I asked what the horse was meant for, and was told it represented all cattle.

The shining face of Belenos, god of Beltane

On hearing such an explanation, the authoress was disquieted. 'Here,' she said, 'was the old pagan worship of Baal if not of Moloch too, carried on openly and universally in the heart of a nominally Christian country, and by millions professing the Christian name.'

Here again, to get to the crux of the matter, Baal needs to be substituted with Bel or Belinus, a Celtic god known through some thirty inscriptions in North Italy, Gaul and elsewhere. Beltane derives from *Bel-tene* or 'goodly fire' and was a time for the ritual purification of cattle. St John is hardly a credible saint of cattle (although often depicted in a coat of sheepskin) and his feast-day, 24 June, falls within the first half of the Celtic Feast of Lughnasa, traditionally extending over a month, fifteen days before 1 August and fifteen days after. One has difficulty tracing his conversion into a fire-saint and the conflagrations of May and June are best seen as earth-urging strategies, the earlier to boost the tender green shoots, and the later to ensure a ripening towards harvest. One presumes the 'white horse', prancing and lunging amid the embers, stands for the continuity of the agricultural cycle. It is the very spirit of survival – the self-renewing flame that springs from the ashes of its own destruction.

CHAPTER FIVE

THE CERNE GIANT

In the sequestered valley, and hard by the spot where Æthelmar's monastery once flourished, the eye is arrested by the apparition of a gigantic human figure, rudely sculptured on the side of a lofty hill, which to a person unaccustomed to the sight is an astounding, and, probably, a repulsive object. There, with outstretched arm and uplifted club, as though he were a tutelary Divinity of the quaint old town of Cerne Abbas, he stands in apparent defiance of the degenerate race below, with whom he owns neither kith nor kin.

(Dr Wake Smart in Warne's *Ancient Dorset*, 1872)

Introduction

Postcards of the Cerne Giant are said to be the only pornographic material the Post Office is willing to handle. He is the most detailed of the ancient hill-figures. Eyes, nose, mouth, ribs, breast, genitalia and notches on his club – all are strongly rendered. The head is round, but not chubby or genial. It is more like the rudimentary features a child might scribble on a sketch of the sun, and the notion that he deputizes for that flaming star is often postulated.

Natives of Dorset have tended to attach more significance to the extended phallus than the club, although the latter is the larger feature. Courting couples walk around him hand-in-hand and pass comment on his manifest virility. Married women, fearing desertion by the spouses, have been known to climb the hillside and ask the Giant to bless their union. If we are to believe folklorists, newlyweds and engaged couples have actually consummated their relationship between the massive chalk thighs.

Above the figure rises Giant Hill crowned by a miniature earthwork known as the Trendle or Frying Pan. In the valley below is the small town of Cerne Abbas, endowed with the ruins of a Benedictine abbey, founded by Æilmar, Earl of Cornwall. Ælfric (d. 1006), author of *Colloquies*, was the most renowned abbot; his piety and erudition contrast markedly with that of Thomas Corton, the last abbot, who was said to have fathered illegitimate offspring and accosted girls in the street. The remains of the abbey lie near the churchyard from which rises a spring of clear water enclosed by a small stone courtyard. St Augustine is alleged to have bidden this fount into being. According to a local guidebook, if you stand here, with your back to the Giant, cupping a laurel leaf, you may be granted a wish.

This would seem to indicate that the hill-figure's unsqueamish virility was regarded as a distraction, an immense graffito that shouted loud preoccupations usually sublimated or bracketed. As Llewelyn Powys observed in 1935, 'Many an honest Puritan must have eyed it askance from under his broad black hat; and during the decades of Queen Victoria's reign it must have offered an uncivil affront to the refined susceptibilities of the ladies and gentlemen, who in comfortable carriages smelling of expensive upholstery hot in the sun, rolled along the dusty roads from Sherborne to Dorchester.'

Today the Giant is owned by the National Trust. The original estate passed through several hands, the last and probably the most notable being the Pitt Rivers family who sold most of their properties in Cerne Abbas in 1919 for £96,767. Lot 1 of the auction included 'Giant Hill with its Sculptured Hill Figure' but at the last moment the Giant was reserved out of the sale and later handed over with an endowment to the Trust.

Site and Appearance

Although the rude, uncouth appearance of the Giant is often emphasized, the carving is graceful and compact. The protective fence makes him appear pinned down Gulliver-fashion and is perhaps an unfortunate necessity. The National Trust tends him lovingly as if he were a small park or garden. No ugly cement blocks are used on the site; every detail is tidily trenched and the setting, on Giant Hill east of the A352 Sherborne–Dorchester road, crystallizes the placid beauty of the sheep-trimmed Dorsetshire downs.

Unfortunately, the figure cannot be properly appreciated from the ground; the angle of the slope, less than 30°, is too gentle. Across the valley, from Weam Hill, it is possible to gain a better impression of his shape and proportions, but from the popular vantage point of the Trust car park (see p. viii), he appears, old, squat, grotesque, like a squashed ogre rather than the virile club-wielder beloved of Wessex patriots. Only from the air can one appreciate the Giant's relationship with the surrounding landscape. The Trendle arises above his head, a delicate, undramatic earthwork; Eastfield Drove – one of the three great open fields of medieval Cerne – runs past his feet; and then, dotted around, are the chalkpits, animal tracks and clumps of tree which characterize this part of the world.

The physical features are obvious or speak for themselves. Notably, the legs and feet are shown in profile, as if stepping to the left, and the elbow carrying the club is unnaturally long and rounded. Furthermore, he is neckless and lacking a navel – a feature investigated by L.V. Grinsell in 1980. Although the legs are drawn sideways, the face and chest confront the observer head-on, but the effect is neither awkward nor distorted, for one takes in the primitivism of technique in much the same way one accepts a relief on an early Greek vase.

A markedly Celtic feature of the Giant is the round babylike head. The nose is formed by a narrow ridge that once splayed out incorporating the eyes and producing the effect – intentionally, it seems – of a subsidiary phallus (although this might be pure neurosis – studying the Giant over long periods tends to produce fixations of this type). More interesting is the fact that a sightline taken vertically up the 30 ft penis aligns true east with the summer sun as it rises above the hills.

There have been several surveys of the Giant. Some of them – notably Hutchins' in 1774 – have omitted the phallus altogether. The earliest is found in the *Gentleman's Magazine* of 1764 and is prefaced by a brief account:

> This monstrous figure, viewed from the opposite hill, appears almost erect with a huge crab tree club in his hand, raised over his head, just going to strike a blow, which seems sufficient to overturn a mountain. As I send you the dimensions of this figure, which I took myself, I hope some of your ingenious correspondents will favour us with an account of its origin and use; it is supposed to be above a thousand years standing, as there is a date between his legs, and the figures are not legible. It is plain there were but three figures, so that supposing the first to be 9, it must be formed a long while ago. Some think it was

Looking up the axis of the
Giant's phallus.

cut by the Antient Britons, and that they worshipped it; others
believe it to be the work of the Papists, as here was formerly an
abbey, but however that be, his dimensions are as follows:

Length of his foot	8
Breadth of the same	8
Ditto of the small of the leg	8
Ditto of the calf	12
Ditto of the thigh	18
Length of the leg and thigh	85
From the top of the thigh to the top of the head	95
Whole length	180
Breadth of the face	9
Ditto of the chin	6
Ditto of the mouth	3½
Length of the nose	6
Breadth of the nose	2½
Length of the face	23½

Diameter of the eye	2½
Ditto of his breasts	7
Length of his ribs	16
Ditto of the fingers	7
Breadth of the hand	12
Ditto of the wrist	7
From the wrist to the elbow	30
From the elbow to the shoulder	44
Ditto of the elbow	19
Breadth of the knots	24
Ditto at other places	7

An authoritative modern account of the Giant's vital statistics appeared in 1926. Sir Flinders Petrie, one of this century's towering archaeologists, plotted some 220 points around the Giant.

> The plan was made by stretching a line down the whole figure, and setting another at right angles across the shoulders, and a parallel line across the legs. Standing at any required point, I held two tape measures; the zero of one was held on a long line by my wife, the zero of the other on a cross line by my son, keeping the tapes square with the lines. I then read off the two distances to the spot on the ground, and plotted it at once on squared paper.

Recent statistics emphasize the accuracy of Petrie's work (and, incidentally, the list published in the *Gentleman's Magazine* of 1764), confirming how little the Giant has altered down the centuries. To summarize the essential dimensions: from heel to crown the Giant is 55 m long, and he is 12 m across at the waist. The club he carries in his right hand is 37 m long, and his phallus extends 7.2 m. He is outlined by a triangular trench some 60 cm wide at the top, by some 60 cm deep at its inverted apex, and 439 m in length.

About 25 tons of soil were removed to create the outline. Allowing for around thirty workers and metal implements, the project could have been completed within two weeks. However, if wood and stone implements and deer antler picks had been used in place of metal picks, the work could well have spread over months. Being an effective portrait but no triumph of anatomical draughtsmanship, the Giant was probably first chalked upon a large stone or a piece of hide and later transcribed on the hill using – like Sir Flinders Petrie – a vertically bisecting line as the reference point for height, size of

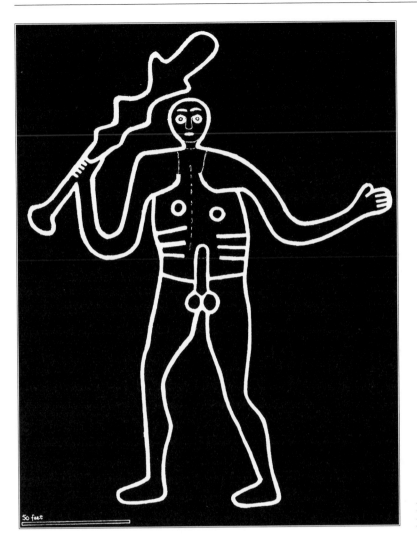

50 feet

Plan of the Cerne Giant from
Flinders Petrie's survey, 1926.

head, waist, breadth of shoulders. The further one veered from basic symmetry, the less reliable this method would become – hence the dramatically disproportionate club and rubbery arms.

THE MISSING NAVEL

Comparing the different representations of the Giant, from the *Gentleman's Magazine* (1764) to recent aerial photographs, one becomes aware of a subtle alteration. Rodney Legg noted in the *Dorset Country Magazine* (April 1978) that 'the navel has since grassed over' and Gerald Pitman later that year observed that it had merged with the phallus. The phenomenon was investigated by the archaeologist and folklorist, Leslie Grinsell, who reported his findings in *Antiquity*, 1980. After analysing the various scourings, he focused on the 1868 renovation, opposed by the local vicar, probably A.H. Bull, who thought that it might corrupt local morals. Did the scourers deliberately contrive the 6 ft enlargement of the penis in order to scandalize the cleric? This is a possibility but on the basis of pictorial evidence Grinsell considered it likely that the omission of the navel and the extension of the private parts dates from 1887 when General Pitt Rivers, the then owner of the Giant, employed Jonathan Hardy to renew the figure. The circular trench outlining the navel had become faint and was mistakenly identified as the tip of the penis. However, as Rodney Castleden (1996) has pointed out, the navel can be picked out in late Victorian or early Edwardian postcards; therefore the most probable date of its loss is the 1908 scouring, after a 21-year interval of infilling and erosion.

SCOURING

Seven years was the interval ascribed to the upkeep of the Giant – a traditional lapse of time, attributed to the Uffington Horse and the renewal of maypoles in the Harz Mountains, Germany. Folklorists have drawn inspiration from this, other septenary invocations being the seven points of the Pleiades, the seven deadly sins, the seven days of the week and the seven stars around the eyes of God. Dr Richard Pococke (*c.* 1754) alluded to the lord of the manor making a donation every seven or eight years to 'have the lines clear'd' and Hutchins (1774) repeated that 'it is repaired about once in seven years by the people of the town, by cleansing the furrows and filling them with fresh chalk'. In practice, however, there was little adherence to mystical numerology and the Giant was renewed at irregular intervals; there were lapses and periods of neglect in which features became blurred.

The first recorded scouring took place in 1868; the *Dorset Chronicle* had drawn attention to the Giant's 'shabby appearance on account of the trenches being choked with weeds and rubbish and the outlines being otherwise defaced'. Orders had been given by Lord Rivers that his 'Mightiness' should have his parts cleaned and restored, a recommendation that upset the vicar of Cerne, the Revd A.H. Bull, who thought that the sight might exert a deleterious influence on local morals. General Pitt Rivers (1827–1900) inherited the estate in 1880. A dynamic and important figure in archaeology, he drew on his own study of firearms and realized that an analogous progression, or refinement, of workmanship can be found in artefacts. Around the time of Queen Victoria's Jubilee (1887) he commissioned Jonathan Hardy to scour the Giant as a festive gesture, enclosing the figure in a six-sided pen to protect it from revellers assembled on the hill around a blazing beacon fire.

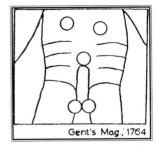

Gent's Mag., 1764

Two records of the Cerne Giant, showing how the penis merged with the navel.

Between 1887 and 1901, no scouring took place. The navel grassed over, although it was just visible in postcards of the period. Seven years later, in 1908, 'a subscription having been raised in the neighbourhood, the Giant was repaired with fresh chalk' (Anon. 1908), and it was about this time, in Castleden's view, the navel acceded to the thrall of the extending penis. By 1920, the National Trust had acquired the Giant from the Pitt Rivers family and, four years later, another renovation was carried out, costing over £5. Shortly after, the idea was floated that a fund was needed to maintain the Giant, and this was endowed by Sir Henry Hoare, the antiquarian and collector, who later complained to the National Trust that the figure was covered with grass, insisting that it was formerly solid white. It took no less an authority than Thomas Hardy to convince him in a letter of 1925: 'The Cerne Giant's figure was never white all over, like King George's near Weymouth, but only the trenches forming his outline. These are fairly deep, and all that can be done to make his shape clear is to keep the trenches cleaned out and spread white chalk over the bottom of them. This will remain white many years if it is weeded over now and then. The interior of the Giant's figure was always green.'

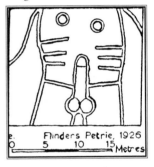

Flinders Petrie, 1926

During the Second World War, the Giant was hidden under brushwood by the Home Guard. In 1945, with the cessation of hostilities, he was repaired under the supervision of Stuart Piggott. Over a decade later, in 1956, a thorough scouring took place, the job being done by E.W. Beard, a firm of building contractors from Swindon who had renovated the Uffington Horse. The effectiveness of their efforts inspired the National Trust to hire them for the restoration of 1979, which took five men eleven weeks. Discoloured chalk was hacked out and replaced with fresh and a narrow-gauge wooden tramway was laid from the hilltop across the figure to ease access.

History and Interpretation

Predictably the explicit appearance of the Giant has attracted advertising promotions and silly season japes. H.S.L. Dewar, the folklorist, wrote of a party of people armed with sacking and paper climbing the figure to cover it with a figleaf. Whether this course of action had any connection with the views of L.M. Middleton of South Perrot, who is quoted as saying, 'Propriety demands that he don a loin-cloth', is not known. This doughty champion of modest apparel clashed with the National Trust, suggesting they should let nature take its course. 'I have now replied', he wrote, 'to the effect that no additions should be made to the Giant. The National Trust should let the grass eliminate his face and genitals, and they should shape his feet so that he is standing with his back to the Sherborne–Cerne road. Then he is artistic instead of ugly.'

In the late summer of 1968, a group of students, carrying pots of white and green paint, re-touched the outline, so that it displayed female organs. And such publicity-grabbing stunts have continued unabated through subsequent decades, with Raleigh bicycles showing their trail bike being wheeled beneath the Giant's arm and Durex manufacturers landing on his fist in a balloon in their 1989 campaign, drawing attention to his contraceptive innocence.

One of the more curious suggestions was that the Giant's lust should be gratified or tantalized by the addition of a female figure. In 1980, Kenneth Evans-Loude, an artist from Devon, proposed that he cut on the hill opposite the Giant the figure of Marilyn Monroe in her notable skirt-fluttering sequence from *The Seven Year Itch*. Despite the fact that the owner of the hill approved the project ('I hope it gives the planners stick'), the Arts Council refused to sponsor the project; as *The Times* commented, 'Some Like it Not'.

The Cerne Grant with Marilyn Monroe.

One local worthy, the Hon. Ophelia Pashley-Cumming, thought that it might prove an enhancement. 'I feel strongly', she declared, 'that Mr Loud-Evans should be allowed to give expression to his impulses on the hill. Personally I have never felt affronted by the Cerne Giant and have no time at all for the simpering old ladies who cluck-cluck every time they pass it. The only residents I sympathize with are the elderly males or tired Dorchester business men who are constantly reminded by their wives and mistresses *en passant* of how far short they fall of the splendid male vigour displayed before them. Every time the Giant is weeded to make his outlines clear there are protests from the prudes: one band of zealots even wanted a spinney to be planted in a strategic position to spare what they called public embarrassment. We soon scotched that but I suppose that the same lot will be pressing for a dirndl skirt on Miss Monroe if the carving is allowed to go ahead.'

Despite so-called 'prudes' and 'zealots', the hearty approach predominates. In this, the Giant features as desire-caught-by-the-tail, a prehistoric seaside postcard, a lumpen yokel to be mocked by sophisticates. An older generation of writers, such as D.H. Lawrence, would attribute this to 'sex-shame' or conditioned prudery, but more likely it stems from conceptual or abstract thought interposing a gulf, or schism, between itself and its origins. The Giant traces the frank outline of biological existence. He is a reminder of the cartoon male, the non-intellectual, headstrong warrior, allowing the force of nature aroused to seethe through him. In modern European and American civilization, these qualities, sublimated and groomed, are marketed in movie halls, boxing rings and tongue-in-cheek advertising. The appearance may be more photogenically streamlined but the message is not, qualitatively speaking, different.

Obscene Jest

Theories concerning the Giant are plentiful and conflicting. The earliest reference is found in Francis Wise's *Further Observations upon the White Horse*. He refers to 'the figure of a Giant cut on a sidelong hill' but defers any judgement because he did not want 'to invade the province of a gentleman [Dr Stukeley] who, as I hear, had undertaken to write the history and antiquities of the county'. Twelve years later, in October 1754, Dr Richard Pococke visited Cerne Abbas and provided a compact pen-portrait:

> On the west side of the hills north of the village is a figure cut in lines. It is called the Giant and Hele, is about 150 feet long, a naked figure in a genteel posture. It seems to be Hercules, or Strength and Fidelity, but it is with such indecent circumstances as to make one conclude it was also a Priapus. It is supposed that it was an ancient figure of worship and one would imagine that the people would not permit the monks to destroy it. The lord of the manor gives some thing once in 7 or 8 years to have the lines clear'd and kept open.

John Hutchins (1774), the historian of Dorset, entered the arena cautiously, stating that the figure was reported to have been cut by Lord Holles' servants during his residence at Cerne but adds that some people 'who died not long before 1772, eighty or ninety years old, when young, knew some of the same age that averred it was there beyond the antiquity of man.' In the rare second edition of his work (1796–1815), he includes a drawing of the porch to the Abbot's Hall at Cerne with the Giant in the background, discreetly fitted out with a loincloth, yet otherwise looking fairly flabby and unappealing.

Denzil Holles (1599–1680) was a wily, high-principled Parliamentarian, who opposed Cromwell's policies during the Civil War, emerging triumphant from numerous scuffles and intrigues. He lived at Cerne Abbas, marrying Jane Freke, a widow, in 1641, and raising Abbey Farm from the remains of the South Gatehouse. It has been contended by Ronald Hutton that the Giant was cut by Holles as a lampoon against his bugbear, Oliver Cromwell, who was dubbed the 'English Hercules', but if satire or mockery was intended, it has taken an awfully long time for the penny to drop

Denzil Holles (1599-1680)

Poet and topographical writer, Geoffey Grigson, thought the carving an 'obscene jest of a ribald free-thinking eighteenth century nobleman making fun of the antiquaries', but Grigson also mischievously suggested that Stonehenge was the remains of a large roofed enclosure. However, the seventeenth-century argument has been revamped, notably by Ronald Hutton, who has argued for the comparatively late provenance of many 'age-old' festivals and artefacts in a series of lively revisionist studies. In the Cerne Abbas Commission of Enquiry 1996, organized by Bournemouth University, he underlined his argument by showing a statue of Cromwell as Hercules – driving home the point that nudity during the Interregnum was no shocking matter – and enlisted the assistance of Dr Keith Walker, an expert on the bawdy verses of Lord Rochester.

A more specific seventeenth-century interpretation attributes the Giant to the Club Raisers. They were an association of Wessex farmworkers who, fearing looting of their property by soldiers during the Civil War, banded together and formed blockades. Owing to the shortage of firearms, they employed cudgels as weapons. They attained the zenith of their influence *c.* 1644, but after a skirmish at Hambledon Hill, in which Cromwell sent in the troops who 'killed not twelve of them, but cut very many and put them all to flight', their revolt lost its impetus. Their 1645 manifesto refers to 'Civill and unnatrall Wars within the kingdon' interfering with 'the true worship of Almighty God'. It is a temperate, pious document in every way and, although odd behaviour is consistent with duress, the Giant is too priapic a figure to express their outlook.

What has given rise to this new wave of scepticism, to this questioning whether the Giant deserves to be classed as 'prehistoric', is the absence of documentary evidence before the churchwarden's 1694 payment of 3*s* 'for repaireing of ye Giant . . .'. This is the earliest written reference; the numerous medieval documents pertaining to the abbey and parish omit to mention the Giant, as do the extensive surveys conducted by John Norden (1617) and Thomas Gerard (1625). However, to quote the neatest maxim emerging from the 1996 Commission of Enquiry, 'absence of evidence is not evidence of absence' (Roy Canham), and it should be borne in mind that many Saxon charters are silent as to the provably historic White Horse, and the Long Man of Wilmington was habitually ignored.

Statue of Oliver Cromwell as Hercules, Highnam Court, Gloucestershire.

THE PHOENICIANS

At a meeting of the Society of Antiquaries in February 1764, Dr Stukeley, the foremost antiquarian of his day, read a paper on the Cerne Giant, noting the dimensions of the figure, praising the skill and optical knowledge implied by its appearance when viewed from the opposite hill, and then hazarding a guess as to his identity:

> Unquestionably it means to represent the famous and first Hercules, the Phoenician leader of the first colony to Britain when they came hither for Cornish tin. It is not to be supposed that it was made in his time, but afterwards, and in memory of him, when the Britons had a notion of the later Theban Hercules, the tamer of wild men, and of wild beasts. But our Phoenician Hercules was a different person, and a different sort of person: as coming from the politer part of the Asiatic world.

This politer type of Phoenician settled on the southern coast of Britain, designed the numerous barrows, earthworks and megaliths, and indulged in solemn sacrificial rites coupled with manly competitive sports such as chariot-racing. The homeland of these Phoenician wanderers was Ethiopia or Arabia, 'and from Arabia our first Britons came, and were of the same patriarchal religion as those Arabian magi, properly Druids, who came to worship our infant Saviour.'

What is one to make of this weirdly subjective verdict? Like many antiquarians, Dr Stukeley had burrowed among the erudite nooks and dark corners of Classical lore in order to find clues as to the origin of British antiquities. Fervently he desired to bring about an ideological marriage between his two overriding passions, Christianity and Druidism, and this was no easy task without forcibly elevating the moral status of the latter. Apart from this aberration, when he actually hazarded a date for the Giant, he was temperate and cautious, ascribing it to the legendary British King Eli, 'father of Immanuence king of the Trinobantes'.

A Phoenician coin denoting dual worship of fire (a lesser manifestation of the sun) and the serpent.

Stukeley was a popularizer of ophiolatry or worship of the sacred serpent. He identified henge monuments as *dracontia* or snake temples, the snake being an object of veneration in the early Egyptian, Babylonian and Hellenic cultures. John Sydenham (1842) applied this quaint reptilian theology to the Cerne Giant, adding for good measure Noah's ark and the accompanying flood.

Sydenham's theory, briefly, is this. Before the flood men worshipped the snake. To punish them for such crass idolatry, Jehovah sent down the flood, as a result of which they afterwards worshipped *both the snake and the flood*. In other words, they deified creatures that were half-fish and half-snake: reptilian water monsters, snaky-tailed mermaids, lumbering Leviathans and a whole gamut of weird aquatic hybrids. For hundreds of years, the natives of Dorset worshipped snaky fishes and fishy snakes until they were overrun by the invading Belgae. The latter were sun-worshippers and everywhere at this period solarite cults were ousting serpent cults. The Belgae imposed their gospel upon the Durotrigian natives: hence the Giant commemorates the victory of the sun over the serpent, and the old name for Cerne, Cernel or 'Cerne Hill', means 'hill of the sun-god', El, Bel, Baal, whose title is reflected locally at El-stone Hill and El-wood.

When, at a much later date, St Augustine visited Cerne, the inhabitants pelted him with fishes' tails or attached them to his gown. Old ways died hard; in the opinion of Sydenham, the natives were reverting to their diluvian-ophite gospel.

THE IDOL SATURN

The monks may have attempted to darken the Giant's reputation. Folklore does not show him as entirely blemishless. He is portrayed as a bedtime frightener of children, an ogre who might eat them up like rashers of bacon if they did not cooperate and go to sleep placidly. Dr Maton (1797) alluded to the tradition that he was carved to commemorate a flesh-and-blood giant who, after glutting himself

The Cerne Giant's leg.

on sheep at Blackmore, rested on the hillside where he was pinned down by locals and slain.

The image of a huge recumbent ogre, drowsing gently, recalls an anecdote of the Greek writer, Plutarch (AD 54–117). In his *Parallel Lives of Illustrious Greeks and Romans*, he alludes to Demetrius whom the emperor had commissioned to explore the islands around Britain: 'Moreover that there was one island there, wherein Saturn was confined by Briareus in sleep; for that sleep had been devised for his bonds; and that round him were many genii as his companions and attendants.' The Greek form of Saturn is Cronos, a name recalling Gogmagog's protagonist, Corineus, whose image was perpetuated on Plymouth Hoe, and Cernunnos, a Gallic god of the animal kingdom, also possessed of healing skills.

In 1772 Hutchins transcribed three mysterious letters cut in the turf between the legs of the Giant which Mr Colley March (1801) translated as J (Jehovah) followed by an N-shaped squiggle (the medieval Saturn sign) and D (Destruxit) or 'God has destroyed Saturn'. Apart from castrating his father, Saturn's infamy was devouring his children as fast as his wife, Rhea, gave birth to them. He created only to destroy, a paradox apparent in the unique conjunction of club and phallus at Cerne.

Dowser Guy Underwood, who died in 1964, spent more than twenty years plotting 'geodetic lines'. He became intrigued by the small mound beneath the Giant's extended left hand and decided that it might be the severed phallus brandished by the god of seedtime and harvest. Over thirty years later, Rodney Castleden, added a new twist to this theory by conducting a resistivity survey on this low boss or knoll. When the results proved confusing, he arranged a close-contour survey, feeding the statistics into a computer, narrowing the interval to as little as 0.03 m, until a splendid *coup de théâtre* swelled up on the screen of his monitor – 'a fist grasping a wild mop of dreadlocks from which is swinging a severed head.'

This alarming discovery is concurrent with Celtic beliefs and practices. Warriors are known to have collected heads of victims and enemies, sometimes grooming and embalming them in cedar oil and showing them off to guests as trophies or emblems of their ferocity. Nevertheless, it demands that the severed head and club be viewed as symbolic rather than internally coherent facets of composition. A sword or axe would be a far more suitable implement for decapitation, but such anachronisms are not uncommon, iconographically speaking.

The objection to this arresting theory must be in the ragged, blurry lines of the resistivity printouts, and the fact that the severed head is subtly rendered in half-profile – an artistic advance on the Giant's pond-flat grimace. Look deeply enough and, yes, there just *could* be a head dangling from the wrist; there *could* be a pair of slitty death-set eyes; there *could* also be the lines of a cloak; but a certain amount of imaginative leeway is required.

Castleden's broader interpretation is compelling. He argues that the Giant, known as Helis, was cut by the Durotriges during the Iron Age as a symbol of ferocity, fertility and healing. Above him was raised the sacred temple of the Trendle, holding a priest's shrine or ritual structure, and below at the foot of the hill bubbled up the sacred spring, a site of physical restoration and prophecy. There was also, quite possibly, a 'sanctuary' or reception area, the remains of which account for the numerous hillocks and earthworks in the Abbey Field. For centuries, the Helis Sanctuary flourished as a ritual

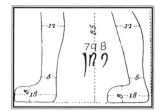

The Revd John Hutchins included a portrait of a gelded Giant in his *History of Dorset* (1774), adding an extra detail: 'Between his legs were copied certain rude letters, scarce legible, which are given here as copied August 1772. It is plain that there were no more than three. Some affirm them to be proof of the great antiquity of this figure, which they refer to Saxon times. Over these were three more figures, probably modern. If these were intended for a date, we may read it 748.' Explanations for the numbers vary, from commemorating the death of the Saxon prince Cenric (AD 748) to recording the last scouring in 1748.

complex, like the temple of Sulis at Bath, a place of pilgrimage and healing, until it was annexed and Christianized by Augustine and his followers. The monks built a chapel over the spring, rededicating it and separating Helis from his power source.

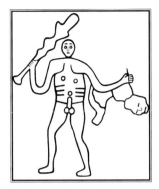

The Cerne Giant: after restoration according to Castleden (1996).

THE TRENDLE

If the spring represents the lower zone of the Giant, the Trendle stands for his brain or mind, the point from which his veneration was ratified. Set just above the head of the nude colossus and terraced into the hill, this small enclosure is double-banked, squarish, and rounded at the north-west and north-east corners. Reputedly the site of the town maypole, it is tempting to relate it to the Giant in much the same way that Uffington Castle – the hub of the scouring festivities – relates to the chalk-carved Horse. However, it is much smaller and had no defensive or corral-like function. The site has never been properly probed or excavated, but it may have contained a priest's hut, or small temple, to Helis–Hercules.

Colley March (1901) quoted Mr Childs, a former sexton of Cerne, who told him that a fir-bole was raised 'in the ring' on the night before May Day: 'It was decorated, and the villagers went up and danced around the pole on the first of May. Nothing of the sort is now done.'

The maypole association is critical. The vertical staff or pillar as an object of veneration is as old as religion. Asherah, or Astarte, the Syrian goddess, was worshipped in the form of a living tree or pole, sometimes carved in the shape of a statue. The single upright bamboo stalk, known as the linga or phallus, was an object of Hindu reverence. The movement of dancers round the maypole can be likened to the apparent revolution of the sun round the earth. The sun-worshippers of Thrace adored the image of a disc balanced on a tall pole. A relic of these sun-images is preserved in the large gold and silver plates adorning altars in Christian churches. Therefore, to some degree, it can be assumed that the upright maypole reflects the Giant's phallus.

However, the importance of this organ cannot be viewed in isolation. Even the erection of the Giant would be a forlorn gesture without a female principle with which to combine.

> Here I come Beelzebub,
> And over my shoulder I carry my club;
> And in my hand a frying pan,
> And I think myself a jolly old man.

The above couplets, noted by Stuart Piggott (1932), connect 'Frying Pan' (the alternative name for the Trendle) with Beelzebub, the stock character in Christmas Mummers' Plays, a blundering, disorderly, club-bearing version of the Evil One. There is also a group of medieval French legends centring upon a spectral, club-wielding giant who dominated a troupe of damned souls, variously titled Helequin, Hierlekin and Helethkin, names conceivably relating to Helith. A variant of 'frying pan' is 'dripping pan', a veiled reference to the female organ.

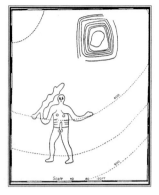

Sketch map of the Cerne Giant and the Trendle.

However, the Trendle is physically shaped like a frying pan, so one need not inflate the sexual symbolism, though it is well avowed that during the early May Day festivities sexual congress was common. Association of the maypole with immoral behaviour led to its banning by the Puritans and to such famous passages of sputtering invective as this by Philip Stubbes:

> Hundreds of men, women and children go off into the woods and groves and spend all nights in pastimes, and in the morning they return with birch boughs and branches of trees to deck their assemblies withal. And they bring home with great veneration the Maie-pole, their stinking idol rather, covered all over with flowers and herbs, and then fall to leaping and dancing about it, as the heathen people did. I have heard it crediblie reported by men of great gravity that, of an hundred maides going to the wood, there have scarcely the third part of them returned home again as they went.

It would be illuminating to learn how these 'men of great gravity' were able to conduct the intimate examinations necessary to procure such statistics. Were they recalling their own halcyon days?

Doubt has been placed on the Trendle as the original site of the maypole by villagers who, three decades later, dismissed Mr Childs' claim. The Trendle, or Frying Pan, they pointed out, contained stumps of a small fir plantation and would not have been suitable for dancing. Instead the maypole was set up in the village beside the town pond.

Confusion may have arisen because of the processional nature of some Maytime ceremonies, starting at one plot and moving on to another. In hot weather, Giant Hill would appear an attractive site to complete the jollification, and it is likely that Mr Childs was recalling the festivity in his own youth. Fertility associations complement the setting. Dorset folklore abounds with tales of young brides, on the night before their wedding, climbing the slopes of Giant Hill and prostrating themselves on the nub of the massive figure.

FATHER BACCHUS

Priapic rites, about which a good deal is known in the Greek and Roman worlds, were practised in Britain, but direct evidence of them is meagre. A startling entry occurs in the Chronicle of Lanercost Priory (1282) and concerns the religious lapses of John, the parish priest of Inverkeithing. During Easter Week, he gathered girls from the surrounding villages and compelled them 'to dance in circles to the honour of Father Bacchus'. At one point he led the party, carrying on a pole 'an image of the human organs of reproduction' stirring the maidens to 'lust and filthy language'.

This echoes the Eleusisinian festival of Haloa, taking place at the bleakest time of the year (around 26 December) in ancient Greece, when maidens and matrons carried models of male and female genitalia and dined off tables laid out with specially baked cakes resembling phalli and pudenda. They provoked each other with the coarsest language and consumed large quantities of wine.

Another festival, coming after Haloa and held in various places all over Attica, was the Country Dionysia, a phallic celebration amusingly portrayed in Aristophanes' play *The Archanians*. Back in the fifth century BC, the playwright saw it as a quaint, slightly outdated ceremony, a throwback to an older, simpler age.

Dikaiopolis: Silence! Keep holy silence! Move forward. You, Xanthias, follow close behind her there. Set the phallus upright.
Wife: Set down the Dorset, daughter, and begin the ceremony.
Daughter: Oh, blessed Dionysus, what a joy it is to lead this procession and other sacrifices together with my wife, my children, my slaves, and celebrate thy festival in my farm.
Wife: Mind your behaviour, child. Carry the basket in a proper manner. Look demure and grave. Mind your gold trinkets – they'll be stolen else.
Dikaiopolis: Follow behind there, Xanthias, with the phallus – keep it up straight! And I'll come up behind and sing the Phallic Song.

Hellenic Greece and Celtic Dorset may be worlds apart, but an identical principle is involved, and if one allows credence to the

The Dorset Ooser. Centuries ago, it was the custom in Dorset for a wild, bull-masked man to caper through the streets of numerous villages, stopping at houses to demand refreshment. This figure was called the Ooser and usually appeared at the end of the year. In Shillingstone it was known as the 'Christmas Bull', a misleading title for what was probably a potent pagan symbol. The last surviving Ooser mask came from Melbury Osmond, about 11 km from Cerne, and was made of painted wood with a horsehair beard.

Scottish debauch, the Cerne Giant could effectively stand in for 'Father Bacchus'. It is noticeable, too, that the Dionysia smacks of harvest festival. Like an ear of wheat, the phallus was a comforting symbol, a lucky charm bringing fruitfulness and prosperity.

THE GARDEN GOD

This point is vividly demonstrated in the Smithers and Burton translation of the Roman *Priapeia*, a collection of short, jocose epigrams to Priapus, the garden god with the outsize phallus. The point about the anthology is not so much its crudity but its heady sensuousness, utterly removed from any sense of sin or hellish retribution. Priapus' bawdiness is the very substance of the land. It flows and energizes the spirit. Notable too is the fact that, in so many epigrams, the member – or *mentule* – doubles up as a cudgel which may be broken off to beat a thief or intruder. In the following, the traveller mocks Priapus' threat to sodomize him as punishment for trespass (the Romans regarded this as a hilarious humiliation) and the god retorts that the strong-armed farmer will belabour him with the same instrument:

I, O traveller, shaped with rustic art from a dry poplar, guard this little field which thou seest on the left, and the cottage and small garden of its indigent owner, and keep off the greedy hands of the robber. In spring a many-tinted wreath is placed upon me; in summer's heat ruddy grain; [in autumn] a luscious grape cluster with vineshoots, and in the bitter cold the pale-green olive. The tender she-goat bears from my pasture to the town milk-distended udders; the well-fattened lamb from my sheepfolds sends back [its owner] with a heavy handful of money; and the tender calf, 'midst its mother's lowings, sheds its blood before the temple of the gods. Hence, warfarer, thou shalt be in awe of this god, and it will be profitable to thee to keep thy hands off. For a punishment is prepared – a roughly-shaped mentule. 'Truly, I am willing,' thou sayest; then, truly, behold the farmer comes, and that same mentule plucked from my groin will become an apt cudgel in his strong right hand.

The richness of atmosphere recalls Keats' *To Autumn* rather than pornography in the modern sense. With a mixture of lyricism and innuendo, Priapus safeguards the fertility of field and orchard, and defends boundaries and acreages. His phallus is about agriculture rather than adultery.

The qualities exhibited by Priapus may be applied to the Cerne Giant. His massive oak-leaf club protects and defends the fertile vale of Cerne. It threatens enemies but, as the Priapus extract reminds us, there was a comic aspect. Despite the citation of sonorous titles like Helith and Hercules, the Giant was kept alive – periodically maintained – because of his appeal to the common man. In essence, he was an honest, vulgar male. Like Robin Goodfellow, he had an element of the trickster. After all, his bauble or plaything was the erect phallus, traditionally the comic tool of the impudent and triumphant clown, jokes referring to which pepper the Elizabethan stage. The emblem still survives in vestigial form in such appurtenances as Chaplin's cane, Groucho's cigar and the suggestively flourished banana.

What is likely is that the May Day emphasis shifted from the phallic fundamentalism of Celtic and Saxon times to something more decorative and feminine, akin to the Roman Floralia, celebrating the return of Persephone to her mother after the blight of winter. Gradually this aspect took over until today one automatically conjures May Queens with charming garlanded attendants – exactly the type of image that provided moments of despondent eroticism for the ageing Thomas Hardy. This change of character was effected when the old festivals returned after the Restoration. The ancient shamelessness was toned down until it acquired the guise of a quaint rustic distraction. Yet still much of the beauty remained, with the maidens going out in the fields to collect the first dew of the month.

> The fair maid who, on First of May,
> Goes to the field at break of day,
> Washes in dew from the Hawthorn Tree,
> Will ever after handsome be.

St Augustine at Cerne

The French hagiographer Gotselin (1058–98) was the first to record St Augustine's visit to Cerne not long after he settled at Canterbury in 1090. Drawing on an earlier source – quite possibly Saxon – he describes the 'demoniac' worshippers of 'Helia' taunting and driving out St Augustine and his band. This account filtered into ampler chronicles, notably *De Gestis Pontificum Anglorum*, written and compiled by William of Malmesbury, a scion of mixed Norman and English stock who died *c.* 1143. His all-digestive *magnum opus* incorporates historical fact, monastic data, lives of saints, reminiscences of the Norman hierarchy and tales, ballads and legends of the countryside.

The episode relating to Cerne tells how St Augustine, after converting the kingdom of Kent, travelled over the remainder of the English provinces as far as King Æthelbert's kingdom extended. Finally he came to 'Cernel', the old name for Cerne, and there he was repulsed and jeered at by the community. Augustine and his acolytes were driven three miles out of the village by the locals who, as a token of disrespect, fastened cows' or fishes' tails to their garments. Shortly afterwards, God assisted him and the people began to relent. Thereupon Augustine, feeling the presence of his Master, proclaimed that the place should be called Cernel, a word compounded of the Latin *Cerno* (I see) and the Hebrew *El* or *Hel* (God). The scoffers then submitted to the True Faith and, to aid baptism, a spring spurted up from the ground: St Augustine's well by the churchyard.

Likewise the author of the *Flores Sanctorum*, in the *Life of St Augustine*, tells us that in AD 603, St Augustine's mission destroyed at Cerne the idol Heil, or Hegle. Furthermore, when the inhabitants fastened tails to his garments, he deflected the peculiarity back on them. 'The

St Augustine's Well at Cerne Abbas.

tradition has descended to this present day,' commented Sydenham (1842), 'among the inhabitants of Cerne and the neighbourhood; and it is still devoutly believed by the common people that the descendants of the tailed race yet exist, bearing the remarkable distinction attributed to them in legend.' (Was this true in the mid-nineteenth century? Did the people of Cerne 'devoutly' believe in their tailed cousins? Or could it be that Sydenham, having a vested interest in tails and finny accoutrements, is cranking the wheel of superstition?)

Walter of Coventry, a thirteenth-century chronicler, recites a fourth version of Augustine's visit to Cerne, adding the telling clause, *in quo pago colebatur deus Helith* – in which district the god Helith was worshipped. Yet again the incident surfaces in *The Golden Legend* (where it is localized at Strode, Kent) and in Camden where it states that Augustine founded Cerne Abbey 'when hee had broke there in pieces Heil the Idol of the heathen English-Saxons, and chased away the fog of paganish superstition'.

LEWD MONKS

Some have translated 'Heil the Idol' as the work of papists or at least commentary on their behaviour – a Chaucerian jest intended to bring the Benedictines into disrepute. A curious story related by Hutchins concerned a pauper in the neighbourhood who 'possessed an old thick folio volume', plentifully illustrated with coins and wood engravings, according to which the Giant was cut at the time of the Dissolution to deride Thomas Corton, the lewd last abbot. The phallus mirrored his lust, the club his meditated revenge, and the shifting feet his imminent departure.

Corton does, indeed, appear to have been informally inclined as a prelate. Four years before the Dissolution of 1539, a disgruntled monk of the abbey called William Christchurch accused Corton of, among other felonies, keeping concubines in a cellar of the abbey, letting the church lands go to ruin, giving gifts to a son by a former concubine, entertaining his concubines at the table, allowing certain monks to play cards all night, abolishing some masses and allowing women to hang around the monastery all day.

Lastly, but more significantly, Corton is attacked for 'imprisoning William Christchurch for writing and speaking against him' and 'expelling him from the monastery', so there was clearly a feud between the men. Eventually Corton was forced to abandon the monastery, but he gained a handsome pension of £100 a year, so life at Cerne Abbey may not have been quite so lecherously picturesque.

If the Giant was not cut by the monks or intended to satirize their practices, it was clearly tolerated. Why? Perhaps their Christianity was of an older brand, where streams, birds and flowers took their place as God's creations, and phallic idolatry, although denigrated, was not harshly censored. A.O. Gibbons (1962), believed that the abbey was deliberately placed in conjunction with the Giant to proclaim a moral message:

Here indeed was an expressible need for a church, which, offering prayer and worship to the true God, should fetter this pagan monster in perpetual thrall. . . . To destroy the Giant as Æilmar could easily have done would not have served the same purpose. To leave him, an outcast in the rain and lonely chill of his own seeking, impotent on the turf, visible to all in his degrading nakedness, could be a lasting monument to the blighting efficacy of Christian prayer.

Gibbons' comment is persuasive, but leaving the Giant on the hillside 'visible to all in his degrading nakedness' is merely doing nothing – maintaining the *status quo*.

ST AUGUSTINE'S WELL

The discovery of a spring – known thereafter as St Augustine's Well – marked the advent of Christianity in the village. Enwalled today in a corner of the cemetery – formerly the abbey churchyard – the pool is sheltered by limes and enclosed by a stone kerb. A secretive place, leaf-fringed and cool, it has never been excavated and may contain votives of earlier periods beneath layers of mud and rubble from the abbey. Formerly it was thought to possess healing properties, restoring poor eyesight, aiding fertility and well-being in women, especially during pregnancy. Just as eyes mirror the soul, fresh water reveals the integrity and purity of the earth. Water was the 'eye' of the land and its emergence from the ground was akin to a blessing, urging settlers to build and drink from the place.

One of the wishing stones – a Catherine wheel? – beside St Augustine's Well, Cerne Abbas.

According to John Leland, antiquary to Henry VIII, the hermit Edwold moved to Cerne, setting up his cell by the 'silver well' or 'fountain' of St Augustine after his brother, Edmund the Martyr, had been killed by Danes. When he died in AD 871, the earl of Cornwall, Æilmer transferred his relics to the local church. In his *Survey of Dorsetshire* (*c.* 1620), Thomas Gerard records that the well was 'heretofore covered with a Chappell dedicated to St Augustine' and that the town itself was 'soe named from the Words of St Augustine who, when he preached Christianity to the Inhabitants of these Partes, pitched down his staff on the Grounde, using these Wordes – *Cerne quid hic sit* – whence immediatelie flowed a quick Fountaine, that served to baptize manie, whom, with this Miracle as well as his Doctrine, hee had converted.'

One of the wishing stones framing the well is carved with a rosette or wheel-shaped design; some see this as a tribute to St Catherine, one of the female saints who absorbed pagan qualities, to whom the shrine above the well could have been dedicated. Despite lack of evidence, the bond between the well and the Giant has developed in the local imagination, the spring supplying the feminine principle to balance the Giant's masculinity.

HERCULES

Over a thousand years after Augustine's mission, local people could inform Bishop Pococke that the Giant went by the name of Hele. Either they were cognisant with Latin and medieval texts or this is an astonishing example of the persistence of folk memory?

The name Hele, Helith or Helis evokes a chain of associations, ranging from 'hell' to 'heel-stone', from 'healing' to 'heathy' or 'hilly' uplands, but no specific British, Gallic or Roman deity. Dorset is rich in 'Hel' prefixes which may reflect such variants or, alternatively, derive from a single pagan figure who lorded over the district. As a proper noun, Helis recalls Helios, son of Hyperion and Thea, who figures in Greek mythology as the sun-god. His worship was extensive, for he had temples in Corinth, Argo, Troezene and Elbis, but he was worshipped most prominently in Rhodes, where the colossus showed him as a naked, well-knit, strongly proportioned figure, reminiscent of the Hercules of classical art. The similarity may not be incidental, for Hercules usurped his role, borrowing the golden cup of the sun.

Celestial Hercules was born at Argos, a name signifying brightness; as a mere infant he strangled the serpents of darkness and, upon attaining manhood, performed twelve consecutive labours (corresponding to the twelve zodiacal signs, or the twelve months of the year, or the twelve hours of daylight) and died a warrior's death. Spreading out the skin of the Nemean lion, using his club for a pillow, he lay down upon the logs of his funeral pyre and let the flames consume him.

It is pertinent to introduce Hercules at this juncture because any large male figure, naked, clavigerous and bearing the title, Helis, might be thought to have affinities with this hero-god? Yet what is Hercules doing on a hillside in the middle of Dorset? Unlike Stukeley, who attributed him to the Phoenicians, Professor Stuart Piggott (1938) believed that he was brought here by the Romans; to him the Giant smacked of the 'clumsily naturalistic yet lifeless convention of Romano-British art'.

General Pitt Rivers, former owner of the Giant and pioneer of modern excavation techniques, made much the same comment in his notebook during the 1880s: 'Figure of Hercules in the British Museum for comparison with the Cerne Giant. The figures have always the club in the right hand; it is usually knotted. The left hand is usually turned out like the Cerne Giant but it nearly always has the

Hercules slaying the hydra.

lion skin hanging on it. The private parts are always shown. Some have a serpent in the left hand' (Thompson 1977).

Several carvings and representations of Hercules, including an altar-piece from Whitley Castle showing an angry-faced infant throttling serpents, and a fragment of castor ware from Welney showing Hercules dispatching the Hydra, emphasize this similarity. Furthermore there is evidence, faintly discernible, that the hill-figure originally supported a lion's skin with his left hand.

Stuart Piggot identified in the Trendle traces of what may have been a priest's shrine, or oratory, and suggested that Hercules, a god of virility and fertility, would have been acceptable to natives becoming used to deities of the Roman pantheon. Speculating further, he linked the Giant with the cult of emperor-worship – with, in fact, the veneration of Commodus, a cruel Roman emperor who, after beating the Scots (AD 184), added the title Hercules Romanus to his name and modelled himself on his hero. First he secured the acquiescence of the Praetorian Guard by gifts of money, then arranged numerous gladiatorial shows featuring himself as the principal attraction. Dressed in lion's skin and armed with a club, he fought with antagonists arrayed so as to represent the monsters of mythology. Although his own club was bulky and solid enough, his opponents were equipped with sponges in place of pieces of rock, and thus an imperial victory was assured. For a period Commodus was tolerated, and then the usual web of conspiracy prepared the way for his removal. After being administered a dose of poison by his favourite concubine, he failed to expire, and the job had to be completed by his favourite athlete, who strangled him.

In his Herculean guise, Commodus was celebrated with statuettes, pottery and castor ware. After his murder, attempts were made all over the Roman world to expunge his memory. This led to the accidental destruction of objects which had no direct bearing on his cult. So if the Giant had been cut to honour the brief, ignoble reign of the emperor, one might have expected the image to have fallen into neglect rather than being maintained with periodic scourings.

A second objection to the Commodus theory is that, although the cult of the emperor could be harshly enforced, the idea of the Giant standing for the manly, civilizing qualities of Rome is laughable. The Romans were not prudish, but would they have encouraged the natives to depict their emperor with a gigantic phallus and idiotic onion-face? One can see it more as a ludicrous, satiric cartoon.

The face of the Cerne Giant
showing his embanked nose.

Nevertheless, the Hercules theory, despite detractors, has weathered well and introduced a more anchored type of thinking. It received a boost in 1979 when, to illustrate Arthur C. Clarke's popular television series, *This Mysterious World*, the BBC commissioned Anthony Clark of the Ancient Monuments Laboratory to do a resistivity test on the Giant. This operates on the principle that soil's resistance to an electric current varies according to its water content and the presence of buried foundations or artefacts. The meter produced a curve of low-resistance readings, looping down from the left armpit and up to the left wrist – a feature he immediately identified with the missing cloak.

If, however, the Giant was originally drawn with the lion's skin, why did the artist entrench the lower line of the left arm – a part that would be blanketed by the draped garment? The end of the club, obscured by the thumb and forefinger, is not carved out. So it is credible that the cloak might have been appended to the figure during the Roman occupation and then left to heal over when the armies left.

NODONS

If the Giant is a native god rather than Hercules, who could he be? During the Second World War, a skillet handle was ploughed up at Hod Hill, near Blandford Forum, Dorset, decorated with a naked man holding a hare in his right hand and a club in his left. His nipples were clearly delineated and a pair of wings sprouted from his shoulder, indicating ornithological affinities. This was Nodons and the hare he grasped – a sacred animal symbolic of spring and corn growth – supplied the overtone of fertility. If the irregular lump beneath the Giant's left arm was a hare, and not, as Anthony Clark's test indicated, a lion's skin, the identification would be clinched.

Skillet handle depicting Nodons found at Blandford Forum.

The temple of Nodons at Lydney was excavated by Sir Mortimer Wheeler in 1932 and exerted a popular fascination. Associated with water – a healing, reviving agent – Nodons featured in the mythology of Ireland, for his sword was one of the treasures of the gods. He also owned a fabulous silver arm. In his role as a divine hunter the Romans equated him with Sylvanus, who was a kind of Latin Pan, a protector of flocks and lord of venery (hunting). Herein might lie the reason why St Augustine's Well was formerly called Silver Well. As for the name Helis, that is a clear allusion to Nodons function as a healer.

In support of this theory, Rodney Legg, the historian of Dorset, reported that, 'in the low sun of January 1969 and again during the extreme drought of 1976, I observed and recorded the outline of what seemed a dog, identical in shape to a Roman bronze terrier found at Wroxeter.' This was a stirring observation, for dogs feature among Nodons' sacred attributes. If confirmed, the presence of a terrier would have consolidated the local connection, but the efforts of others to trace this animal by resistivity readings and prolonged scrutiny have, as yet, yielded nothing.

THE GOOD STRIKER

If the identification with Nodons is inadequate or only partially satisfactory, to whom else in the Celtic pantheon does the Giant relate? His Jupiterian stance suggests a powerful, all-father figure, a vegetation god combining the qualities of warrior and procreator. He bears little resemblance to the horned and anthropomorphic deities often associated with the Celts and stands as an example of man making god in his own image. In many ways he is typical of the

Dagda, the all-purpose god who served as a father-protector, lord of the underworld and bestower of fruitfulness, not dissimilar to the Gallic divinity, Succellos, the 'Good Striker', who wielded an enormous mallet instead of a club.

In addition, one might cite how the early Teutonic tribes worshipped a god called Donar, a strong and massive figure. His groves were situated deep within the forests; the Romans identified him with Hercules. Today the memory of him survives in Germany as the folklore giant, Rubezaal, who carried an oak tree as his club.

Is there a Celtic equivalent of Donar? In the *Mabinogion* story, 'Lady of the Fountain', there is a portrait of a big, swarthy, one-eyed man who wields an iron club. His position is keeper of the forest and, when asked to demonstrate his powers, he belabours a stag; the animal lets out a mighty bellow whereupon all the creatures of the forest, including lions and vipers, gather round and pay him obeisance.

This brutish wild man in his woodland setting suggests a link between Hercules-Donar and the antler-crowned Lord of the Beasts, Cernunnos, who is strikingly depicted in silver relief on the Gundestrup cauldron. In the past, some have argued that 'Cerne' denotes a local grafting of Cernunnos, but the name appears to derive from the winding stream and it is also pertinent that the name of the local tribe, the Durotriges, signifies 'dwellers by water'.

Cerne began as a spring-line settlement. The magical efficacy of water is everywhere apparent – in the town pond with its Muscovy ducks, in the busy Cerne River with its watercress beds, in the well of St Augustine with its curative properties. It was a clement, fertile valley, well-stocked for fishing and hunting. With the large-scale annexing of the downs and open tracts during the Late Iron Age, military strength became a priority in a region that was highly prized. There was jostling for strategic positions; grazing territory and boundaries had to be tightened, raiding parties repulsed. The threatening stance of the Giant – all bluster and exuberance – mirrored this instability as much as his primitive weaponry denoted the limitations of the Durotriges during the Roman invasion. Their method of warfare was 'ritualistic' and the awesome ramparts of Maiden Castle are a triumph of obsessive and sustained effort rather than military architecture; once breached, the immense ditches, timber gates and winding ways would obstruct defender and assailant alike. The complex system could be turned against itself.

Eminently practical, the Romans isolated and unmanned those structures capable of blocking their political objectives and allowed the rest to thrive and develop. The Giant, unlike the hillfort, did not fall into the former category – hence the invading legions came, saw and conquered, but did not vanquish a principle that they shared and honoured as much as their enemies.

Conclusion

The most influential argument concerning the identity of the Cerne Giant is the one refined by Stuart Piggott, identifying the figure as Hercules and relating it to the second-century cult of Commodus. There is much to be said for this. Hercules was a Roman god acceptable to the native Britons. Immensely strong, good-humoured, virile, he distinguished himself as a tamer and slayer of wild beasts. He was not a distant or disdainful god either, possessing the common touch, and he wielded a club – a utensil familiar to the pagan Celts. The posture of the Giant is comparable to several Roman statuettes and reliefs of Hercules; furthermore, the evidence of the missing lion's skin, hinted at by resistivity tests, appears to endorse the claim.

The counter-argument, held by the present author, Bernard Pickard, Rodney Legg and Rodney Castleden, sees the Giant as a Celtic god, a warrior-protector, fertile and ferocious. Briefly the reasons are threefold:

1. The Giant is an example of the native art of turf-cutting. This is hardly a mode of worship the Romans would inspire. And what of depicting the emperor with an enormous upraised penis? This is surely an odd feature.
2. Commodus' reign was brief and unpopular. Statuettes and altars dedicated to him were destroyed and removed after his death. Why, then, should the Giant be maintained nearly two thousand years later if it was only a temporary expression of a Roman cult?
3. The Giant is an expression of an ancient phallic religion dating back thousands of years before the arrival of the Romans. The proximity of the maypole underlines this fact. Trying to yoke the Giant to the Romans is a distortion of a principle that can be traced back to Neolithic times.

It may be, with the refinement of silt-dating techniques, that the answer is not far away.

CHAPTER SIX

TROJANS OF ALBION

Brutus, far to the west, in th'ocean wide,
Beyond the realm of Gaul, a land there lies,
Sea-girt it lies, where giants dwelt of old,
Now void, it fits they people: thither bend
They course, there shalt thou find a lasting seat;
There to they sons another Troy shall rise,
And kings be born of thee, whose dreadful might
Shall awe the world, and conquer nations bold.

(Milton's adaptation of Geoffrey of Monmouth)

Introduction

Although our knowledge of the Plymouth Giants consists of inadequate scraps, they have attracted interest and commentary because of their relationship to the Matter of Britain and the riddle of Gogmagog. They create a bridge between Devon and Cambridgeshire (where another giant was carved on the Gogmagog Hills) and point to a hitherto unsuspected function of such artefacts – namely as harbour markers, warning or welcoming signs, aptly situated near strategically important sites. Gogmagog was, if you like, a ruder version of Rhodes' famous Colossus.

Site and Appearance

No longer visible, the Gogmagog Giants were cut overlooking Plymouth Sound below Charles II's Royal Citadel which incorporated into its walls the ancient chapel of St Catherine (1370). South of the chapel was a Giant's Grot or cave which became the site of the magazine. The figure faced the sea on the only slope sufficiently steep and high, slightly west of Fisher's Nose promontory and

The Citadel, Plymouth. The giant figures of Gogmagog were carved on a slope leading up to this fortress, overlooking the Hoe.

near the entrance to Sutton Harbour. Across the water lies Mount Batten, a former Iron Age settlement where five gold coins and eight silver coins of the Dobunni were found, and to the north stood the fourteenth-century castle.

The images of the Giants were carved on hard grey limestone. Theo Brown (1970) argued that the outlines were reddened with earth to make them stand out. Aside from the information that they wielded clubs, nothing is known about their appearance except that one was considerably larger than the other which may have been added later.

It is supposed that the construction of the Citadel caused the disappearance of the Giants, blocking off the steep slope and reconstructing parts of it. The fortress was built in response to the Dutch war which was more concentrated in the North Sea and eastern Channel. In 1665 the commission was issued approving the project. The engineer – Sir Bernard Gomme – modified his plans and extended the 6 m high walls to take in Drake's old fortress (1592–5), incorporating granite doors from the older structure. The Citadel was fitted with 152 gun emplacements as opposed to the old fort's 67. The foundation stone inscribed 'Jo, Earle of Bath 1666' is still intact, and the gateway, attributed to Thomas Fitz, is a splendid essay in baroque architecture. In 1683 Samuel Pepys, the Secretary of the Navy, looked over the Citadel and wrote that, 'De Gomme has built very sillily'. The King visited the fort in 1671, some forty years after the last known reference to Gogmagog.

History and Interpretation

When Geoffrey of Monmouth (1100–54) published his stirring and fabulous *History of the Kings of Britain* the impact of this book was enormous, although some realized that its value was more literary than soberly historical. The early section, concerning the displacement of the aboriginal giants by invading Trojans, has fascinated the antiquaries of Devon because it is localized around Totnes, which features as a landing-place for the Continental invaders. Plymouth also has strong affinities with the legend, claiming to be the scene of the wrestling match between Corineus and Gogmagog.

The implantation of the Biblical names Gogmagog or Gog and Magog is a source of puzzle and confusion. And what, precisely, is their link with Göemagot, the title Geoffrey prefers? Links have been postulated between such names and places like Ugborough, Ogbourne St George and festivals like Hogmanay – a chain of guttural cross-fertilizations slip off the tongue, but how reliable are they? Ardent literalists have claimed Gog and Magog as early rulers of Britain, but such concepts belong to more spacious historical ages when no pettyfogging division existed between flatulent legend and puncturing fact.

Today harsher standards prevail and scholars tend to dismiss Gogmagog as a chance collusion of Biblical and Celtic lore, viewing the wilder flights they have provoked as obfuscations and irrelevancies rather than clues to Britain's distant past. The present writer does not take this view but assails the tangled undergrowth, and no doubt emerges as prickly and nonplussed as his predecessors.

Geoffrey of Monmouth, the twelfth-century Benedictine chronicler, attempts to supply the British with an impeccable classical lineage. He portrays them as descendants of Brutus, son of Sylvius and grandson of Ascanius, the son of Aeneas. The Britons are the progeny of Trojan heroes of whom Homer sang and share a common ancestry with the Romans who, according to the equally inspired Virgil, are directly descended from Aeneas. The latter left the smoking ruins of Troy bearing his aged father upon his shoulders and founded a new kingdom in Italy. Trojan ancestry was considered a mark of good breeding and claimed by the Franks, the Saxons and the Normans.

Brutus' beginnings were ill-starred and disaster-prone. His mother died while giving birth to him and, at the age of fifteen, he accidentally killed his father while hunting and was expelled from

Italy. He journeyed to Greece, where he located another tribe of exiled Trojans, and they quickly elected him as their leader. After various adventures in Greece, he set sail across the Mediterranean and landed on a deserted island where there was a temple to the goddess Diana. The interior held a statue of the deity and Brutus fired questions at it and received the following answer: 'Brutus, there lies an island beyond France, guarded on all sides by the sea, which was formerly the abode of giants, and it is now uninhabited and fit for thy people. Seek it. It will be a lasting seat for thee and a second Troy for thy descendants, to whom the whole world will be subject.' The island was later known as Britain, and Brutus sallied forth once more, acquiring en route four more tribes of expatriate Trojans, led by Prince Corineus, a stout warrior who lusted after combat with giants.

Corineus' aspirations were destined to be placated. When Brutus and his cargo of heroes landed at Totnes, Devon, they learned that Albion, although fair to look upon 'with fish in its streams and wild beasts in its forests', was the abode of a dwindling tribe of giants. The leader of the giants bore the resounding title Göemagot and was capable of wielding a small uprooted oak as lightly as a hazel switch. He and his band of titans attacked Brutus and his men while they were holding a thanksgiving ceremony at Totnes. Corineus straightaway seized his opportunity and engaged Göemagot in a wrestling bout.

> At the beginning of the encounter [writes Geoffrey of Monmouth], Corineus and the giant, standing from front to front, held each other strongly in their arms, and panted aloud for breath; but Göemagot presently grasping Corineus with all his might, broke three of his ribs, two on his right side and one on his left. At which Corineus, highly enraged, roused up his whole strength, and snatching him upon his shoulder, ran with him, as fast as his weight would allow, to the next shore, and there getting on top of a high rock, hurled down the savage monster into the sea, where falling on the sides of the craggy rocks, he was torn to pieces and coloured the waves with his blood. The place where he fell, taking its name from the giant's fall, is called Lam Göemagot to this day.

The wrestling match swiftly passed into legend and numerous chroniclers and poets drew it into their imaginative designs.

Michael Drayton incorporated it into his poetic topography *Poly-Olbion* (1612):

> Upon that lofty place at Plymouth called the Hoe
> Those mighty wrestlers met, with many an ireful looke
> Who threatened as the one the other tooke.

TOTNES AND PLYMOUTH

Geoffrey tells us that the Trojans landed at Totnes and were attacked during a celebratory banquet. Totnes lies at the highest navigable point on the River Dart and became a place of importance when Æthelstan (d. 939) established a fort there. Early medieval writers, however, used the name Totnes to indicate not merely the settlement but also a large area of the South Hams, from Berry Head to Prawle Point, and it is a strong possibility that Geoffrey intended to denote the broad district.

Despite the generalized application of its name, Totnes took its Trojan heritage seriously. At 37 High Street is a waterworn granite boulder alleged to mark the spot where Brutus, alighting from his vessel, proclaimed:

> Here I am and here I rest
> And this town shall be called Totnes.

Regrettably this association cannot be treated with due gravity. Probably the Brutus Stone is the old 'bruiter's stone' from where the medieval crier called out his *bruit* or news. Alternatively it may have been the 'brodestone' or boundary stone which figured prominently in fifteenth-century litigation, for it marked the point of divergence of a stream issuing from a well. The stone indicated where the water ceased to serve the townsfolk and drained off into the castle moat.

If Totnes featured as the site of the thanksgiving feast, Plymouth, to the west, was where the fight took place. *Lam Göemagot*, where the giant was dispatched, is believed to be the present Lamhay Hill, an eminence leading to where the Citadel overlooks the Sound. Across the water, at Torpoint, is a small promontory called Deadman's Point, an interesting coincidence in that a giant of the ogreish, child-eating variety, who formerly enjoyed a bleak reputation in the Gorran Haven district, was bled to death by a wily doctor at Dodman's Point. The word 'dod' is Old English for a snail; Alfred Watkins revered the name and formulated a special theory identifying it with the medieval surveyor whose twin staves produced an effect similar to the snail's cocked horns.

Map of Plymouth Hoe indicating likely site of missing giants.

Aside from supportive topographic features, Plymouth may have actually celebrated the wrestling match between Corineus and Göemagot by large-scale artistic portrayal. What is known is that there was fomerly a hill-figure overlooking the Sound which either directly referred to the combat or gathered the association down the years.

Richard Carew, an Elizabethan historian writing in 1602, states that two figures were incised upon the turf above the estuary: 'Upon the Haw at Plymouth, there is cut in the ground the portraiture of two men, the one bigger, the one lesser, with clubbes in their hands (who they term Gogmagog) and (as I have learned) it is renewed by the order of the Townsmen, which should infer the monument of some moment.' Westcote (1630) similarly refers to the 'portraiture of two men of the largest volume, yet the one surpassing the other in every way', and adds, 'These they name to be Corineus and Gogmagog.'

An old Audit and Receiver's Book belonging to the Corporation of Plymouth confirms both reports. The figures indeed existed and, as Carew remarked, were cleaned and scoured at the cost of the ratepayers:

1486	Item paid to Cotewyll for ye renewing of ye picture of Gogmagog upon ye howe.
1500–1	Item paid for making clene of Gogmagog apon ye howe.
1529–30	Cleansing of Gogmagog 8d
1541–2	Item paid to William Hawkyns, baker, for cuttyng of Gogmagog, the picture of the Gyaunt, on the hawe.
1566–7	20d new cutting of Gogmagog.

One notes a discrepancy. Carew and Westcote mention two figures, yet the Audit Book entry alludes to the 'picture of the Gyaunt' in the singular. Were there two figures or one – or was a second giant added later, as Morris Marples suggests? Carew resided at Anthony House, on the other side of the Sound, and could certainly be considered a reliable authority – yet the question persists. Furthermore, does the doubling of the cost in 1566 reflect inflation, a thorough re-cutting (as opposed to a cleaning), or the addition of a second giant?

And what of the name, Göemagot or Gogmagog? Is he a figment of Geoffrey of Monmouth's highly coloured imagination or was he a known figure in Celtic lore? Geoffrey was evasive on the subject of his source and claimed that the *Historia* was a translation of an old book in the British tongue passed on to him by Walter, Archdeacon of Oxford. It is clear that the *Historia* assimilates many stories from the Celtic lands and preserves significant folklore. Yet, although it exerted the widest possible influence, it was intermittently denounced as a work of no scholarly merit. William of Newburgh decried the whole enterprise not long after its publication: 'His entire book is little more than a farrago of trashy and insolent lies against the Welsh.'

CUDGELLING

So Geoffrey's romance both amplifies and obscures the problem of Gogmagog? The difficult questions remain. Was there one figure or two? Were the impressions upon the Hoe constructed in a sudden burst of patriotic frenzy – to celebrate Geoffrey's vivid narrative – or did they exist before he ever put pen to paper? What is their age? Have they any relationship to the club-bearing giant of Cerne Abbas? More problems are raised than resolved in such enquiries.

One aspect of the Hoe figure – the possession of clubs – harks back to an old country tradition. William Barnes records how in summertime the Dorsetshire villages would amuse themselves with feasts. After consuming the old English fare of beef and plum pudding, they would enjoy the sports of single-stick playing, cudgelling or wrestling. In cudgelling, as the name implies, the weapon was a stout cudgel, and the player defended himself with another, which was crowned by a large hemisphere of wickerwork. The latter was called the pot, and the object of each participant in this match was to fetch blood from his opponent's head 'whether by taking a little skin from pericranium, drawing a stream from his nose, or knocking out a few of those early inventions for grinding – the teeth.'

Thus the giants upon the Hoe relate to a tradition far older than that inaugurated by Geoffrey. Clubs were used as weapons and sporting items long before the advent of metal and doubtless a Neolithic origin could be claimed – if not established – for such pastimes. Yet in view of the singularly unhelpful nature of the evidence, it is wild guesswork to adduce a prehistoric orgin from a mere descriptive detail.

Nevertheless, there are points which contradict the legend of Göemagot and Corineus. Why did Carew describe both figures as holding clubs? One might have supposed that, if the citizens of Plymouth had decided to illustrate this legend, they would have delineated the two combatants clearly, contrasting the knightly bearing of Corineus with his ogreish assailant, Göemagot. Also, one would have expected some sort of documentary record to survive if the cutting had been sponsored by the townsfolk. Geoffrey's *Historia* became a celebrated medieval classic, much reprinted and hotly argued over, so why this vague phraseology, 'whom they term', if the Hoe carvings were a straightforward commemorative relic? It is notable that the giants of London originally had the legendary titles, Hercules and Samson, and then later, as a deeper sense of nationalism took hold, they merged into the specifically British Gogmagog and Corineus.

An argument could be made for the cutting of the 'Gyaunt' some time after 1437, when an act of parliament granted mayoral privileges to Plymouth, previously governed by the Prior of Plymton's courts. The gesture underlined the community's newly acquired independence, a legendary association providing texture and lineage to an identity that had not yet hardened in the civic mould.

THE GUARDIANS OF LONDON

The adventures of Brutus did not end with the demise of Göemagot or Gogmagog. Further laurels awaited him, for he now set about his task of founding a new Troy. The site he selected lay on the River Thames and was called New Troy or Trinovantum. He reigned over the capital for twenty-four years and had three sons, Locrinus, Camber and Albanactus. After his death, Locrinus reigned over England, Camber over Wales, and Albanactus over Scotland.

Tradition states that Brutus lugged a stone across the seas from Troy. He incorporated this into the Temple of Diana which he set up in London shortly after founding the city. The stone – known as the London Stone – is said to reflect on the fortunes of the capital. St Paul's Cathedral has been cited as the original location of Brutus's Dianic temple and Milman (1868), in his *Annals of St Paul's*, relates how a statue of the goddess was found between the Deanery and Blackfriars and a stone altar of Diana, in 1830, at Goldsmiths' Hall in Foster Lane.

Gog and Magog, London
Guildhall, 1953.

The latter were relics of London's Roman rather than Trojan past and, like the Plymouth relics, tend to blur the line between fact and folklore. Yet elsewhere the tradition persists – a variation of Geoffrey's legend maintains that Brutus captured two of the giants and, far from dispatching them to eternity, took them with him to London and appointed them doorkeepers of his palace, allegedly on the site of the Guildhall which today displays the huge carved images of Gog and Magog.

So Göemagot is reincarnated as two personages, Gog and Magog, occupying London's most venerable reference library containing printed books on topography, history, genealogy and heraldry, together with a huge collection of prints and maps. Here the two giants, guardians of the threshold, stand 3 m tall, fashioned out of dowelled and glued limewood planks. They are the work of Mr David Evans FRBS and were unveiled on 8 June 1953.

The modernity of these giants need not deter students of tradition and folklore, for they replaced an earlier pair of figures destroyed during an air raid in December 1940. The incinerated giants had predecessors whose great age and decrepit deportment encouraged rats and mice to gnaw at their entrails. Even they had a history exceeding their individual lifespans, and a brief chronology should suffice to indicate the role of giants in London's celebrations:

1413   Henry V, passing over London Bridge on the way to his coronation, is greeted by the City's first recorded giant. Two years later, after the triumph of Agincourt (1415), he is greeted by a male and female giant at the Southwark gate entry to London Bridge; the male held the city keys, as if porter of London.

1421   Henry V returns to London with his new queen, Katherine, after their marriage in France. At Tower Bridge, two giants bow before the royal couple.

1432   After his coronation in Paris, Henry VI proceeds to London Bridge accompanied by civic dignitaries. A giant with a drawn sword, reflecting the power and majesty of the City, stands mounted upon a tower to receive him.

1522   Emperor Charles V visits London. At the drawbridge gate, on London Bridge, two giants, this time specific personages – Hercules and Samson – greet him at the threshold.

1554   King Philip of Spain, accompanied by Queen Mary, pays a visit to London. After receiving the symbolic mace from the Lord Mayor, the royal couple repair to London Bridge where, near the drawbridge, they are confronted by the giants Corineus Brittanus and Gogmagog Albionus.

1559   Coronation of Elizabeth I. Gogmagog and Corineus are set up in the Temple Bar where, holding Latin verses, they confer their goodwill on the Queen on her way to the abbey.

1559   Puttenham, writing of the London Midsummer Show, draws attention to 'great and ugly giants marching as if they were alive and armed at all points, but within they are stuffed full of brown paper and tow, which the shrewd boys underpeering do guilefully discover and turn to great derision.'

Gog and Magog destroyed in the Blitz, 1940.

1666   The Great Fire destroys the pair of giants which were probably stored in the Guildhall.

1672   The Court of Aldermen decide 'That the two Gyaunts now preparing to bee set upp in the Guildhall shall be used upon the next Lord Maiors Day for such purpose as his Lordshipp shall thinke fitting, his Lordshipp now ingageing to restore them againe in Good plight and condicion as they shall bee when hee shall receive them.'

1700   Edward Ward comments scathingly on the giants of the capital: 'I asked my Friend the meaning and design of setting up those two Lubberly Preposterous Figures, for I suppose they had some peculiarly end in't. Truly, says my Friend, I am wholly ignorant of what they intended by 'em, unless they were set up to show the

City what huge Loobies their Fore-fathers were, or else fright they stubborn apprentices into obedience.'

1706   Mr Olley, the clerk of the City's works, was ordered to see that the giants, who were now in an advanced state of decay, were either restored or replaced. Having been feasted upon by vermin, they no longer stood upright, and the carver, Richard Saunders, was commissioned to do the task.

1710   Von Uffenbach describes Saunders' creations: 'The two giant forms, bearing a shield opposite the entrance, which one is led to imagine something quite out of the ordinary, are most wretched. The sight of them would make anyone laugh, for the bodies are quite monstrous, while the legs are like those of a dachshund.'

The giants of Richard Saunders, seemingly the subject of much robust jocularity and abuse, survived well over 250 years until the air raid of 1940.

OGMIOS

Before discussing the significance of the Giants, it is helpful to gain an idea of their appearance. Gogmagog, of barbarous aspect, was the more formidable of the two, equipped with bow and arrow and a spiked globe known as the 'morning star'. Corineus, the Trojan hero, was attired after the fashion of a Roman warrior, with a sword and spear. An effective portrait of them can be found in John Noorthouck's history of the capital (1773):

> On the opposite side of the entrance into this hall, a little to the right, is a flight of steps leading to the offices, over which is a balcony or gallery supported by twelve iron pillars in the form of palm trees. From the middle of the balcony projects a square clock elegantly carved round the case, with the figure of Time on the top. But the most extraordinary decorations of this balcony are two uncouth gigantic images, which stand one at each end on the outside of the rails. These enormous figures are made of pasteboard and painted in ancient military dresses: the one holds a spear in his hand, hanging by a chain from a long staff; and are supposed to represent an ancient Briton and a Saxon.

One of the liveliest commentators on the giants was the folklorist and Atlantean, Lewis Spence (1928) who recalled how, as 'a gaping

PUNCH'S PENCILLINGS.——N° LXIX.

BROUGHAM AND THE CIVIC GIANTS.

"A few nights ago he made dreadful sparring with his old civic friends, the Guildhall giants."—*Vide page* 116.

Punch's view of Gog and Magog.

urchin', he would gaze fascinated at the garishly painted colossi and sense a deeper philosophy of tradition behind them.

Citing Doctor Henry Bradley, Spence derived London from the Celtic 'Londinos', meaning 'fierce'. Furthermore, the legendary title of the region Cockaigne (after which Cockneys are named) has been translated as 'the land of region of Gog'. In *New View of London* (1708), Hatton states that the name Gog and Magog frightened some apprentices 'as little children are at the terrible sound of Raw-Head or Bloody-Bones' – could this terror be rooted in folk memory, harking back to a time when sacrifices were made to a pair of grim tutelary deities? Do the deposed idols, Gog and Magog, constitute the original 'fierce ones' who presided over the twin hills of Walbrook beside the Thames?

Originally, Spence surmised, the giants would have been put together from wickerwork, like the basket idols of the Druids, and this could identity Gog with Ogmios, the Celtic Hercules, 'who garbed in lion-skin, and with club in hand, drew all men after him in chains and demanded more than the occasional human holocaust.'

Rousing prose – but Londinos? Gog and Magog? Cockney? Walbrook? Awesome leaps are involved as Spence interweaves dissimilar titles in an evocative tapestry of lore and legend and, surprisingly, omits to mention that London has been derived from Lugdunum (Lugh's place or dominion) and Billingsgate from Belenus' Gate. If the names Gogmagog and Corineus could be traced earlier than 1554, his case might have fared better, but Gog and Magog cannot be fixed in a London location, and the stirring rhetoric does not reverberate much beyond the margin of the page.

The whole issue is gloriously confused by the appearance of Gog and Magog in the Bible. Ezekiel predicts their destruction by the Jews and mention is made of them in Revelation. Gog was the chief prince of Mesech and Tubal, a country north of the Caucasus or Mount Taurus, and Magog features as another name for this region. Elsewhere Magog is identified as one of Japheth's sons, a progenitor of the Scythians, a nomadic tribe which displaced the Cimmerians from the Eurasian steppes in the eighth century BC and whose influence is detectable in Celtic art.

It is clear, however, that London's Gogmagog appears to have been modelled on the passage in Ezekiel, for the weapons are rendered faithfully: 'And I will smite the bow out of thy right hand, and I will cause thy arrows to fall out of thy right hand.' Even his spiked globe, the 'morning star', recalls the Luciferian brilliance of pagan gods and kings. So, in all events, it must be conceded that widespread Bible-reading assisted in the promulgation and popularization of Gog and Magog and perhaps obscured the native Göemagot.

Conclusion

Geoffrey of Monmouth, compiling his *Historia*, imposed a fluent narrative upon a corpus of fact, anecdote, folklore and Welsh and Breton legend. His work is only part imagination, for he did possess topographic knowledge and documentation no longer extant, and this he employed to endow his chronicle with verisimilitude.

The present writer contends that the place called Lamgöemagot or Göemagot's Leap bore that name, together with the carving of the battling giants, before Geoffrey started to compose his history. The turf-cut giants were part of the palladia of Plymouth, old pagan tutelary deities who in the course of time became deposed, their original significance forgotten, yet still retaining a kind of mascot status. They were collectively called Gogmagog; the name, ostensibly Biblical, may have a Celtic lineage and there are several parallels. Doctor Borlase, in his account of Irish dolmens, refers to Gig-na-Gog, the presiding giant of an Irish barrow lying on the road to Beardville.

The British ogre Göemagot met his death at the hands of the Brutus's lieutenant, Corineus. The introduction of a Trojan hero into the narrative can be seen as a literary fabrication on the part of Geoffrey of Monmouth. Originally the Plymouth Giants celebrated the triumph of light and fertility over darkness and death. They were a pictorial record of an archetypal encounter such as took place between Zeus and Saturn, Baal and Mot, Horus and Set – conflicts later epitomized by the dragon-slaying knights of Christianity.

The Trojan line of interpretation became accepted when the old stories had faded from memory. A similar process was repeated when Francis Wise, examining the Uffington Horse, proclaimed it the work of King Alfred. Were it not for the fact that the Horse survives today, and possesses features inconsistent with Wise's interpretation, his views might have acquired permanent validity. Likewise, had the Plymouth Giants survived, Geoffrey's attractive fiction would be discarded and the figures would be related to the Cerne Giant. Hence, taking this view, the Gogmagog and Corineus fable is an example of a medieval reading superimposed on an artefact so old that nothing survives to clarify its origin.

Two giants, one bigger, one smaller, were cut upon the Hoe. No second figure was added. The single fragment of contradictory evidence is the missing 's' where 'gyaunt' is employed in the singular. Allowing for grammatical imprecision, this hardly presents a serious case. If a second figure had been added, in order to endorse Geoffrey's stirring chronicle, one would have expected firmer, more conclusive commentary from the Devon antiquaries of Elizabethan and Stuart times.

This is a personal view, for there is a dismal paucity of evidence concerning the Plymouth Giants. Not so much as a bad sketch survives to indicate their general appearance. Any direct connection between them and the Cerne Giant is impossible to establish, but it is of incidental interest that Mr Napper (1889) identified the Dorset figure as Gogmagog, citing not only the Hoe carvings but also two ancient hollowed-out oaks guarding each side of the road near Glanvilles Wootton. These were known as Gog and Magog, a name shared by another pair of oaks at High Stoy, on the Minterne to Evershot road, and yet another couple of trees at Glastonbury, Somerset, rumoured to be vestiges of a Druidical grove.

HERNE THE HUNTER

So Gog and Magog are connected not only with giants, hills and dark demonic agencies but with strong, durable oak trees, associated with the mysterious golden bough, the sacred mistletoe of Baldur. The oak was the tree by which Socrates swore, and the priestess of Zeus had her shrine beneath an oak at Dordona in north-east Greece and interpreted the rustling of its leaves as answers to her questions.

Not only Zeus but Baal, the god of idolatorous Syrians, incarnated himself as an oak spirit. His acolytes performed sacrifices 'under every leafy oak, wherever they offered pleasing odours to their idols' (Ezekiel 6.13). The oak is the tree of Maytime, and locally appointed May kings and queens, often depicted as wild men and women, were traditionally garlanded with oak leaves. Neither is it coincidental that the Cerne Giant's club mimics the shape of an oak leaf.

The word 'Druid' has been translated as 'knowledge of the oak'. Maximus of Tyre observed that the Celts venerated the tree as a symbol of Zeus–Taranis. Obviously it embodied a deity, a growth principle, which had several manifestations. One of England's most famous trees was the Herne Oak in Windsor Forest. Herne was a former keeper of the forest park who, like Odin, hanged himself on a tree. His ghost, associated with times of national crisis, has been described as 'a wild spectral object, possessing a slight resemblance to a human being, clad in the skin of a deer and wearing on its head a sort of helmet, formed of the skull of a stag, from which branched a pair of large antlers.' Shakespeare was acquainted with this handsome apparition and evokes it in *The Merry Wives of Windsor*.

There is a tale goes that Herne the Hunter
Sometimes a keeper in Windsor Forest,
Doth all winter time, at still midnight,
Walk round about the oak with great ragged horns.

Tradition states that Herne would be seen standing or crouching near his favourite tree, as if about to spring on a victim, or otherwise galloping round the trunk, festooned with chains and accompanied by a pack of howling dogs. Here folklore seems to have connived a marriage between the antlered Celtic god, Cernunnos, and Odin leading his Wild Hunt.

And what of the stag's horns – how do they fit in? Herds of deer once roamed freely through the forests of England and formed the staple diet of Robin Hood. Every year the beast sheds its antlers and rapidly grows a new pair, gaining extra points, until it takes on a splendidly regal look. It is likely that the Celtic tribes intimately linked the stag's branching horns with the spreading boughs of the oak. The deer was the monarch of the forest animals, and the oak was lord of all vegetation.

One more significant point is that the oak was believed to be the tree of the thunder-god because it was frequently struck by lightning. Most likely, this reflects upon its size and distribution but the tree can be seen as a kind of omphalos, or magnetic centre, where Thor, Gogmagog, the Cerne Giant, Cernunnos the stag-god, Odin and the chain-rattling spectre of Herne unite their manifold principles.

GOG AND MAGOG, AFTER THE LORD MAYOR'S DINNER.

CHAPTER SEVEN

THE WANDLEBURY

ENIGMA

Take heed you find not that you do not seek.

(Old English proverb)

Introduction

South of Cambridge, rising almost imperceptibly to the height of 76 m (250 ft), are the Gogmagog Hills, today crowned by an extensive golf course. The name is first recorded in 1574, compared with the earlier 1486 allusion to the Giants on Plymouth Hoe. The derivation is not clear but the earliest mention (1576) refers to 'Gogmagoghills'; later variants are 'Hogmagogge' (1667) and 'Hogmagog'. In his paper, 'The Linguistic Status of the Wandlebury Giants', Richard Coates (1978) drew attention to the parallel of the word *hodmedod* or *hodmandod*, meaning snail, once common in Cambridge, and invoked the concentric rings of Wandlebury Camp as comparable to a snail-shell pattern.

Wandlebury Camp, or Wandlebury Rings, as it is commonly called, is the major earthwork of the hills, a former outpost of the Iceni, consisting of two massive banks and ditches enclosing a circular space. Unfortunately the camp was incorporated into Lord Godolphin's landscape garden during the eighteenth century. The inner bank was levelled and pushed into the ditch, and the outer bank was breached in several places. This operation may have destroyed the giant human figure carved on the turf which the late T.C. Lethbridge, an archaeologist of controversial repute, attempted to restore.

Site and Appearance

The figure is no longer visible. According to John Layer (1640), the original Giant was cut within the trench of Wandlebury Camp in the Gogmagog Hills. This seems to indicate the turf ramparts between the ditches – in which case the figure must have been fairly small, and it is difficult to imagine how it could be viewed from a distance – or within the earthwork itself. Nothing is known about its appearance. One gathers from at least one reference that it was more laughable than alarming. It became overgrown or was effaced during the building of a landscape garden, some two hundred years ago.

History and Interpretation

At the turn of the century the children of Cherry Hinton, two miles north of Wandlebury, were warned not to play in the chalkpit above the village because Gog and Magog were buried there. Also they may have been told of a golden chariot buried at Fleam Dyke, near Murtlow Hill, three miles east of Wandlebury. Such fabulous yarns are pertinent to the region, for, although scenically unspectacular, the Gogmagog Hills, Cambridgeshire, are veined with rich lodes of legend and lore centring upon their enigmatic name, the figure of the vanished giant, and the big Iron Age encampment which ceased to be occupied *c.* 250 BC. In fact, it was the association of these heights with giants and supernatural agencies which provoked Dr Fritz Heichelheim, who had made a study of small crude bronze Hercules statuettes found in the Cambridge district, to connect Wandlebury with the cult of Hercules–Commodus which he believed had a significant following in Roman Britain (1937).

According to Gervase of Tilbury, the name Wandlebury is derived from the tribe of Vandals, transferred there by the Emperor Probus in AD 277. However, Reaney, in his study of Cambridgeshire place-names, derives it from Wendlesbirri or 'Waendal's fort'.

The first published reference to the Wandlebury Giant is found in a work by Bishop Joseph Hall, appearing in Frankfurt in 1605 but quickly followed by an English edition: 'A Giant called All Paunch, who was of incredible Height of body, not like him whose Picture the Schollers of Cambridge got to see at Hogmagog Hills, but rather like him that ought the two Apple Teeth which were digged out of a well in Cambridge, that were little less than a man's head.'

William Cole, the antiquary of Cambridge, gleaned the bishop's account and enlarged it with his own childhood recollections of the figure: 'When I was a boy, about 1724, I remember my Father or Mother, as it happened, I went with one of them to Cambridge, the road from Baberham lying through the Camp (now blocked up by the house and gardens inclosed in it of my Lord Godolphin), always used to stop and show me and my Brother and Sisters the figure of the giant carved on the turf; concerning whom there were many traditions now worn away. What became of the said teeth I never heard.'[1]

Yet another Cambridge historian, John Layer, was familiar with the Wandlebury Giant and commented in 1640: 'I could never learn how these hills came to be called Gogmagog Hills, unless it were from a high and mighty portraiture of a giant wch the Schollars of Cambridge cut upon the turf or superficies of the earth within the said trench, and not unlikely called it Gogmagog, which I have seen but it is now of late discontinued.'

The accounts fail to match. Bishop Hall implies the figure is unimpressive, William Cole gives the impression of a remarkable figure of some antiquity, and John Layer emphasizes the Giant's high and mighty dimensions but attributes it to the horseplay of undergraduates. The scholars of Cambridge did assist in the scouring of the figure, and probably relished the drinking and cavorting, but Layer's account of their cutting the figure somehow lacks authority.

A curious legend attached itself to Wandlebury Camp which runs thus. Once the arena was ruled by a dark night-rider whom no mortal could defeat in combat. Anyone brave enough to test his prowess had to ride into the camp on a moonlit night and cry 'Knight to knight, come forth!' The warrior would appear on his sable charger and joyfully embrace the challenge.

A Norman knight called Osbert, who was quartered at Cambridge, decided to oppose this weird spectral horseman. He rode into the camp, shouting the challenge out loud, and the warrior galloped forth to meet him. Shields and levelled lances clashed and sparked, and bloody blows were parried and returned. Osbert, with a skilful spear-thrust, managed to unseat his opponent. As a token of victory, he seized the steed of the black horseman and began to lead it away.

---

[1] This recalls Hunt's anecdote about the workmen on Plymouth Hoe coming across the gigantic molars of Gogmagog while laying foundations for the Citadel. Identical whimsies, it seems, surround the titan-deities of these islands.

Thereupon the fallen warrior picked up his lance and hurled it at him. The missile embedded itself deeply in Osbert's thigh. The Norman knight retired to Cambridge with the captured horse, but upon the following dawn the animal had vanished and was seen no more. The years passed by, and upon each anniversary of the moonlight tournament, Osbert's thigh wound opened and bled afresh.

It has been maintained that this legend was an attempt to explain an immensely complicated set of hill-figures which were rediscovered and ingeniously interpreted over thirty-two years ago. Elements of the legend preserve time-honoured themes: the recurrent stigmata, the arrogant protagonist and his eventual defeat, the deserted camp beneath the waning moon, details which can be readily paralleled with ancient myths invoking sky-storming warrior gods, the defeat of the demon of darkness, spilt blood to placate the moon-goddess presiding over the encampment, and the mysterious vanishing horse, formerly a manifestation of the other world.

Having set down the basic source material, this seems the apt point to deal with that highly unorthodox, sometimes derided, yet intermittently stimulating and enjoyable archaeologist, T.C. Lethbridge. He made a valiant attempt to slice the Gordian knot of Gogmagog. Many think he had less success in the enterprise than his numerous devotees claim, but nevertheless he deserves a proper hearing in any book on hill-figures.

THE MISSING GIANT

In the autumn of 1954, Tom Lethbridge, director of excavations for the Cambridge Antiquarian Society, embarked on a search for the missing Wandlebury Giant. His intention was to excavate the grassed-over carving and try to relate it to other such figures. His initial interest in the Giant had been aroused by Sammy Cowles, who was a monkeyish museum assistant with a penchant for such grisly duties as boiling flesh off New Guinea skulls. He told Lethbridge that, as a child, he had spoken to an old man who remembered from his own childhood days being able to see the Giant from Sawston. This anecdote encouraged Lethbridge that, whatever infilling had taken place during the past hundred years, the hill-figure was capable of restoration.

After studying the various descriptions of the Wandlebury figure, Lethbridge examined the southern slopes facing Sawston, no longer visible from the Cambridge–Linton road, the view being obscured by a broad belt of beeches planted over a hundred years ago. His preliminary investigations revealed 'a low mound of made-up soil, containing small lumps of chalk, on the end of a small spur projecting southward from Wandlebury' which he concluded was formed by the tipping of scouring waste over a long period. He then proceeded to test the ground with a heavy sounding-bar, which he would hammer into the ground, attempting to probe any areas of disturbed chalk. Soft patches could indicate the trench formerly outlining the Giant, and by planting sticks in these areas an idea of its original shape might be established.

The sounding-bar has never been considered part of the archaeologist's equipment, and for this reason many experts have questioned both Lethbridge's method and results. They distrusted him because, having no first-hand experience of his unorthodox technique, they were unable to confirm or deny his findings. For Lethbridge, although an original thinker with Arctic expeditions and Hebridean voyages to his credit, was viewed as *persona non grata* by his more conventional, or, according to one's way of thinking, less wrong-headed colleagues. His reasoning differed from theirs and was characterized by imaginative leaps and bounds, the confident gathering-together of loose strands of speculation, and the rooted assumption that, despite far-flung distribution and contrasting customs, there was an underlying unity to the religious beliefs of Europe and Asia, which, by inspired deduction and informed comparison, could be plainly set forth.

Working with the sounding-bar proved arduous and backbreaking. The reverberations of the implement brought up blisters 'the size of hens' eggs' on his palms, and Lethbridge confessed it was a job for a man twenty years younger. His efforts were poorly assisted by the groups of doubting archaeologists, bevvies of apathetic bystanders, pushy busybodies and semi-delinquents who, to force a little meaning into their lives, deliberately removed his marking-sticks. A note of hurt indignation creeps into his writing at this stage, but he managed to concentrate fully on the matter in hand and keep sounding with the bar until a curious pattern became apparent.

To Lethbridge's puzzlement it resembled something like a man in a bowler hat, an image that fitted into no known canon of prehistoric art. Deciding that assistance would be helpful at this juncture, Lethbridge did a quick sketch and posted it to Sir Thomas Kendrick at the British Museum. The latter replied with a brief telegram:

'Rear quarter of an animal. Walking (not galloping) white horse. May the lord be with you.' Encouraged, Lethbridge resumed work with the crowbar. The shape of a female became gradually clear, obviously the horse's rider, and another drawing was dispatched, which, on this occasion, was received by Cyril Fox, an authority on Celtic art. He sent back a cheering telegram: 'Female with two horses, probably Epona. Congratulations.'

The Wandlebury goddess and her horse.

This discovery came as a shock. Lethbridge had expected to find one giant of the male gender, and instead he had uncovered a female giantess, identified with the Celtic horse-goddess, Epona.

When he re-applied himself to his soundings, the pattern started to develop further elaborations. The form of a chariot began to emerge on the hillside (legend has it that a golden chariot lies buried beneath the hill) together with a pole connecting it to the horse's legs.

However, yet another find was forthcoming. His persistent efforts exposed a second hill-figure which turned out to be a gigantic sword-wielding warrior, of distinctly Celtic aspect, grasping a small circular shield, beneath which a close-fitting tunic flowed, gashed here and there with various wounds. Unlike the goddess-giantess, this figure rang true. The first design had consisted of a muddled assemblage of ectoplasmic loops and whorls (recalling faked spiritualist photographs or one of Picasso's more playful phases), but the warrior proclaimed itself an effective piece of representational art.

Figure of a Celtic warrior with small round shield and short sword, as plotted by Lethbridge from soundings and test cuts.

On the debit side, although more believable pictorially than the goddess, the Celtic warrior was not excavated but merely plotted out with sticks subsequent to positive soundings with the bar. This cursory treatment was accorded to the third hill-figure located to the left of the goddess, a sun-god, delineated in wild lines and swanlike curves with flying cloak and crazed, windswept expression.

Lethbridge was faced with a problem more considerable than he had anticipated. His quest for one hill-figure had culminated in the discovery of a hillside mural showing three figures, artistically dissimilar and probably dating from different periods. His job now was to establish their relationship with one another and to decipher the religious codes that engendered them.

Although his researches, as finalized in the book *Gogmagog*, led him down tortuous by-paths of folklore and archaeology, his conclusions were neither overtly fantastic nor even unorthodox. He identified the giantess as Magog, a horse-goddess known as Epona to the Celts, Diana to the Romans, who combined the familiar roles of earth mother and moon-goddess. Lethbridge tentatively maintained that

the Iceni tribe constructed the Wandlebury fortress and decorated it with her image *c.* 200 BC. When the Catuvallani tribe displaced the Iceni during the first century BC, they fashioned two complementary figures, the cloaked sun-god together with the warrior-god with his sword, shield, scars and tunic.

ANCIENT BRITISH DEITIES

Lethbridge's basic argument is that certain religious images, whether of the sun, the moon, or club- or sword-wielding giants, have a common Indo-European ancestry. Horse-figures share this. The Trojan horse was originally a ceremonial figure and the ancestor of the numerous hobby-horses of Britain and Europe. The equine emblem implied the fertility of the earth mother, later venerated as a moon-goddess. She is to be found repeatedly, in the naked and blackened Godiva parading through Southam, in the statuettes of Epona holding the keys of heaven, in the weird Horse of Uffington and in the lucky moon-shaped horseshoe. This moon-goddess was superseded by the sun-god in his numerous manifestations, Balor, Bel, Belinus, Lucifer, Apollo, Gog, all of whom are closely related. Where other archaeologists emphasize the bewildering and apparently formless variety of Celtic deities, Lethbridge briskly simplifies the pattern to familiar sun, moon, blood, fire and fertility archetypes.

He concludes that Gog and Magog are not mere biblical infusions but ancient British deities representing masculine and feminine principles. Gog is a version of Ogmios, a Herculean divinity equated with the glare and dazzle of the sun – hence the word 'goggle'. Magog, known variously as Mag, Meg and Matrona, was the moon 'under whose pale light the lovemaking took place and the children were born'. He finds Magog's name embedded in the nearby hills: Meg's Hill, Mag's Hill, Margaret's Hill, several having a triple-breast shape, a peculiarity shared by the goddess he uncovered at Wandlebury.

Although he was the more physically active in demonstrating it, the theory was not entirely devised by Lethbridge. Many years earlier Lewis Spence had argued that Gog was short for Ogmios, the Celtic Hercules who founded the Ogham alphabet, and that Magog was his female counterpart, conceivably related to Ceridwen, the Celtic goddess of agriculture and inspiration.

T.C. Lethbridge thought this warrior graffito, carved in nearby Wallington church, might be a sketch of the Wandlebury Giant. (Copy by Ross Parish)

Today very little is left of Lethbridge's excavations. Few traces remain of the giantess earth mother Magog, whom the anthropologist Margaret Murray examined admiringly, except as one writer put it 'overgrown depressions and mounds in the ground, neglected by all but the mystic and curious'. Nevertheless, a certain aura and mystery hangs around the spot and it continues to gather a lore of its own; neo-pagan pilgrims leave offerings on the breast of the goddess. The former editor of the *Ley Hunter*, Paul Devereux, described how, when flying over Wandlebury Camp, 'an expensive newish camera fell apart at the precise moment when infra-red pictures of the Gog Magog figures were to be taken' (*Ley Hunter* 84). The camera had worked perfectly before take-off, so one must conclude that the old gods were at their mischief.

Conclusion

Lethbridge's achievement is almost impossible to assess. Either one has confidence in him or one has not. To a layman, he appears knowledgeable, practical, experienced, and talks very much as if he is a man on the spot and in the know.

Yet what of the opinion of official archaeologists? They may on occasions be merciless to an ill-informed non-archaeological writer trespassing on their territory, but regarding Lethbridge (who, despite his faith in dowsing, the paranormal and odd folkloristic backwaters, did have some standing as a professional, or at least semi-professional, archaeologist) they have tended to preserve a dignified silence. If they considered his claims unfounded, they adopted the gentlemanly damnation-by-overlooking tactics rather than indulging in open derision.

Hoping to get some sort of indication of Lethbridge's standing as an archaeologist and, in particular, as a rediscoverer of lost hill-figures, I wrote to the late Professor Glyn Daniel for information. In a short but kindly letter, I was informed that *Gogmagog* was not reviewed in *Antiquity* – no one, in fact, was asked to review it. He described it as an unfortunate book and believed 'that he was not finding any genuine antiquities but probably confusing geological features'.

Who then is right? The problem is appallingly difficult but not entirely lacking in comic aspects. There is Lethbridge, a dynamic and erudite man, portly and assured, standing among heaps of excavated grey and brown sludge, veined with gleaming swathes of fresh-cut chalk, pointing proudly at his hill-figures as a major archaeological find, while other equally learned men stare uncomprehendingly at the same pattern, seeing them as arbitrary doodles of the frost and rain. Lethbridge built on the foundations of his discovery a whole mythology, a set of exciting transcontinental links and patterns, and what is more he relayed the information in a firm, emphatic, no-nonsense style calculated to inspire the reader's confidence. It all, of course, leads to the overwhelming question: do people looking for hill-figures invariably tend to hallucinate and indulge in a type of automatic drawing? Are they led hopelessly astray by plough-marks, tiny water-cut gullies, small chalk pits and depressions? Without any precedent it is a vexing problem to establish how exactly a hillside slope, of a certain gradient, exposed to thousands of years of weathering, along with agricultural interference, should look when stripped of its turf. Even geologists would find it difficult to define a norm and contrast it with an artificially imposed pattern.

A PARTIAL VIEW

Nearly all books that singlemindedly expound a theory exclude evidence that would disrupt or seriously damage an effective presentation of their case. In a sense, *Gogmagog* can be seen as a PR exercise in which most of the cracks are smoothed over and hardly a strong objection voiced. I have loaned several learned friends my copy – after reading it, nearly all have been charmed and convinced by the author.

However, they have not examined the case for the prosecution. Lethbridge's account is extremely partial. That the story can be told with a quite different emphasis can be gathered from the article written by W.A. Clark (1997), present warden of Wandlebury Rings, who relates the whole affair with a mixture of curiosity and irony.

In *Gogmagog* Lethbridge dates his preoccupation with the Giant from 1954 but does not mention his original involvement in the excavation of Wandlebury Rings in 1955. Clark reminds us that the search for the Gogmagog was triggered when Lethbridge, tiring of the 'humdrum digging and barrowing of large quantities of soil', decided to push ahead with a pet project. Abandoning the team to which he was attached, he asked the Cambridge Preservation Society, the new owners of Wandlebury, for permission to look for the lost hill-figure. They acceded as his method – pounding an iron bar into the ground – was not likely to damage the ancient monument. When he began prospecting, however, friction arose between him and those continuing work on the hillfort. In one of his letters he refers to his iron bar landing on 'A.N. Other's foot', but he carried on undeterred and soon had charted the outline of a figure.

He submitted his drawing to the CPS secretary, asking permission to dig and bring his 'god' to light. There was initial approval – hardly anyone had opportunity to muster a coherent objection. Together with his friend Tebutt and a small team of helpers, Lethbridge quickly dug out the 'Goddess' and afterwards contacted *The Times* who announced his discovery of a 'previously lost, three thousand-year-old hill-figure'.

After such publicity, what forgiveness? Besides, archaeologists needed to confirm Lethbridge's outline. The CPS examined the figure and found themselves puzzled rather than appeased. Eventually the Council for British Archaeology appointed a committee to investigate the matter. From this point, mockery, doubt and counter-argument began to surface. In February 1956, three specialists examined Lethbridge's 'Goddess' and concluded that he had 'excavated a natural phenomenon of polygons, caused by periglacial conditions during the last ice age'. Such features are common in East Anglia.

Their report embarrassed the CPS who thought it best to turf over the 'Goddess'. However, Lethbridge quite naturally objected to smothering the 'great British antiquity' and issued a pamphlet attacking the proposal. With the publication of *Gogmagog* (1957), there was a shift towards Lethbridge's forcefully argued thesis, and several friends and academics made encouraging noises. But then a distinguished archaeologist and friend of Lethbridge's, who had been unavailable at the time of the February inspection, read *Gogmagog* and surveyed the site. Totally unconvinced, he insisted that his report be presented separately from those of his more sympathetic colleagues. At this juncture, whatever moderate enthusiasm the CPS retained for the 'Goddess' drained away.

Since then, the buried 'Goddess' has been tested by magnometer and resistivity meter without any supportive evidence emerging. Furthermore, W.A. Clark measured the relative depth of the excavation, most of which did not fall dramatically below the plough-line. Some 30 per cent of the carving – around the torso area – was markedly deeper; the latter anomaly, in Clark's view, was caused by trees that formerly grew there having collapsed during a gale. The quantities of small round pebbles buried in the hollows – Lethbridge thought them Iron Age slingstones – were probably of natural origin.

More damningly, it seems he had selected the wrong place to dig for the Giant. He discounted John Layer's description of the carving being 'within the said trench' and did not mention – or ignored – Dr Dale (an antiquarian who visited Cambridge 1722–38) who stated that the figure was 'cut on the turf in the middle of the camp'. Above all, he preferred Sammy Cowles' memories of the old man seeing the figure from Sawston. If the Giant could be picked out from there, it must have been on the slope and not inside the Camp. This is sound reasoning, but why value it above Layer and Dale?

If the figure had been cut inside the earthwork, this might raise problems about an Iron Age dating. Lethbridge (who had a very practical side) must have thought that a large hill-figure would pointlessly complicate the operation of a hillfort. The ditches would prove an obstacle, and it would have to be protected from straying livestock and tramping feet. In such an odd position, the design was likelier to have been cut in medieval times, when the fort no longer had a practical purpose. Intent on finding a Celtic antiquity, similar to that of Cerne Abbas, Lethbridge chose a more prominent position.

On finding the figure, his thinking abruptly switched from the tentative to the categoric:

As late as December 1956, Tom was writing, 'It is anyone's guess who this chap is. Mine is that he is a Sun God.' The fact is that only days later Tom had cut a couple of nipples into the outline and called it a Goddess. I think that puts the whole thing in perspective. Dr Bushnell remembered Tom from their student days as a great joker. During a site visit he was asked by Tom what he thought about the figure. The good doctor's reply was, 'Well Tom, I think this is your best jape so far.' He said that Tom never spoke to him again.

(Clark 1997)

One can sympathize with Lethbridge. Having exposed his figure and committed himself to its existence, he was unlikely to rescind his declaration or admit to doubt. The more he pushed ahead in the face of opposition, the more Gogmagog was transformed from a provisional antiquity into a projection of his personal standing. What began as a stimulating foray had become the mirror of his reputation, and he could not endure the thought of it being smashed.

CHAPTER EIGHT

THE LONG MAN OF

WILMINGTON

The Long Man may originally be the work of ancient priests, bored monks, conquering Romans or Saxons or an eccentric squire. The Cerne Giant may have been cut by Durotrigians, Romans, monks or Holles's servants. I do not actually think that the figure's origins are of primary importance. Both archaeologists and members of the public do ask, 'When was it built? What is it?', and will continue to do so, but the problem is probably more interesting than the answer. Indeed it may be that we need these prominent mysteries to prevent our getting over-mighty and filled with certainty about ourselves and the world.

(Martin Brown 1996)

Introduction

Unique among hill-figures, the Long Man of Wilmington holds a pair of staves or wands in his outstretched hands. He is the tallest of the giants, 70.3 m (231 ft), and is said, on the authority of local wiseacres, to be a portrait of the tallest person who ever lived. Also known as the Lone Man, the Lanky Man and, if overgrown, the Green Man, his posture is meeker than that of the Cerne Giant and far less detailed. Only his staves vaguely speak of something tangible: a traveller, a sage, a magus, the Hindu deity Varuna – all these suggestions have been advanced. For the Long Man epitomizes the central problem of identifying hill-figures, being vaguely evocative of many things in general and specifically evocative of nothing in particular.

The figure is outlined with white bricks and is elongated to compensate for the foreshortening effect of the hill slope. His staves are 70.3 m (231 ft) and 71.8 m (235 ft) long, and it has been claimed than he is the world's largest representation of the human form.[1] His lofty cranium has been used for weather forecasting.

> When Firle or Long Man wears a cap,
> We in the valley get a drap.

When clouds cover the figure's brow, rain can be expected down below.

The Long Man is enhanced by an adjoining Benedictine priory which gave shelter to Eleanor, daughter of King John and wife of Simon de Montfort. The idle monks of Wilmington, in common with the lecherous monks of Cerne, have been credited with cutting the figure. According to tradition, the Long Man once bore a cock to his right.

By comparison with the Berkshire Horse and Dorset Giant, the Sussex hill-figure was late in achieving recognition. Speculation about the former led to its rediscovery as an important prehistoric monument. In 1874, when its outline became blurred, it was re-trenched and the Duke of Devonshire paid for a surround of bricks to highlight its shape.

Site and Appearance

The Long Man is one of the most accessible of hill-figures. Facing slightly east of true north, he lies on the slope of Windover Hill, behind the village of Wilmington, Sussex. Only six miles south-east is the large town of Eastbourne, and the main A27 from the coastal resort curves through Polegate and strikes west to Lewes. A turning to the left passes through Wilmington and skirts the base of a high hill sprinkled with tumuli. This is Windover – crowned by a distinctive long barrow – and the Long Man may be approached from public paths running to the base and top of the figure. Today one finds him fenced in for protection against archaeological zealots and vandals. Another innovation is that he is marked out with 770 white concrete blocks, replacing the earlier bricks removed in 1969.

---

[1] The world's largest carving of the human figure is the Giant of Atacama, northern Chile, on the Sierra Unica, 120 m high with a panther-like head, boots and a crown.

The side of Windover Hill showing the Long Man. An eighteenth-century chalk quarry is situated to the right of the figure. The broken ground above his left shoulder is formed by a Neolithic long barrow and Bronze Age bowl barrows. (photograph courtesy of Martin Brown)

The Long Man adorns the northern part of a rounded massif of chalk about four miles square. There are several of these detached blocks of chalk, all caused by rivers breaching the escarpment of the South Downs, and the hill-figure occupies the easternmost of them. The Cuckmere River dawdles and twists in its shallow valley and reaches the sea near the famous Seven Sisters cliffs.

This, then, is the geographical setting, but the visual impact of the figure is another matter. To gaze upon the Long Man is to experience a special type of frisson. The steep turf rampart rising to the calm crest of Windover creates that faint chill of apprehension one feels when immensities whittle us down to our all-too-human stature. Time past broods here as a forceful presence. For thousands of years, men pastured their cattle on these hills, hunted, fished, hewed down trees and planted corn. When they died, they were interned in those chambered barrows that stand out on the skyline today. The Long Man seems to speak out for the mystery of their absence, to epitomize the enigma of time distant, being more evocative than the Cerne Giant – whose general meaning is bluntly obvious – and haunting by virtue of those omitted or lost features. Eyeless, noseless, mouthless, he is like a face waiting to be born or a revelation that is imminent. More dauntingly, he can also be compared with an empty frame, a vessel into which one can pour one's obsessions or biases about the past. Lovers of Sussex have come to see him as the familar spirit of the Weald, the phantom essence of all those chalky epochs, the lingering spirit of Downland Man etched upon the green. In a memorable passage, invoking the Colossus of Rhodes, the statue of Athena on the Acropolis and the huge image set up by Nebuchadnezzar, Arthur Beckett extols the long-standing enigma to which he was to devote so much attention and newsprint:

> Arousing myself from these speculations I turned to look at the landscape. Over Mount Caburn lay Lewes and, leftward, Firle Beacon, with an outline like a human arm placed akimbo. Distances were lost in the liquid blue, and from the blue above a lark showered its song on the world of the Downs. Dark woods gleamed in a sudden glare of the sun. The grey scar of an old chalk-pit lay on my left. Behind me was the lonely Long Man asking the traveller – like the Sphinx – to solve the dark mystery of its origin.

This is fanciful-sounding yet true, true of all hill-figures – but particularly of the Long Man. To immerse oneself in the question of his identity is like walking perpetually in a mist. Strange shapes loom out of the grey vapour – exciting, plausible comparisons – but if you stare hard at them, they dwindle and fade, leaving you with little but a fleeting imprint. J.B. Sidgwick (1939) experienced something akin to this when he wrote: 'When was it cut? By whom? Whom does it represent? Is it a religious emblem, and if so of what religion? An endeavour to answer these questions takes the enquirer back through the dark by-ways of folklore, mythology, archaeology and early history, but it leads to no final conclusion.'

To return to basics, if one studies the Long Man closely, one sees that he is not carved on an even scarp face. Ice had gouged shallow amphitheatres in the Downs, and the figure is set slightly back. To his right is a modern quarry; dotted around and above him are the round barrows, flint mines and lynchets that characterize the region. The slope on which the Long Man is cut appears very regular – artifically flattened in the view of some – and makes an average angle of 28°. Despite the scrupulous care and the allowance made for foreshortening, the giant's proportions are not quite perfect, appearing correct only from the air. And his unique setting in a gentle embayment makes him impossible to pick out from certain angles; thus, as Rodney Castleden (1983) has observed, his site is 'curiously ambivalent in that it both exhibits and conceals'.

The Long Man. The effects of erosion caused by sheep and cattle are apparent as lines running across the figure. (photograph courtesy of Martin Brown)

EARLY NOTICES

It is not known whether the undeveloped, inexplicit quality of the Long Man is the upshot of deliberate design or partial obliteration. The original appearance of the figure has been a subject of much controversy. Until recently the earliest known sketch was the one made by Sir William Burrell in 1776. However, in 1993, a new drawing was found on a map at Chatsworth House, showing the land and properties owned by Spencer Compton, who inherited the Manor of Wilmington from his father, the Earl of Northampton, in 1681. When Spencer Compton died without issue in 1743, the manor reverted to the main line, and later, by marriage, to the estate of the Dukes of Devonshire.

Surveyor, John Rowley, was hired in 1710 to map his client's estate, noting field-names, acreages, lanes and drove-ways. The Long Man is outlined in plot 2, 'Court Laine with the Great Sheep Down', on the sheep down, a slightly chubby figure with bulges where the ears should be and a conical head. The shape is not clearly picked out, being rendered in dotted lines, with the staves significantly longer. The eyes, nose and mouth are marked; there are even hints of kneecaps and pectorals; the stance is symmetrical, both feet facing outwards. Unlike the gently sidestepping present-day figure, the posture is confrontational, like a warrior guarding the hill or blocking the way. He does not suggest a sun-god or a mystic mediator but a protector or guardian.

Sir William Burrell's sketch, 1776.

This contrasts with Sir William Burrell's sketch appearing nearly seventy years later. It shows a figure quite different from Rowley's outline. Clothed instead of naked, he holds a rake in his right hand and a scythe in his left. The general impression is of a shambling agricultural labourer, and a caption accompanies the sketch: 'The above is a sketch of a rude figure cut out in the chalk 80 feet high on the side of the Downs opposite Wilmington Priory. The spot being covered with grass may be plainly discovered by the colour of the grass.' One presumes the clothing to be a 'seemly' addition, deferring to the Age of Elegance, for there is no evidence for it from any other source.

Presumably Sir William intended '80 yards' or 73 m, the statistic appearing subsequently in Royer's guidebook (1787) and the Reverend Stubbing Shaw's more authoritative description of 1790:

> On one side of [the Downs] is a curious representation of a figure of a man in the different tincture of the grass. The length of the figure is 240 feet; and each hand grasped a scythe or rake in a parallel direction with the body, but these latter are not so visible; the whole shall be shewn in a picturesque view of this place in the future. This, no doubt, was the amusement of some idle Monk belonging to the neighbouring cell. It is formed by a pavement of bricks underneath the turf, which gives it this difference of colour. In time of snow, it is still more visible.

Referring to the 'pavement of bricks', John Rowley's 1710 outline was dotted. This may not reflect the surveyor's inability to define the outline or, in the words of John Farrant, that he 'saw the shadows cast by indentations in the grass produced by a lesser depth of humus, rather than a clear outline in chalk or subsoil', but the fact that he viewed the figure closely and, seeing the effect was obtained from an irregular outline of bricks, conveyed such an impression. Richard Gough (1806) also alluded to 'a pavement of bricks under the grass', but it is unclear whether he actually saw it.

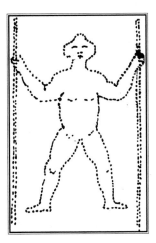

John Rowley's drawing of the Long Man, 1710.

Following Royer and Shaw, notices began to proliferate, though later writers made much the same points, often drawing attention to propitiatory conditions aiding the figure's visibility:

> A rude, gigantic figure of a man, 240 feet in length, has been cut on the hill to the south-east of the monastery; and tradition subscribes the work to the idleness and ingenuity of its inhabitants. The figure stands, or rather reclines on its back, for it is on a steep declivity, with arms extended upwards, and a long staff in each hand parallel to the body. The outline is so slightly indented in the turf that to a close inspection it is imperceptible: but when viewed from a distance with a strong side-light, i.e., either in the morning or evening, it may be plainly seen; and yet, even then, the unpractised eye will have some difficulty in tracing out the figure, of which the lower parts are at all time extremely indistinct. The thawing of a slight snow brings it out into the boldest relief.
>
> (G.M. Cooper 1850)

During the second half of the nineteenth century, the Long Man became an object for sightseers to admire and antiquaries to speculate upon, but little fresh information emerged and, even to this day, the debate revolves around the reliability of a handful of early testimonies and sketches.

FACE AND FEET

Did the Long Man have clearly defined features? In 1926, when Sir Flinders Petrie conducted his survey, he noted, 'The eyes are marked by plain hollows; the nose is a boss, possibly with recesses for nostrils; the lips are a long boss of turf.'

Another moot point, the source of much debate, was the Long Man's feet. Some, like the Revd G.M. Cooper, have preferred to leave them shrouded in mystery, but others are convinced that a surgical alteration took place. When the outline was restored in 1874, was the position of the feet altered? Rowley's drawing suggests that both feet pointed outwards, and Burrell's confirms this, but shows the left foot inclined slightly downwards. This hardly squares with the objection framed by T.C. Woodman (1900) who wrote that 'this most interesting piece of antiquity has undergone a most deplorable restoration some twenty years ago', adding, 'The feet of the figure have been quite altered, now they are sideways, formerly they were foreshortened, and the form was coming straight forward.'

The Revd T. Bunston delivered a popular lecture on the Long Man to the Literary and Social Guild, Hailsham, 27 February 1912, stating that the lower part of the figure was altered and the feet originally pointed downward. The most recent chronicler of this debate, E.W. Holden FSA (1979) was 'inclined to accept that the restoration of the left leg and foot was mistaken and that the left foot should either point north-west or west, or that both feet originally pointed down hill.'

Furthermore Rowley's drawing, while marking facial features, has no rake and scythe, implements later taken up by Burrell (1776) and Shaw (1790). Neither is there any sign of the cock that James Levett claimed to have seen in 1873 to the right of the figure. Why these discrepancies? Could it be that the hungry perception, yearning for greater completeness, supplied extra details? Variations in light, the dryness of the grass, the sudden melting of snow – such factors seem to have 'developed' the general visibility of the Long Man and of those supplementary features which, presumably, were not outlined by a 'pavement of bricks' or identification would not have presented such a problem.

Aside from face and feet, some like Phené have claimed that 'slight but beautiful intaglio and cameo effects' have become obliterated. There is also confusion about the staves. Were they originally spears, crosses or agricultural implements? Some commentators have ignored that they cross the hands and read them as the door jambs of the sky. Hence, in such a context, the Long Man becomes Baldur the Beautiful, opening the doors of the firmament, flooding warmth into the land after the blight of winter.

And then there are features of which there is no trace, yet whose presence would seem, naturalistically speaking, feasible. For instance, it has been suggested that the Long Man once possessed the potent generative organs of the Cerne Giant, but the monks of Wilmington, finding them disquieting, stole up the hillside one night and removed them.

Any massive ancient chalk figure is liable to be grasped by self-promoters as a venerable billboard to which may be attached more less durable causes. This was made plain in July 2007 when the stylists, Trinny and Susannah, invited 100 women to decorate the Long Man by giving him temporary pigtails, breasts and hips. Arthur Pendragon, a 53-year-old Druid battle chieftain, responded: 'We pagans are very angry. We would not in our wildest dreams consider putting female breasts and clothing on effigies of any Holy Prophets, be it Jesus Christ, Buddha or any other revered figure of faith. Why then does ITV commission Trinny and Susannah to do so at the Long Man of Wilmington?'

THE 1874 RESTORATION

In 1874 voluntary work was undertaken to cleanse and restore the Long Man. The project was financed by the Duke of Devonshire and supported by the Revd W. de St Croix and other antiquaries. Yellow bricks – 7,000 of them, according to the record – were used to outline the figure and carried up the slope in large trolleys often 'manned' by children who assisted the workmen; apparently the children used to crowd into a trolley going downhill and, by their weight, pull up another trolley loaded with bricks.

The *Eastbourne Gazette*, 29 April 1874, reported: 'In the work which has lately been carried out, it was necessary to remove the turf in some places and in doing so fragments of Roman brick were discovered, which would clearly point to a much earlier than Norman date.' No specimens of these bricks were retained, however, and so it is difficult to confirm such a dating.

The restoration was not long-lasting. Fifteen years later, in 1889, the vicar of Wilmington, W.A. St John Dearsley, complained that the Long Man had been invaded by weeds and rubbish; furthermore, rabbits had been dislodging the bricks and 'excursionists' rolling them down the hill. A committee of restorers was formed, again financed by the Duke of Devonshire. They considered scouring the trenches down to the clean chalk, but decided that the soil was too deep; besides, the figure traditionally had a brick surround. A local farmer advised white glazed bricks to replace the old. Eventually he was commissioned to do the work, but only where repair was necessary.

THE 1969 RESTORATION

Soil is akin to a dynamic organism, never static on hillsides, but subject to gravity, weathering, excavation by mammal, insect and earthworm, water erosion, frost and ice – all of which will cause it to slip downhill, creating low ridges called 'terracettes', plentiful at Wilmington and Cerne Abbas. This downhill movement will eventually obliterate trenches – already vulnerable from the tendency of crumbled matter from the sides to fill them. Upkeep of hill-figures thus becomes a periodic expense and responsibility which some landowners prefer to transfer to the state or an interested party.

In 1925, the Duke of Devonshire passed the Long Man over to the Sussex Archaeological Trust which is currently responsible for its maintenance. During the Second World War, the white bricks were painted green, so that they would not help enemy bombers. By 1969, however, the damage had become extensive, with bricks missing and broken, and it was decided to remove the Victorian bricks and substitute them with pre-cast white cement blocks to obviate the need for regular painting.

The top of the Long Man's head showing the concrete blocks which now form the outline of the figure.

Seeing this as a suitable time to resume enquiry, the Sussex Archaeological Society made some experimental cuts across the original trenches. Nicks were made by the right shoulder, on top of the head, over half-way down the right stave and across the right shin. Briefly, they found the hard chalk lay 25–38 cm down. The surface comprised turf and grey-black topsoil underlain by chalk rubble, chalk silt and crumbs and finally the bedrock. The longest cut (2.8 m) was made in the right stave. It uncovered a depression, 40 cm wide and 5 cm deep in the base chalk, suggesting that a channel had been dug out sometime in the past; similar evidence was found in the cut made in the right shin, tentatively confirming the original was an 'incised' outline.

In the stave and shoulder cuts, pieces of fired clay were found. They were examined by Dr I.W. Cornwall, of the Institute of Archaeology, London. The specimens found in the stave cut contained 'numerous splinters, thin, acute-angled, sharp razor-blade flakelets' which were almost certainly the result of 'mechanical crushing or pounding of coarser grains.' These had been deliberately added to the clay as a 'filler'. As for the clay in the shoulder cut, this was a 'fine-grained porous, pinkish-red fired body' containing 'small rounded masses of up to 1.5 mm in diameter, of grog, broken pottery, these generally also of a rather less ferruginous fine, silty clay than the ground-mass.'

Dr Cornwall's report was sent to Professor B.W. Cunliffe at the University of Southampton. The presence of fired clay had given rise to the suggestion that the artefact might date from the Beaker period, an opinion with which the Professor did not concur: 'We spent some time the other day,' he wrote back, 'looking at your samples from the Long Man. The general opinion was that there was nothing Beaker about them. No one had seen anything from Beaker contexts like them. My own feeling is that they are fragments of Roman tile. Grog is sometimes used in Roman tile, the colour and texture are right and one of the pieces has a good surface exactly like the finish of Roman tiles. One cannot be certain but we all felt it was the most likely explanation.'

The fired clay, then, is of crucial importance. If it could be positively identified as Roman, dating and defining the Long Man would be made easier. Is he a Roman god? Or was his outline emboldened or repaired during Roman times? Alternatively, is he a native Celtic god to whom the Romans once paid homage?

As for the restoration itself, the Ministry of Public Buildings and Works made a grant of £250 towards the cost. The Sussex

Archaeological Society asked Mr Ben Walker & Son, Selmeston, to estimate and advise on the work. The white concrete blocks replacing the old bricks weighed 72 lb each and measured 60 cm in length. A trolley was loaded with them and winched up and down by two tractors at the bottom. There being no purpose-built vehicle in existence, a special Long Man prototype was designed from the chassis and towbar of an old electric milk-float covered with the framework of an iron bedstead, part of a stable door and boards; the wheels were taken from a discarded lawnmower. The total cost of work was £800.

RESISTIVITY SURVEY

In 1969, not long after the laying of the concrete blocks, a member of the Sussex Archaeological Society, Mr K.W.E. Gravett MSC, FSA, conducted a resistivity survey using a Martin–Clark meter with four electrodes, arranged in a square 2½ ft wide and forming a table on which the instrument was mounted. As the slope was as steep as 40°, it was not easy to direct the survey, and the erosion was too bad in parts to plot anything at all. However, the tops of the staves and the head were investigated for anisotropic anomalies, and the outline of what might have been a plume was found curving from the top of the head; also traces of a possible scythe blade were found at the top of the left stave and the teeth of a rake on the right. This was only a partial investigation; nothing definite emerged, save confirmation that the Long Man may have altered considerably, but Mr Gravett cautiously concluded 'that such anomalies are not certainly archaeological and should be confirmed by excavation before acceptance.'

Plan of resistivity survey, 1969.

WINDHOVER BARROW

Above the Long Man is the largest burial mound in Sussex, Windover Long Barrow, a long thin cylinder of raised turf, some 55 m long and 15 m wide, with an unusual feature at its southern extremity, a small round knoll, obviously part of the barrow, yet intentionally separated from it. Is there an intrinsic relationship between the barrow and the Long Man? Are they coeval, employing complementary symbolism. Is the long thin mound, with its rounded tip, implicitly male. 'The phallic form of the long barrow', to quote Castleden (1983), 'is as consistent with Neolithic beliefs as the hemispherical, pregnant-belly form of the passage-grave;

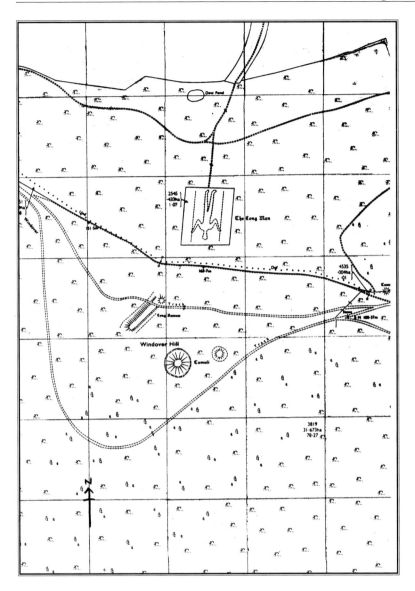

Position of the Long Man on
Windover Hill.

both shapes show a trust that death and burial would result in some
kind of regeneration'.

Side-ditches run parallel to each side of the tomb; these latter
may have been used for shallow burial before the storage of bones in
the tomb. A related feature is the cursus leading to it, an embanked
freeway running south-east up the hill and tapering near the summit.
Arduously hammered out with antler picks nearly 3,500 years ago,
these lateral enclosures are an enigma. Some fifty of them have been

137

identified over Britain, the longest being in Dorset and the most intriguingly patterned at Rudston, Yorkshire, where four of them intersect near a single large megalith.

The apparent pointlessness of these painfully extended earth-shifting marathons has baffled practical minds – indeed, Stukeley, at a loss to divine a practical function, likened the Stonehenge cursus to a noble racecourse. This is one of the many wide-of-the-mark speculations, for cursuses appear to have been primarily neither defensive nor domestic. When excavated, the ditches have been shown to contain pits filled with potsherds, domestic litter, animal bones, and tidily organized flint hoards but nothing pointing to a single integral function. There was a large conference about them in Dorchester in 1988, the outcome of which was the rapt articulation of puzzlement.

The Windover cursus runs for some 100 m up a steep gradient. The sides are traced by shallow ditches 2 m wide. The impression is of a wide-armed sweeping openness. Was it a communal gathering-place? Was it astronomical in intent? Or was it a coffin road, a *temenos* or holy precinct, along which the dead were borne to the barrow on the crest of the hill? In the past, it might have formed a dramatically stage-managed walk, staked out with pylons and timber and stone impedimenta.

If the Windhover Cursus is a road of the departing spirit, Windover Barrow is the temple of death, of organic dissimulation, where the picked bones are stored for eternity, while the Long Man, carved out of the bones of the land, symbolizes the perpetuity beyond the grave, the god who shines at dawn and dies at dusk, but whose presence is continuous and stable as a star.

This Neolithic argument, advanced forcefully by Rodney Castleden, is persuasive. The austerity of the figure inclines one to relate him to a period of primeval simplicity. Early pastoralists farmed, fished and sowed here, and the Long Man, so bare of historic trappings, arises naturally in the context of long barrow, causewayed enclosure and flint quarry. It might be possible to place him as the culmination of a long sequence of earth sculptures or land monograms. Yet, beyond proximity and perceived pattern, no indisputable connection emerges. Neolithic sites have thrown up squat goddesses, chalk phalluses and hermaphroditic 'dollies' – but not a scraping or carving directly recalling the Long Man.

The problem arises from trying to establish to what degree monuments grouped together are linked by intention. Consider the juxtapositions of a modern town. A Georgian square edges up to a tower block, a Gothic cathedral dominates a housing estate, a bank stands next to a bingo hall, a Saxon moot adjoins a municipal car park. A similar medley of periods and functions may be found in a prehistoric landscape, yet because the base materials – turf, chalk, timber and sarsen blocks – remain consistent, one more readily assumes an overall unity.

Furthermore, itemizing the round barrows, lynchets, huts and farmsteads dating from the Bronze Age in the vicinity of Windhover, and adding to that list the memory of the hoard of bronze axe-heads and cutting-tools found in an urn at Wilmington in 1877, a further probability emerges – of the Long Man being a Bronze Age priest or warrior. The solar connection is appropriate; the figuratively assured outline denotes growing artistic sophistication. The accompanying poles are 'tools' of authority, ritual implements. There are stave-holding chieftains from Sardinia and spread-armed ingot-bearing figures from Cyprus which one could invoke for comparison. Yet here again, an objection interposes, for much of Bronze Age work shows a tendency to abstraction, a stylized angularity, quite unlike the smoothly moulded Long Man.

History and Interpetation

Ingot bearer, Kourion (Cyprus).

Claiming prehistoric ancestry for the Long Man is made awkward by the fact that not a single famous antiquary observed or assessed him. There is no mention in Camden, Leland or John Aubrey. He is ignored by map-makers, churchwardens, early surveyors and, even after his presence had been recorded, he continued to be overlooked by writers of guidebooks until late in the nineteenth century. There is no record of scouring or money being put aside for maintenance. The Long Man only became visible, so to speak, just when he was about to become invisible.

No hard early information exists. Oral tradition preserves the story of two local giants, one living on Windover Hill, the site of a barrow, the other at Firle Beacon, which similarly possesses a barrow or 'Giant's Grave'. They enjoyed a relationship of fierce discord, throwing rocks at each other across the Cuckmere Valley, and one struck the Windover Giant. So there he lies, the image of the Long Man, on the steep hill slope. This crumb of folklore gave rise to the idea that the hill-figure stands for a Neolithic chieftain buried on the summit of Windover. A further possibility is that the rival giants are descendants of Andred and Andras, presiding deities of the Weald, a name repeated in the Forest of Anderida and the Saxon fort of Andredesceaster. The giants may have had a significance akin to Gogmagog and Corineus or the struggling Gemini twins.

Aside from this, there is little else save scattered memories recorded in the closing decades of the nineteenth century. In *Folklore* 89, a local stated that the Long Man was called the Wilmington Giant and a Roman was buried in a gold coffin under him. He also remembers being told in 1891 'that the Long Man carries spears, not staves, in his hands, and that an upright line (which I was unable to find) runs from top to bottom of the hill a little to the east, and another a little to the west, of the figure.'

THE ROMAN LEGIONS

Everyone enjoys the challenge of unravelling a mystery, particularly if the available information is so meagre that free play of imaginative fancy, yoked to a modicum of historic detail, can be allowed. When awareness of the Long Man came to the fore, an explosion of debate ensued, inaugurated by Arthur Beckett in the *Herald* magazine. From July 1923 to February 1924, many theories were aired and later summarized by Sidgwick in 1939.

Appearing in the same volume (13) of the *Sussex County Magazine* as Sidgwick's article, another plausible hypothesis made its debut, based upon the fact that soldiers, when not deployed fighting or defending, have been known to show a creative streak; this may be inferred by regimental badges cut on the hillside of Fovant, Dorset, and other memorials, both secular and religious, found in Britain and Europe.

In the fourth century AD, Sussex was the focus of important mercantile activity and was densely occupied by Roman troops. Under Julian the Apostate, who was emperor AD 360–63, some 800 wheat ships were dispatched from Britain to supply garrisons stationed in Gaul. Taking up a suggestion first advanced by A.D. Passmore (1937), comparing the Long Man to a coin showing the emperor Ventranio holding in each arm the standards of his authority, Mr Heron Allen (1939) suggested that it was about this period that Roman soldiers, under the Count of the Saxon Shore, who were quartered in the Pevensey–Richborough–Dover area, cut the figure of the Long Man after arriving from Boulogne. The staves are comparable to the *labarum*, the Banner of Christ

Denarius of Vetranius showing the *labarum* or Banner of Christ.

that features on numerous coins after its adoption by Constantine in AD 312:

> The original standard, the Vexilium, consisted of a long gilded spear from which hung (bannerwise), a square of purple silk or cloth. Later this square was attached to the spear like a modern flag, bore the Christogram, the Sacred Monogram Chirho P/X, and under the Emperor Jovian (AD 363–4), when Christianity was established as the state religion, this became the general standard of the army.

So the Long Man can be viewed as an image of Constantine the Great, Rome's first Christian emperor, together with the *labarum* which, owing to time and weather, has suffered partial obliteration. It was carved in the pious hope of impressing upon native Britons the value of the True Faith.

The case is well stated and the likeness of the coins conspicuous. Folklore lends it dubious credence with the story of the Roman soldier buried beneath the figure, and there is the more substantial report of 'a pavement of Roman bricks' being uncovered during the 1874 restoration.

Roman-British relief sculpture of Mars, from Cadbury Camp, Avon. It bears a fleeting resemblance to the Long Man which is situated in a heavily Romanized part of the Weald.

MAHOMET AND ST PAUL

A more nebulous explanation than Heron Allen's – but one that utilizes religious imagery all the same – was proposed by the Revd Chancellor Parish, vicar of Selmeston, who amassed invaluable collecteana relating to the Long Man. He first set down the popular belief that the Long Man was flanked by the outline of a cock on his right – the bird was faintly discernible until the 1870s. This yielded the explanation that the Long Man was Mahomet, founder of Islam, who was born of poor parents in Mecca, AD 571. The cock was the fabled giant rooster encountered by the prophet in the First Heaven and was cut by prisoners of the Crusades of the twelfth and thirteenth centuries who were employed to work on the land by the monks of Wilmington.

This long shot can be matched by suggestions that the giant is St Paul who, like Mahomet, was associated with the cock, and that the nearby Polesgate derives from 'Paul's Gate'. There is a legend that the saint did missionary work in England; the monks of Wilmington cut the Long Man in honour of their distinguished forbear. The rake and scythe are blurred impressions of crosses at the top of staves.

BEOWULF

The vicar's theory was based upon pagan imagery imported from another land. We find a similar case, developed from Norse mythology and fixing on a seventh-century plaque found at Torslunde, Sweden, showing a bearded figure (Beowulf?) in a horned helmet grasping a spear in both hands and standing next to an armoured monster (Grendel?) with which he is engaged in combat. The Long Man, then, is Beowulf; the memory of the cock standing to his right preserves the image of Grendel. This whole idea, leaning literally on the chronology of the legend, is supported by the presence of Knucker Holes in the district, deep pools in the chalk deriving from *nicor*, an Anglo-Saxon word for water-monster, recalling Beowulf's gory underwater combat.

It is supposed that the Long Man was carved at the instigation of Elle, the Saxon leader who defeated the Britons at Mercredesburn (AD 485) on the River Ouse. Thus, like the Uffington Horse, the Long Man becomes a badge of victory. But why select Beowulf? The earliest extant copy of the manuscript dates from AD 1000 and is heavily Christianized. Beowulf's exact significance, or popularity, before that period can hardly be established.

A modification of the Saxon theory translates the Long Man as the insignia of King Harold II, who was slain at Hastings. He is a Saxon foot soldier, and the two staves formerly stood for his drawn sword and scabbard. Now the white horse was traditionally an emblem of the Saxons, and the white horses of Wiltshire are placed near the boundaries of the ancient Saxon kingdom of Mercia. Might not, then, the Long Man, together with the horses, define the limits of King Harold's kingdom?

Yet another variant refers to the Burrell manuscript, identifying the Long Man as a Saxon haymaker, denoted by the rake and scythe, and yet another deifies him as Baldur the Beautiful, opening the celestial doors, releasing the channels of light and growth after the blight of winter.

AFTER STRANGE GODS

Sir Flinders Petrie (1926) dismissed the idea of a Long Man cut by Saxons or Danes – immigrants from cold countries would ensure that their gods were warmly clad. His imagination ranged back to the Bronze Age tribes camped around the Rhine and Danube. After mingling with the Indo-Iranians, they learnt of strange new gods, Indra, Mithras, Varuna, and conveyed them to other lands: 'If these had come westward with the Bronze migration, Varuna might be the origin of the Wilmington figure, which has already been supposed to be opening the gates of heaven; it looks to the north, the region of Varuna, and Varuna was the god of the ten months of gestation.' Varuna, in Hindu mythology, was the rain-god, lord of all rivers and the sea; his name corresponds with the Greek Ouranos (Uranus). Generally he is represented as a white man, four-armed, riding a sea-dragon, holding a noose in one hand a club in another – details that hardly inspire confidence in Sir Flinders' audacious theory, but nothing can be entirely ruled out, for the early inhabitants of Britain derived from a variety of influxes and invasions.

Varuna, the Indian God of Waters.

HERALD OF HIGH SUMMER

Curiously, medieval and late-medieval interpretations of a secular nature have never touched the Long Man. Apart from the monastic theory of origin, little conjecture of an origin later than Saxon has appeared. No writer has forcefully put the case that he might be a folly, an ingenious doodle, or a straightforward illustration of a religious theme, such as Samson pushing apart the pillars of the temple of the Philistines. The scholarly approach prefers to relate him to a landscape context rather than a social or imaginative context.

The enigma he poses was engulfed in the mists of prehistory by the appearance of *The Wilmington Giant* (1983), an impressive study by Rodney Castleden, lecturer, part-time archaeologist and, more recently, the author of an exciting, many-angled study of the Cerne Giant (1996).

Showing an intimate acquaintance with the South Downs, he placed the Long Man in his environmental context, summarizing the various theories, including the suggestion that the area around Windhover is the setting for an episode in the *Petit Saint Graal* (*c.* 1200): Peredur, the hero of the story, is sent to a mound beneath which is carved the figure of a man. The allusion is interesting, whether or not it refers to the Long Man, for it seems to confirm that carving figures in the earth was a known custom.

Basically Castleden's approach is holistic. He sees the Long Man as integral to the landscape and relates him to various far-flung features, including oddly enough a smallish mound by the castle at Lewes in which he finds astronomical significance. The Windover burial mound is referred to as the 'Windover Phallus' – as if it is intended to supply the virility the Long Man conspicuously lacks. Artefact and landscape are elevated to the symbolic plane and interrelated in a tapestry of association. If things are presented a little too neatly – as if the features had been set out on some Neolithic drawing-board and then placed accordingly – the book is otherwise a delight: meticulous, packed with detail and iconography, charmingly illustrated and written with feeling.

Rodney Castleden's conclusion is that the Long Man stands for the Neolithic sun-god 'arriving to bring High Summer through the ritual gateway to the world of men.' The Long Man as the spiritual embodiment of John Barleycorn is an effective concept, and given that the Uffington Horse dates from the Bronze Age, the likelihood of the Long Man being Neolithic seems no longer far-fetched. Such a long ancestry would dramatically vindicate the persistence of tradition.

WARRIORS OF ODIN

Despite Sir Flinders' sartorial stricture – that an unclothed icon was unlikely to have derived from Nothern Europe – the case for a 'cold' origin of the Long Man warmed up in 1964, when the Anglo-Saxon cemetery at Finglesham, Kent, was excavated by Sonia Chadwick Hawkes. Among other items, a bronze belt buckle was disclosed, about 8 cm long and overlaid with thick yellow gilding. The buckle was triangular in shape and decorated with the figure of a warrior with his legs slightly bent at the knees, holding a spear in either hand with the shafts canted at the top. The man was nude except for a horned helmet tipped by a pair of curving birds' beaks and a broad belt with an oval buckle, beneath which a demure but distinct penis was evident, confirming the essential pagan quality of the design.

The archaeologist husband of the excavator, Christopher Hawkes (1965), compared the Finglesham warrior with the Long Man and found striking points of resemblance. He noted that both men conveyed a similar step movement, a shuffle to the right with both feet flat, and both held staves where canting was evident. Sylistically the Finglesham belt buckle reflected the Swedish influence – a feature evident in the finds at Sutton Hoo. Christopher Hawkes suggested that the Finglesham warrior and the Long Man represent Odin, god of inspiration, magic and battle, and testify to the infusion of Swedish culture into Kent and Sussex.

Finglesham belt buckle.

Odin commanded the allegiance of a special class of warrior, light-armed, ferocious, who fought naked or clad only in a cloak. 'The beserks' was the name assigned to this formidable soldiery who, according to Snorri, were as strong as boars and fierce as wolves. When possessed by the ecstasy of bloodlust, neither fire nor iron could deter them for they were the fury of Odin incarnate.

The numerous symbols of Odin reflect his many facets and include the horse and the eagle, indicating his power to move across earth and sky, the three-way knot, signifying his ability to bind, the maiden who holds a cup or chalice welcoming the heroes to Valhalla, reflecting his chthonic or underworld aspect, and the raven and the wolf, recalling his shape-shifting magic and latent ferocity.

An important possession of Odin's was his personal spear, Gugnir, the flight of which decided victory when armies opposed. He guided them to or deflected them from their targets, and his handmaidens, the pitiless and predatory Valkyries, watched over the battlefields, assessing the carnage and executing the god's inscrutable will.

> We weave, we weave the web of the spear,
> As on goes the standard of the brave.
> We shall not let him lose his life.
> The Valkyries have power to choose the slain.

The Long Man, then, may depict one of Odin's special warriors in ceremonial headgear and carrying the symbolic spears. Conceivably the bird motifs on the up-curving horns refer to the Valkyries, alleged to be able at will to change themselves into birds of prey.

The Christian missionaries who entered Sussex were headed by St Wilfrid (AD 634–709). He was a peppery but likeable Northumbrian, a musician and a lover of architecture and fine art. When he came to Sussex, the countryside was suffering a famine, the upshot of three years' drought, and Wilfrid was said to have endeared himself to locals by teaching them how to fish. If ever his mission was confronted with the image of a naked, armed warrior, it is possible that their moral and aesthetic susceptibilities may have been upset. So, after removing the sexual organ and horned helmet, they transformed the spears into crosses by horizontal strokes.

Horned dancers from the Sutton Hoo helmet.

HUMAN HOLOCAUSTS

The Finglesham argument is bold and persuasive, although it involves a plea for extensive alteration rather than attempting to explain the figure as it stands. Neither does it account for the 'Roman bricks' beneath the turf or compare the Long Man with his counterpart at Cerne Abbas. This is surely relevant, for the carvings may be coeval and complementary.

Comparison with Odin, however, is enlightening. The Norse god was equated with the Roman Mercury, and Wednesday or Odin's Day was called *Mercurii dies*, *mercredi* in French. The following tenth-century homily (translated from Kemble's *Solomon and Satan*) demonstrates the likeness.

> Once there lived a man
> who was Mercury called;
> he was vastly deceitful
> and cunning in his deeds;
> he loved well to steal
> and all lying tricks;
> the heathens had made him
> the highest of their gods,
> and at the crossroads
> they offered him booty
> and to the high hills
> brought him victims to slay.
> The god was most honoured
> among all the heathen;
> his name when translated
> to Danish is Odinn.

Describing religious customs of the Celtic tribes, Caesar provides a gruelling description of how they construct 'figures of vast size, formed of osiers, they fill with living men; which, being set on fire, the men perish enveloped in the flames'. Strabo, reporting the same custom, added that the figures were filled with 'wood for fuel, cattle and several kinds of wild beast'. In 1872 Dr Phené, an architect and antiquary, cited these passages, arguing that it would hardly be possible for such heavy-laden colossi to stand upright. He theorized that the holocausts did not take place in the tall-standing idols of the popular imagination but in huge arenas – vast enclosed cages fashioned in the shape of giants.

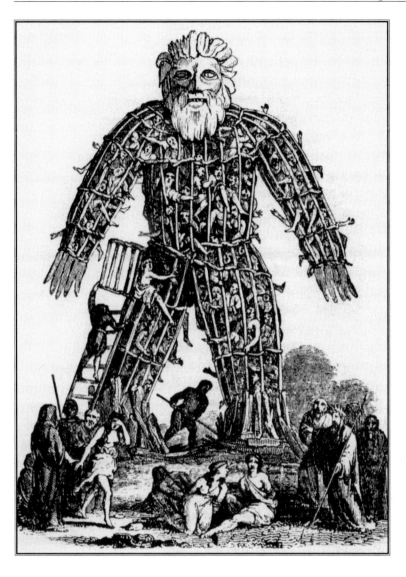

Caesar and Strabo describe basket idols in which humans and cattle were burnt alive.

In the immediate vicinity of Caesar's landing is such an image, 240 feet high, and on so steep a slope of hill as to look almost upright; this figure, fenced around, in the manner customary with the Britons in their defences in the woods, and which is still retained in a more simple form by the hurdle pen in Sussex, would have represented an almost upright human figure, and at the same time an arena.

Probably this contention is inaccurate. The holocausts did take place in upright wickerwork idols, for similar receptacles feature in seasonal processions in Celtic lands, and there are accounts of cats being fired in such containers by French peasants hoping to destroy the evil eye. Yet had Carthaginian horrors on the scale Phené evoked repeatedly taken place, one might have expected the sites, instead of being 'ritually clean', to be strewn with the charred bones of humans and animals. Moreover, there would have been no need at all for such details as staves or facial features. However, it is not impossible that sacrifices were made around the Long Man and the Cerne Giant. The figures *could* have signposted where the basket idols were erected. If this sounds sensational, one can only retort that, in some circumstances, sensational practices were the rule rather than the exception.

'Among the gods they worship Mercury,' writes Caesar of the Celts. 'There are numerous images of him; they declare him inventor of all arts, the guide for any road and journey, and they deem him to have the greatest influence for money-making and traffic.'

The Long Man has aspects of the wayfarer. He is situated on the slope of a high hill where, to quote again from the homily, 'The heathens . . . brought him victims to slay'. Also, he is found in an area which, during Roman times, enjoyed intensive trading with the Continent. Furthermore, it was claimed by the Revd Chancellor Parish that a cock stood to his right, a bird sacred to Mercury in his manifestation as Asclepius, god of healing. The cock, the goose and the hare were revered by the early British; a relief from York depicts Mercury holding a *caduceus* or snake wand, in his left hand, and a purse in his right, on which side he is flanked by a cock.

Apart from his underworld contacts, Mercury was celebrated as the god of limitary lines and boundaries. The Celtic Mercury is sometimes equated with Esus, 'whose strange shrine makes men shudder', but such comparisons can be misleading, polytheistic societies being so accommodating in the attributes they attach to a god favoured in a particular locality. Suffice to say that if the Cerne Giant, with his vengeful club and intimidating virility, represents passionate dynamism, the Long Man, with his symmetrical staves and androgynous aspect, stands for balance, caution and reflection.

Judging from the plenitude of surviving inscriptions, Caesar may have been referring to Lugh or Lugus as the Celtic Mercury. The latter's festival in Ireland was held on 1 August. Commonly known as Lugh Lémhfadha or Lugh of the Long Arm or the Long Hand (*manu* in Latin means hand: Long Man = Long Hand?), aside from being a master craftsman, he was seen as a solar deity, a harvest-god, able to command day and night – an image not incompatible with the stance of the Long Man. Not much of this squares up with the Classical conception of Mercury. The latter, however, did have a pastoral aspect, as a protector of cattle and crops.

Despite his importance, not a great deal is known about Lugh, who may well preserve the character of a Bronze Age god. The early drawing by Rowley reflects Lugh's power and status and the staves, or measuring rods, his skills as judge and mediator. The bulges at either side and at the top of the head hint at the presence of a helmet; Mercury's helmet was an adjunct of his speed and dexterity. This is the identification the present author favours, principally on stylistic grounds. A markedly literal drawing, the Long Man appears to integrate the art of the Classical world and might, as the pottery finds suggest, predate the Roman invasion and link up with his cousin at Cerne.

Mercury presided over boundaries and markstones, and if the Long Man's staves pertain to this specialization, vestiges may survive in the rites of Rogation or Ascensiontide. Led by priests and dignitaries, there would be processions around parish boundaries. The cavalcade, holding long sticks or peeled willow wands, marched from markstone to ditch, from coppice to stone wall, stopping to dress a holy well and everywhere being greeted with gifts and friendship. Children would be rewarded with sweets or nuts or, alternatively, thrown in ditches, doused in streams, kicked, rolled and beaten, in order that they remember the precise borders of their village. The atmosphere was one of celebration and playful rough-and-tumble, depending on the temper of the times. In some parishes it was considered pagan and undignified; in others, more severely religious variants were introduced, sometimes involving cross-cutting in the turf. It is likely that this fundamentally agrarian rite was honoured in Romano-Celtic Britain and later adapted to the Christian calendar. However, so many layers of custom have overwritten the original ceremony that it is impossible to draw any firm comparisons.

Rodney Castleden drew attention to evidence of a soil-cut trench being in place prior to the bricking of the outline, leaving the likelihood of an earlier origin open. Also Martin Bell showed him a Neolithic flint scraper he had recovered from one of the excavated trenches to which little attention was paid at the time. Was, he asks, the 1545 bricking 'an attempt, just like the 1873-4 bricking, to rescue a deteriorating image in the grass that was in danger of disappearing.'

Conclusion

Of all the hill-figures, the Long Man has posed problems of the greatest complexity. No one has satisfactorily established his original appearance, the degree to which he was altered in the past and the function of the pair of staves. Another problem is the credence one can attach to the contrasting sketches of John Rowley (1710) and

Sir William Burrell (1886): the earlier is a convincing variation on what one sees today, but the latter is a baggily clothed, scraggy peasant with eyebrows, eyes, nose and lips and a head of hair.

In the view of Christopher Hawkes (1965), the rake and scythe were the remnants of Christian crosses which had been imposed on the original spearheads of Odin in much the same way as Celtic saints made their marks on the upright standing stones of prehistory.

Mr Heron Allen (1939) forged a powerful case for the Long Man's Roman origin, comparing the staves to the *labarum* (Banner of Christ) appearing on coins of Constantine the Great. Other details, such as the discovery of grog in 1969 and the allusion to 'Roman bricks', seem to support this date. Comparing the cluttered appearance of the image on the coin with the present-day Long Man, one must accept that the figure has been drastically denuded.

Taking up the argument developed by Phene, the present author maintains the Long Man's origins are essentially Celtic, like those of the Cerne Giant, and relate to the cult of Lugh or Lugus, in which the principles of light and fertility are yoked to mediation and balanced judgement.

But many of these ideas seem less credible after the findings of a team of researchers, led by Prof. Martin Bell, an archaeologist of Reading who, in 2002–2004, carried out a series of tests on the figure. He subjected to thermo-luminescence dating fragments of orange-red brick that once enclosed the Long Man and were a source of dispute among antiquarians. The mean date the tests supplied was AD 1545, later than many imagined, confirming the figure was paved and hinting at a genteel, decorative function – an Elizabethan chalk folly to enliven a bare slope on a gentleman's estate? Professor Bell analysed chalk fragments washed down the slope, finding little evidence of activity on the hillside during the Iron Age, Roman occupation or Medieval period, broken by a dramatic disturbance around 500 years ago when a layer of chalk rubble swept down the hill. This, he believed, was caused by displacement of material during the cutting and embanking of the Long Man.

CHAPTER NINE

FALLEN IDOLS

> O! 'tis excellent to have a giant's strength,
> But tyrannous to use it like a giant . . .
> (Shakespeare, *Measure for Measure* II, ii, 107)

The most powerful hill-figures, aside from the horses, portray giants or men of extraordinary stature. At Cerne Abbas and at Wilmington, and formerly at Plymouth Hoe and Wandlebury, such figures are perpetuated in the turf, and there are fantastic tales of sheep-swallowing and boulder-slinging to account for their presence. So perhaps it is useful to look at this folklore in a more analytical way to try to understand what fostered the concept of giantism.

In general, the appearance of oversized heroes coincides with earlier stages of civilization when the mind was prone to the literalistic or anthropomorphic personification of natural events – a gale caused by Zeus sneezing or a tidal wave by Poseidon whipping up the sea. They are the upshot of man projecting his psyche into realms outside his influence.

The first reference to giants in the Bible occurs in Genesis where the Hebrew word *nephilim* is used. The word is applied to the sons of Anak, who dwelt about Hebron and were described by terrified spies; compared to them, they were as grasshoppers. A race of giants called the Rephaim is frequently alluded to in the Bible and in Genesis appears as a distinct tribe of whom Og, King of Bashan, is said to be the last. Other races of giants are mentioned, such as the Enim, the Zuzim and the Zamzumin.

The origins of giant lore are vague but the idea appears to be linked to a massive patriarchal divinity, a dominant all-father figure, someone who with capable hands crafted the shape of the earth, fashioned the cliffs and mountains and, when distressed, unleashed the elements of rain, wind, thunder and lightning upon the population below. Thor, Odin, Zeus, Jehovah, Tiwaz and Horus were notorious sky-stormers, standing for the benign and adverse forces of nature. Many of these deities had their residences upon mountain peaks and dwelt amid climactic turmoil.

There are subordinate processes by which giants would appear to be created. T.C. Lethbridge interpreted Geoffrey of Monmouth's giants, of whom Göemagot was the leader, as little more than an adverse reaction to a rival. Enemies prowl and persist in the consciousness and memory finally transforms them into giants of repellent aspect – tales of gigantic Saracen warriors loomed large at the time of the Crusades. Lethbridge illustrates this, stating that a well-known giant's cave in the Western Isles of Scotland turned out, upon investigation, to be a former stronghold of pirates.

Many writers of folkloristic leanings are intrigued by the association of giants with megalithic remains. Anthony Roberts (1978) drew attention to their prominent role in landscape myths and believes them to be the archetypes of the great megalithic surveyors (Watkins' dodmen – see Ch. 11) who supervised the shifting of huge sarsen blocks and harnessed the currents of vitalizing energy which, in the view of some earth mystics, are the basis of early religion. This is an intriguing notion but weak in that myths are not datable and a critical investigation of the episodes of boulder-slinging slapstick and genial dim-wittedness can hardly be said to conceal ineffable wisdom. To Roberts, giants recall an age of wisdom and spiritual prosperity: 'It's a glimpse of that Golden Age of harmony and ecological equilibrium between humanity and its natural habitat, so well recorded by Hesiod, Plato and other intellectual giants of Antiquity'.

Broadly speaking giants, like dinosaurs, fall into two distinct categories. First there are the man-eaters or ogres; secondly there are the lead-footed bumblers whose exploits, like those of the Wise Men of Gotham, are therapeutic to read about in that we recognize, whatever our intellectual failings, certain lofty pinnacles of inanity will forever defeat us.

The following story, drawn from the Bristol region, serves as an example. The giant Gorm was walking along carrying a shovelful of earth when he tripped up. The soil slipped off his shovel, creating Maes Knoll. At the same time his gigantic spade cleft the ground, forming the Wansdyke. He got up and was frightened to see Vincent, Lord of Avon, who had been awakened by all the racket, galloping towards him. So he bolted in the other direction – but he did not get

The giant Bolster (after Cruikshank) and his unfeasibly long stride.

far. Tripping over his toes, he fell slap into the middle of the Bristol Channel: his bones made the islands of Flatholm and Steepholm.

The story cocks a snook at the science of geology – millions of years of erosion and deposition are accounted for in a pleasantly flip and offhand way. However, from this illustration, typical in many ways, it can be seen that the activities of giants are fairly limited. They are forever walking about with huge spades, throwing rocks at one another and striding over the countryside, presumably creating large depressions wherever they step. The association with large rocks and massive piles of earth invites the question as to what extent, during the Dark Ages and earlier, people actually did assume that the earthworks and standing stones of Britain were the result of men of superhuman strength and stature.

Obviously many of the tales were light-hearted and not intended to be taken seriously, but comedy, by definition, is a parasitic response usually preceded by seriousness. Clearly, at an earlier date, such tales were gravely related to children and adults. Only after a long period of time could the mockingly subversive reaction set in, to render afresh stereotypes by emphasizing their ridiculous aspect which, during the course of time, has become glaringly apparent.

The giants, then, before lapsing into figures of fun, constituted old, deposed deities, formerly presiding over things on a cosmic scale. All over Britain exist impressive natural features, Cheddar Gorge, the Wrekin, Cader Idris and St Michael's Mount, which are attributed to the Devil (often a brand-name for paganism in its multiple aspects) and men of giant stature. King Arthur often prominently reclines in these geological marvels, for his valorous reputation soon swelled to outsize proportions.

The huge effigy of St Christopher at Salisbury Museum was carried around the city in the Midsummer Pageant of the Guild of Merchant Tailors (1496). Before his conversion, it was said St Christopher was the giant Reprobus who used to devour his victims.

THE GIANT WANDIL

A fragment of folklore – first published in the *Countryman* – features the giant Wandil, a little-known English monster, quite feasibly related to the giant of the Gogmagog Hills, Cambridgeshire: 'The giant Wandil stole the spring, so winter grew longer and harder till it seemed the world must die. At last the gods caught Wandil and made him give up the spring. Like them, he was immortal, but they threw him up into the sky and he became the constellation Gemini. When his eyes, Castor and Pollux, glare down, as on the night of our encounter, there will be a keen frost, and there was.' This is how T.A. Ryder recorded the legend as it was told him by an old man living in Stroud.

The story appears to enshrine elements of Greek myth and its zodiacal overtones might appeal to those who seek evidence of early man's interest in astronomy, but one notes that Wandil's behaviour is akin to that of the dragon, a greedy hoarder of treasure and goodness, a bringer of blight and cold. The Cerne Giant, while flagrantly brandishing his potency, guards it with his murderous club. He is not only a life-giver but a death-dealer.

The ambivalence is apparent in the other horses and giants displayed on English hillsides. All seem to combine suggestions of fertility and death, agriculture and strife. The Cerne Giant, as we have seem, amounts to a blatant marriage of virility and violence. The Red Horse of Tysoe, dedicated to the Saxon sky-god Tiwaz, is concerned with fertility and aggression; similarly the Uffington Horse emphasizes speed, power and pride. Even the gentlest of the hill-figures, the Long Man of Wilmington, has been linked with Odin on the strength of a belt buckle found in a seventh-century grave at Finglesham, Kent.

So it would seem that the hill-figure deities possess darker aspects and their ritualized maintainence can be seen as acts of appeasement to powerful, enduring deities and may have been accompanied by ceremonies both sacrificial and festive. For the hill-figures of England, though sometimes thought of as mere curiosities, are larger and more impressive than, for instance, the squat and unlit Romano-Celtic temples and flourished long after such structures had fallen into neglect. Obviously many became overgrown and vanished, but the fact that some of them have survived must be an indication of their former importance. Perhaps they once had the status of cathedrals, vast open-air shrines, massive icons, around which people could gather and touch the form of the god they worshipped.

NATURE WRIT LARGE

One cannot put a certain date to these unique artefacts, but they echo the earliest epochs when men were pastoral nomads and did not require wood and stone structures to house their gods. Instead they worshipped the designs of nature: rocks, trees, evocatively shaped mountain peaks and the animals that ranged about them.

When the first flint blade exposed the gleaming chalk, someone must have become aware of the possibilities of turf-cutting, and it is likely that both Neolithic and Bronze Age Man cut numerous hill-figures and that the ones surviving to this day, although possibly cut by their descendants, are relics of the earliest culture of these islands.

There is tangible proof, for instance, that Bronze Age tribes knew how to use chalk to excellent effect. When they consigned one of their dead to a barrow on the downs, they placed the body in a pit which they overlaid with turf. After building up the sides with sarsen revetments, they capped the mound with a fresh-hewn layer of chalk, visible across the Downs for miles. This is a merely one minor example, but it is feasible that the prehistoric landscape of Britain featured whole chains of hill-figures depicting birds, beasts, gods and goddesses. These decorated the hillside below the monuments and barrow cemeteries and portrayed the deity honoured at that place or to whom the ceremonial structure was dedicated.

Could this Brittany standing stone, twinning Mercury and Hercules, be analogous to the Long Man and Cerne Giant?

This idea would have appealed to the late Harold Massingham, who stated in *Fee Fi Fo Fum* (1926) that giants originated in the Neolithic period. They were a distorted legacy bequeathed to the Celtic peoples by the megalith-builders and the story of Gogmagog and Corineus records the ousting of the Wessex Culture by waves of foreign invaders. He styled the giants as 'the supernatural impersonation of old mining kings of the archaic civilisation, bequeathed to the Celts in demonic guise' – a concept utterly charming in its audacious unprovability.

And what of the general meaning and purpose behind these figures? The giants and horses cut on English hillsides are best viewed as the powers of nature writ large. They are magical attempts to amplify vital life-principles for strength, fertility and health, and if they were aligned with stellar azimuths, as John North has argued (see Ch. 11), they are placed so as to draw power down from heaven to earth. Giantism can be viewed as a strategy to regulate destiny by conjuring an image of hoped-for or needed qualities to counter the batterings of fate and circumstance. Any member of a hillfort tribe, whose life was constantly threatened by sickness, cold, hunger, failing harvests and enemy attacks, would have deemed the massive virility and fearsome aspect of the Cerne Giant a mighty asset; the swiftness and dexterity of the Uffington Horse represented another 'ideal' in an age when slowness or infirmity might result in being permanently disabled by a spear or sword thrust.

The tales of giants, as they have been passed down and preserved, are often debased fragments of fancy and foolishness. The ancient figures of Cerne, Wilmington, Plymouth and Cambridge, however, personified the natural law, the spirit of the self-renewing earth, and

are the human form of those old, dark gods to whom man formerly
yoked his destiny. In troubled times they served as dependable points
of reference, constant elements, and were tended as sacred groves or
gardens. To an extent all lives need structure and ritual to enforce
meaning and value, and seasonal celebration was the foremost pattern
in primitive times and still survives for good measure in festivals like
Christmas, Harvest Thanksgiving and Easter.

CHAPTER TEN

THE CHILTERN CROSSES

The Wayside Cross! From mound to mound; from rifted rock to lofty hill; there stood in solemn stone the trophy of old Syra, above some scene of battle, some Saint's or Warrior's grave, to be the southing signal of the solitude, the welcome beacon of the wayfaring man.

(R.S. Hawker's introduction to Blight's *Ancient Crosses of Cornwall*, 1872)

Introduction

Two prominent crosses are stamped upon the Chiltern Hills, the spectacular Whiteleaf Cross and the Bledlow Cross, designed after the Greek form and less chronicled than its larger neighbour.

Although the idea of a cross as a uniquely Christian symbol has become indelibly printed in the mind, the shape has numerous pagan prototypes: Egyptian, Chaldean, Celtic and Roman. Among the ancients a piece of wood fastened across a tree or post formed a cross, on which were executed criminals of the most dangerous character. The custom of making the sign of the cross may be traced to the third century when the Emperor Constantine had crosses erected in public places, palaces and churches. He adopted the emblem (*labarum*) in consequence of a dream representing it as a sign of victory. In his time also, Christians painted it at the entrance to their houses as a sign of their faith, and subsequently churches were, for the most part, built upon a cruciform plan. However, the fact that it was monopolized by the Christians cannot obscure evidence that it was used emblematically long before the Christian era, in the same way as vestiges of belief in a trinity of gods, in a war in heaven, in a paradise, in a flood, an immaculate conception and the remission of sins by the shedding of blood, are to be found diffused among widely separated peoples. The general meaning of the sign seems to have been *life* and *regeneration*, and since its adoption by the Christians it has undergone numerous modifications.

This brief discourse on the evolution of the cross serves as an indication of the quality of argument that can be brought to bear upon the Chiltern carvings. For while both of them retain ecclesiastical associations, no direct evidence links them with the monkish conclaves of Risborough and Missenden, both of which lie in the vicinity and which have been cited as their inspiration.

Sir Flinders Petrie measured both the Whiteleaf and Bledlow Crosses. He discovered they were cut in multiples of 58 in – a unit which applies to the Long Man and is repeated at Stonehenge. This led him to doubt the Christian origin of such figures: 'It has been naturally supposed that these monuments are Christian in origin. This is not at all certain, for the Greek Cross is not used in Western Christianity. Further, the pyramidal base seems unknown; Byzantine coins from the sixth to the thirteenth century often bear the cross on steps, but never above a slope.' This erudite overview makes no allowance for the often dramatic variations in size which such monuments undergo during the course of the centuries, including the effects of weathering, turf-creep and soil erosion, factors undermining one's faith in a precise unit of length.

The Bledlow and Whiteleaf Crosses abut on the Icknield Way, an ancient traders' route used by the Roman military and the early British. Items such as flint from the mines at Grimes Graves, tin ingots from the granite and limestone uplands, and wool bales on packhorses were conveyed upon this well-worn track along which are scattered various prehistoric relics. The Whiteleaf Cross adjoins a long barrow and is aligned with other sites of antiquity: Grim's Dyke, the barrows on Five Knolls Hill, Dunstable, and the earthworks on Pulpit Hill. Might it not, then, have been cut as a Bronze Age monument, a phallic mark of some sort, similar in intent to the *hermae* of Greece, which, after widespread conversion to Christianity, was conventionalized to a cross by the monks of Risborough or Missenden?

This singular line of argument has been applied less convincingly to the Watlington White Mark, a turf-cut obelisk about 26 m long in the vicinity of the crosses. The apex of this tidily tapered chalk stripe points south-south-east; at the midsummer equinox the rising sun appears to strike it – so was this too, originally, a solar-phallic symbol? Or was it merely, as others claim, the work of Edward Horne, who had it made in 1764 to beautify his estate?

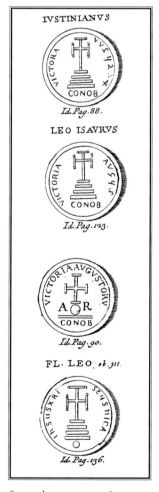

Stepped crosses on ancient coins evoking Whiteleaf Cross.

Finally, let us deal with a theory of more recent origin, first presented by Payne in *Records of Buckinghamshire* (1896). He suggests that the crosses served the purpose of 'military beacons' during the Civil War by signposting the route from the Vale of Aylesbury through Harpenden and Missenden to the Parliamentary headquarters at Amersham.

> It may be added that the Cross is evidently connected with an ordinary fire-beacon, the earthen mound of which, on the crest of the hill, is well known to all who visit it. Possibly the chalk Cross was first suggested by the exposure of the chalk when the sods were cut to form the beacon mound. When this beacon was lighted by kindling a bonfire on top of the mound, the white surface of the Cross must have been vividly illuminated, thus clearly identifying it to distant observers.

Payne is eloquent in telling us how dramatic the Cross might have looked, but he provides no evidence of the Whiteleaf or Bledlow crosses being used for such a purpose. The best he can do is cite 'Beacon Hill' in the parish of Lewknor, on which the Parliamentary forces were seen after sunrise, prior to Prince Rupert's encounter at Chalgrove Field (1643) in which the patriot John Hampden was fatally wounded. From the timbre of his prose, one judges that Payne is a Royalist whose enthusiasm for the period is clouding his judgement, especially when he styles Whiteleaf Barrow as a 'bonfire mound'. Although it is conceivable that plain, bold, blunt-cut crosses might have appealed to Cromwellian austerity, they seem irrelevant to the issue of conducting a war and, in any case, might equally have aided the Royalist cause.

FAIRY CIRCLE

Like other commentators, one senses that Payne became mildly fixated with the monument. This may well be because the Cross's setting is 'charged' with a timeless quality, distilled from a permanent wind, the susurrus of leaves and the ever-folding horizon. Standing in the clear patch of ground above the Cross can give rise to oceanic states and mystical experiences, and the clairvoyant, Ann Petrie (1984), identified a 'fairy circle' or natural ring there. She visited it one morning when the woods were empty:

Empty? No. They were full of nature spirits, fairies, elves, gnomes, pixies and imps, and we simply sat and waited. Gradually the whole forest started to move and vibrate. The leaves of the trees became silvery and almost transparent and, as our vision went into a different state of consciousness, it seemed that nothing solid was before us but everything was a sea of movement and shimmering light.

To those unable to tell an elf from an imp, such a tribally precise encounter invites scepticism. Yet Petrie deserves a sympathetic response. In prehistoric times, elevated sites like Whiteleaf and Bledlow, with their barrows, sarsens and deep-cut tracks, had a profound effect. As well as being routes of commerce, they were places of silence and reverie, spirit grounds, and there are people today for whom this association is still potent.

The Whiteleaf Cross
Site and Appearance

Any traveller approaching the steep escarpment of the Chilterns, near Monks Risborough, cannot fail to be struck by the sheet-white apparition of a huge pyramid-based cross, cut deeply into the green turf, glaring against the murky blur of the beechwoods shading the hill slope. Today it measures approximately 24 m across with arms 7 m wide, but weathering has vastly increased its dimensions. In the nineteenth century this process was accelerated by visitors of a sportive disposition, who, to amuse themselves and onlookers, slid down the shaft of the cross on faggots. The base of the cross is known locally as 'the globe'.

Occupying a gradient varying from 25° to 45°, the cross faces west, and the Icknield Way skirts its base. Dominating the Vale of Aylesbury, it can be seen as far away as Headington Hill, Oxford, and the Revd Francis Wise – a lynx-eyed antiquary if ever there was one – claimed he could identify it from Uffington Castle. To view it up close, one takes the path behind the Plough Inn, Monks Risborough, and ascends between grey trunks of beeches to the ridge of Whiteleaf Hill where the Cross – the most spectacular of the Chiltern hill-figures – sprawls and spreads like a potentate. It is well maintained by the estate wardens. Scrub has been kept at bay, but not unexpectedly the chalk has weathered unevenly – deeply gouged in places and shallower in others.

The Whiteleaf Cross.

From the monument the view is superb. One can identify the villages of Aylesbury and Thame, Quainton, Long Crendon and the witchert villages – named after a thick, white, sticky local clay – of Haddenham, Dinton and Upper and Lower Wichendon. The countryside is streamered and chequered with rambling woodlands, coppices and rich meadows, and in the villages building materials vary from thatch and timber to wattle and daub, from russet brick to local flint and chalk.

No one knows who conceived and carved the Cross but most authorities agree that it constitutes a remarkable and impressive sight whether viewed closely or from a distance. Warton (1815), the historian of Kiddington, thought it was of great age and recalled 'a savage idea of sepulchral pomp', and the Revd A. Baker (1855), displaying greater devotional fervour, described it as 'an awful and almost spectral apparition of the Sign of the Son of Man'.

To the south, traces of a prehistoric Cross Ridge Dyke mark the hill and, immediately above the Cross, there is the mound of the Whiteleaf Long Barrow, 22 m long by 18 m wide, excavated by Lindsay Scott in the late 1930s. Kidney-shaped, surrounded by a circular ditch, two large 'bites' indent its western side – the scars of antiquarian zeal. Beneath the mound were found the postholes of a wooden burial chamber, containing the left foot of a middle-aged man, the rest of the bones being scattered in the forecourt. Pieces of more than fifty neolithic pots were found and also hundreds of flints. The pots were thought to have been broken at the funeral feast and later scraped up and incorporated within the building of the mound.

Approximately 100 m north of the Cross, there is a low ovoid barrow with a cross-shaped trench and, 100 m north-west of this, the conical mound of a round barrow, 14.5 m in diameter and about 1 m high that 'seems to have been deliberately positioned to take advantage of the false crest at the northernmost edge of the ridge'. This bowl barrow was first identified by Dyer (1959) and is not very easy to pick out because of the sloping ground surface.

History and Interpretation

The Whiteleaf Cross has produced theorizing of the same order of tortuousness as the Uffington Horse and the Cerne Giant. It all began innocently and classically enough with Francis Wise, who, typically beleaguered by Saxons and Danes, believed the Cross commemorated a victory of the former over the latter. The detritus of mortal combat survives in the name of a nearby village, Bledlow, derived from Blodlaw or Bloody Hill. Wise suggests that King Edward the Elder, son and successor of Alfred, having repulsed a predatory incursion of the Danes into Buckinghamshire in AD 921, celebrated this minor triumph by having the Cross cut out in the turf, Christianity being so firmly rooted by then that white horses were becoming passé.

Local inn sign.

> After the death of King Guthrum which happened in AD 890, the Danes encouraged by receiving fresh supplies of their countrymen returned to their old trade of plundering and harrising the country. In the year 905 we read of them marching through the Mercian Kingdom as far as Cricklade in Wiltshire. . . . In the year 921, they are said to have carried off a great many prisoners, and a vast booty of cattle between Ailesbury and Bernwood forest in Buckinghamshire, which extended almost to Oxford. That the Saxons might be provided against these sudden inroads, it was necessary for them to have fortified places upon their great roads; and the remains of one of these appears at Princes Risborough just under the Cross, which the common people now call the Black Prince's Palace, and for my own part, I make no doubt, but the Cross was made in memory of some victory gained by the troops quartered at that place.

In one of those grasshopperish leaps of logic that can delight by their unexpectedness or astonish by their temerity, Lipscombe (1847) derived Whitecliffe from *Wiglife*, grandson of Odin and father of Hengist and Horsa. Alongside this ebullient insight came calmer material, stating that the parish of Risborough, in which the Cross is situated, belonged at the time of Domesday to Archbishop Lanfranc. At the time of the Conquest, Algar Stalre, standard-bearer of Christ Church, Canterbury, held Risborough. In short, Lipscombe argued that the ancestors of Algar carved the Whiteleaf Cross to celebrate the conversion of the heathen Britons.

THE WHITE CLIFF

Early references to the Cross are either non-existent or ambiguous. There is a mid-sixteenth-century allusion to 'Whitt Light' hill, suggesting radiance. However, this presumes that 'light' means light-coloured and is not a derivative of *lig* or 'flame' in Old English.

Before spelling out his 'military beacon' theory, E.J. Payne discusses an alternative name featured in Gough's edition of Camden (1806), 'Whitcliffe Crosse'. He believes Whiteleaf to be a corruption of the more gutturally explosive 'Whitcleaf', the 'cliff' element being common in placenames: Clifton in Bristol; Cliveden in Bucks; Clevedon in Somerset – the place where the 'cliff' ends and forms a 'dun' or valley. Furthermore there is the tendency of titles to absorb geologic colouration: e.g. Redcliffe, common in regions of Devonian marls and sandstones; Black Rock, near dark shale and basalt; Whitecliffe, by gleaming outcrops of chalk:

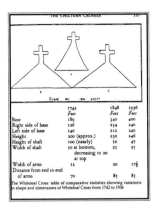

	1742 Feet	1848 Feet	1936 Feet
Base	189	340	400
Right side of base	126	234	240
Left side of base	140	212	240
Height	200 (approx.)	230	246
Height of shaft	100 (nearly)	50	47
Width of shaft	50 at bottom, decreasing to 20 at top	25	25
Width of arms	12	20	17½
Distance from end to end of arms	70	85	85

The Whiteleaf Cross: table of comparative statistics showing variations in shape and dimensions of Whiteleaf Cross from 1742 to 1936

The Whiteleaf Cross: contrasting statistics.

> The Cross is evidently named from THE WHITE CLIFF which it surmounts; and the lowest part of this White Cliff, abruptly rising from the road, is obviously due to the gradual wearing down of the road itself. This road was originally a track-way leading from the village of Monks Risborough to the downs and woodlands where the villagers, long before Julius Caesar landed in Britain, depastured their sheep, goats and pigs, and cut timber and brushwood for building and fuel. By the attrition of years, a long cutting was formed in the base of the steep chalk hill; this is the original 'White Cliff,' and it is doubtless, at least in its rudiments, nearer two than one thousand years old.
>
> (E.J. Payne 1896)

This trackway became an important line of communication – here the second element of the name enters. Cross is a common suffix, denoting a place of convergence, a crossing point, like Butler's Cross, Handy Cross, Potter's Cross and Gerrard's Cross, between Beaconsfield and Uxbridge. These junctions were often marked by hand-crosses or posts supporting cross-boards, beneath which potters and traders exhibited their wares. The Whiteleaf Cross, which, in Payne's view, formerly had a stepped base, could have been a prominent version of a hand-cross.

THE SAXON CHARTER

A Saxon charter of the Whiteleaf area dated AD 903 provides evidence of a more negative character. There is no allusion to the Cross. Furthermore, Whiteleaf Hill is called *easteren hrisan byrge*, 'the eastern hill covered with brushwood'. Later the hill became known as Whitt Light (1541) and Whitcliffe. Morris Marples (1949) cites this as evidence that the Cross may have a sixteenth- or seventeenth-century origin – that it is the original cliff tailored artistically to the shape of a cross – but he assumes that 'cliff' implies exposed rock when the word is often used in the sense of declivity or scarp slope. Also Saxon charters are notoriously reticent concerning hill-figures; neither the Uffington Horse nor the Cerne Giant is detailed in any early documents. Perhaps they had become objects that were too familiar for special notice.

However, this 903 charter, while not providing direct evidence of the Whiteleaf Cross, includes a reference to a well-known landmark called 'Weland's Stoc' which was approached by a 'straet' or paved footpath, indicating a monument of some moment. In Old English the word *stock* or *stoc* signified a wooden post or pole, but in a looser sense it seems to have been a term applied contemptuously to pagan monuments or graven images: Milton referred to our ancestors' worship of 'stocks and stones', and Kipling echoed him.

Weland, or Wayland (see Ch. 1) belonged to the Norse pantheon of super-heroes. His *stoc* may well not have been a wooden post but a large upright stone, a hefty phallic pillar, on which he was alleged to have stood to mount his horse. Until the last century there was a great stone on Sedgemoor, Somerset, called the Devil's Upping Stock. The *stoc* occupied a prominent position and, judging from the existence of a paved way, was much patronized by locals. Women may have anointed it with oil or, to ensure a healthy childbirth, slid down it on their bare bottoms. Consequently, so the argument goes, the medieval monkish conclaves at Risborough or Missenden, to effect the people's spiritual education, had the stone broken up and then substituted the handsome chalk cross. The adoption of pagan shrines for Christian purposes is too well known to require extensive justification here.

MONKS AND PURITANS

Despite the multitude of ingenious suggestions, it must be borne in mind that the monument is a cross, not a phallic pillar. Whatever the motive behind its construction, one is left with an essentially Christian symbol, and it is therefore logical to look to that religion for its primary inspiration. Following this more obvious line of argument, three explanations offer themselves: that the Whiteleaf Cross was cut by the monks at Monks Risborough; that it was cut by the occupants of Missenden Abbey only six miles distant (the abbey was dissolved in 1539 and a similar fate would have befallen the conclave at Risborough); or, thirdly, that the Cross was cut during the Puritan Interregnum when many innocent country frolics were banned. If one takes this latter view, the Whiteleaf Cross can be dated to the mid-seventeenth century. It may have been cut by country folk – possibly at the instigation of a pious local cleric – whose normal outlets and celebrations had been abolished. This would explain its sudden chronicling midway through the eighteenth century and also account for the absence of any previous reference.

SCOURING

Scouring the Cross was never a rowdy occasion on the scale of the Uffington or Cerne revels. Nevertheless, Dr George Lipscombe, the local historian, assures us that in the nineteenth century the cleaning of the Cross 'is now borne by the neighbourhood and never without a merry-making'. Lipscombe, incidentally, was a medical doctor who was passionately involved in antiquarian research. He used up every penny he had to bring out his magnum opus, *History and Antiquities of the County of Buckinghamshire* (1847), and died a pauper. One intriguing point is that he mentions the Oxford colleges lending a hand in the scouring; this information has a mild sociological interest – was assisting scouring festivities a nineteenth-century student's equivalent to participating in a charity walk? Traditionally the owners of the Hamden estate, on which the Cross is situated, are responsible for its upkeep. This dates back to 1826, when George Robert, Earl of Buckinghamshire, had the Cross weeded and re-cut as stipulated by an Act of Parliament of George IV.

Kate Bergarmar recorded (1972) that scouring was carried out under the supervision of the head forester of the estate, Mr D. Watt, and took three men eight hours to complete. Today the Cross is a listed ancient monument.

Current Opinion and Evidence

The most radical re-appraisal of the Cross's use – by John North (1996) – ignores symbolism, or the slightest possibility of it being a Christian monument and concentrates on sightlines in relationship to other landmarks. For instance, a mound north of the Whiteleaf Long Barrow has a cross-shaped trench imposed on it.

It may be the base of a windmill or, alternatively, a round barrow. Below, branching from the road, an old path runs parallel to the Icknield Way before taking a sharp upward turn, exactly between the mound and the prominent knoll of Risborough Cop. From here, the Cross and mound align. This divergence was intended to provide a viewing platform for Arcturus rising above the mound as early as 1360 BC. 'How such a point', asked North, 'could ever have been determined except by chance over such hilly ground is hard to imagine. The symmetries of the situation speak strongly for this as the ideal place of observation.'

Where some interpret the eccentric winding of an old track as arising from changing landforms and foci of significance, North explains such kinks and irregularities in terms of sightlines and azimuths developed over thousands of years by priests of a star cult. He believes that widening the base of the Cross provided further vantage points for stellar sightings, the original draughtsman's intentions being preserved in Francis Wise's sketch of 1742, when the diameter of the base was half that of the present-day. Subsequent Victorian scourings enlarged it so drastically that this function was subsumed.

Similarly Whiteleaf Long Barrow can be seen to align with the lower part of the Cross and the main road up the hill (Peter's Lane) which cuts across the Icknield Way. From the crossing-point, the barrow could be identified in 3140 BC with Procyon, the lesser dog-star, rising above it. Down through the centuries, this gave way to the Pleiades (2480 BC) and then Aldebaran (1620 BC) or the eye of Taurus.

North's intensely statistical argument pushes the Cross back deep into the shadows of civilization. His revisionism is more precisely argued than that of his predecessors, but is not entirely radical. In *Chiltern Country* (1940), H.J. Massingham placed the origin of the Cross firmly in the Bronze Age and postulated an astrological or phallic function. However, that was typical of that elegant and genial writer saturated in the diffusionist theories of Elliott Smith and his protégé Perry. However, the writer Ian Rodger recently put the notion to the test. He had been studying the Whiteleaf Cross from his home in Brill and decided that it was a landmark of the old pagan Celtic year, aligning with the dawn rays of the sun as they crept over the Chilterns on 31 October. In 1980, when he took sightings, the alignment did not fall on Whiteleaf but on Beacon Hill – thus an old theory was scotched.

The Bledlow Cross

Site and Appearance

Four miles from the Whiteleaf Cross, on the north-west face of Wain Hill, is another Chiltern cross, known as the Bledlow Cross. It is regularly shaped in the manner of the cross of St George or the Greek Cross and lies on the old 500 ft contour line. In the vicinity are Roman remains and a number of burial mounds.

A popular approach to this monument is by taking the B4009 road from Chinnor to Princes Risborough. About one mile along this route, before the Skittle Green crossroads at Bledlow, take the road to the right, signposted 'Wainhill Only'. This leads to the hamlet of that name and peters out into a bridlepath. Not far from here, only about 200 yd off the path skirting Great Bledlow Wood, the Cross is carved into the chalk. Since it is not exactly in pristine condition, being encroached by beech scrub and juniper, it is often necessary to prospect around to find it. The arms extend approximately 22 m and are some 4 m wide. Generally it is far less dramatic than the Whiteleaf Cross, although its woodland setting is agreeable.

History and Interpretation

Nothing is known about its origin. Although Francis Wise (1742) makes much learned ado about the battle fought at 'Bledelawe or Bledlow', he is unaware of its being the site of another cross. Similarly J. Collins of Newport Pagnell, writing to William Stukeley in 1757, alludes to 'a Danish camp at Bledlow, near Prince's Risborow; and about two miles east of that place, on the side of a chalky hill, called White Leafe, a large white cross cut in the side of the hill', but makes no reference to any neighbouring monument.

The first unequivocal reference to the Bledlow Cross is found in a copy of the *Gentleman's Magazine* (1827):

Bledlow Cross: top, from the *Gentleman's Magazine*, 1827; bottom, G. Marples' sketch, 1936.

On the Bledlow Hills is to be traced the figure of a cross cut in the chalk, but from its having been neglected many years, is now nearly obliterated by the grass and weeds growing on it. A gentleman, who visited it a few days ago, and who is somewhat of an antiquary, had the curiosity to measure its dimensions, and to examine it very narrowly. He supposes it to have been made by the Saxons about the time the Whiteleaf Cross (from which it is not very distant) was formed; the mode of working seems to have been by digging squares of six feet, of which there are five, both in the perpendicular and the transverse lines, making a cross of 30 feet long in both lines, and of the width of six feet.

All this information was examined in an article published in *Antiquity* (1937), written by W. Lindsay Scott, the archaeologist who excavated the long barrow above the Cross. He believed that the only possible way to avoid the conclusion that the Bledlow Cross was cut between 1757 and 1827 is 'by assuming it was so overgrown on the former date as to be then unknown and that it was found and cleaned at some time prior to 1827, by which date it had again become partially overgrown'.

Only one piece of evidence exists that might counteract this argument. In the Calendar of Patent Rolls, September 1350, there is an entry recording the names of various felons who are to be brought before the bailiffs of Edward, Prince of Wales. Among them is 'Henry atte Crouche of Bledelowe' or 'Henry at Bledlow Cross' – a probable early reference to the hill-figure. The snag is that 'atte Crouche' – an old way of spelling 'cross' – is also a surname, and 'Henry atte Crouch of Bledelowe' may be a form of 'Henry Attcross of Bledlow'. This need not totally destroy the case, for names are rooted in details of localities: Attcross could still mean at the Bledlow Cross in the same way that John Hill implies John-who-lives-on-the-hill.

The Revd A. Baker (1855) subscribed to the monkish theory of origin for both Chiltern crosses. He described the Bledlow carving as 'a second cross, traditionally coeval, incised upon a still more prominent hill'. At that period it was a sorry sight, looking ragged and forlorn, and it occurred to him that it might be the precursor of the more stately symbol at Whiteleaf: 'May this not have been the original memorial, and have suggested the position of the other, as on a more conspicuous spot, where it would have served the further purpose of a wayside cross, the monks being the authors of this monument? A right of sanctuary, or demarcation of Church lands, may have been included in the intention.' The reasoning is sound but not convincing. Large chalk-cut crosses make confusing substitutes for boundary markers and inelegant wayside shrines. Medieval monks used their time cautiously and practically, creating objects of utility and craftsmanship. The cutting of a chalk cross seems more like the communal pursuit they would foist upon an unlettered peasantry too much addicted to maypole dancing, Obby

Oss risking and bonfire burning. Since the clergy were well aware that the traditional lore of the countryside was liable to be observed despite their censorship, they may have decided to divert it into a harmless outdoor festival of their own, the cutting and seasonal weeding of a large cross, an activity not unlike dressing a holy well.

Arms of the Bledlow Cross
(Marples).

And, of course, the Bledlow Cross stands in a region redolent of the passage of centuries. 'If ever there were a few square miles of countryside,' wrote a local topographer, 'which should cause an imaginative traveller to recall Byron's *Where'er we tread is haunted ground*, it is the Bledlow neighbourhood.' Tools of the Old Stone Age, long barrows of the Neolithic, bell barrows of the Bronze Age, Iron Age habitations, a Roman villa and Romano-British settlements – all have been located here. The palimpsest of history overwrites the work of each generation and the shadow of time lengthens.

LEGEND

There is a legend connected with the Bledlow Cross noted by Elizabeth Cull (1977), stating that anyone who runs up and down and across the arms of the Cross barefoot will be invested with fresh energy to complete his or her walk. This interesting oddment may conceivably relate to a primitive tradition connected with the place. Standing stones are said to possess reviving or healing properties; touching them establishes contact with their special magic. Unfortunately this fragment of folklore is undatable and, while it is to be expected that any long-standing hill-figure should pick up its quota of fabulous yarns, further data are required to create anything substantial.

Conclusion

Despite the fact that neither Stukeley's correspondent (1757) nor Francis Wise (1742) was aware of its existence, the present author inclines to the same view as the Revd Mr Baker, namely that the Bledlow Cross is the oldest of the Chiltern crosses and that the reference to 'Henry atte Crouche of Bledelowe' is an authentic fourteenth-century allusion to the monument. This then was the first of the crosses, cut before 1350, and it served as a preliminary model for the more spectacular version at Whiteleaf. It was cut at the instigation of monks, rather than by them, in a remote wooded place, the site of a former pagan shrine. Pious natives did the work, although it was supervised by the monastery. Cross-cutting in the soil, which sometimes took place during Rogation ceremonies, affirmed contact with the land while not harking back to country customs with pagan overtones. The Cross is best understood as a compromise between the old pantheistic religion and the church-based Christianity which was to infiltrate every aspect of daily life. The Bledlow Cross was scoured fitfully and, after the cutting of the Whiteleaf Cross in the seventeenth century, became overgrown and was ignored for a period, its reputation being almost totally eclipsed by its massive neighbour. Hence it remained unknown to Wise and to Stukeley's correspondent in much the same way as the Long Man remained obscure until attention was drawn to other hill-figures. This argument, admittedly flimsy, seems to me as substantial as the argument which places the Bledlow Cross after 1757. Between 1742 and 1855 Francis Wise had publicized such monuments, Baker and Lipscombe had conducted enquiries into both crosses and the *Gentleman's Magazine* had featured items on the Cerne Giant and the Bledlow Cross. The first mention of the Bledlow Cross was in 1827, some eighty-five years after Wise; there seemed to be no local knowledge of its being cut within living memory. In other words, allowing for the relative fame of the Whiteleaf Cross and the fact that such landmarks were beginning to stir up interest, one might have expected to find some notice in Buckinghamshire or national periodicals after 1757 describing the cutting of another large Chiltern Cross. This lack of information seems to support its great age.

Ditchling Cross (Sussex)
Site and Appearance

This is cut in the turf of the South Downs above Plumpton Place about five miles north-west of Lewes. No visible part of the cross survives today. It occupied the high ground on the old 600 ft contour line and was of the Greek type, the arms measuring approximately 30 m across. It was surveyed by W.J. and W.A. Jacobs, May 1923, and the plan (reproduced here) appeared in the *Brighton and Hove Archaeologist* of 1924.

History and Interpretation

The Cross is said to have been cut by the monks of the Priory of St Pancras, Lewes, to honour the memory of those who fell in the Battle of Lewes, 14 May 1264, when Simon de Montfort led his army against Henry III, son of King John, who had been taxing the country heavily

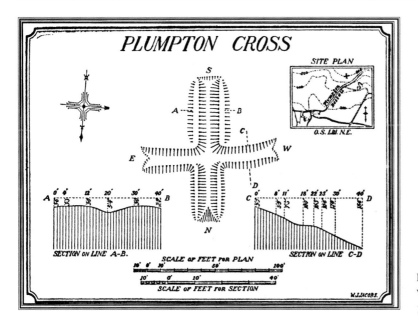

Plumpton Cross, surveyed by
W.J. and W.A. Jacobs, May
1923.

and conferring positions of privilege on foreigners. This angered the
barons. They maintained that the King was flouting rights established
in the Magna Carta and tried to submit their grievances for arbitration.
The Bishops of London and Worcester were sent as conciliatory envoys,
but they were received uncivilly by the King, and their efforts proved
fruitless. Simon de Montfort therefore felt justified in having recourse
to arms. With an army largely consisting of peasants, he marched
against the King, and, by a combination of luck and adroit strategy,
managed to win the day. The victory was commemorated in grand
style some 660 years later, on 14 May 1924, when a flock of Sussex
dignitaries and citizens attended the unveiling of a memorial which
had been erected in the centre of the Cross by the Brighton and Hove
Archaeological Club. Mr F. Harrison, a local historian, made a speech
providing a full outline of the battle and the facts and traditions
surrounding the Cross. One can do little better than quote from it at
length, for it covers the ground admirably:

> Those who ask what evidence there is for connecting this cross
> with the battle, I will say at once – direct evidence, none; indirect
> evidence and tradition, yes. I wonder whether those who put the
> question are aware that there is doubt whether the place-name,
> Mount Harry, has any connection with the battle.

A learned and well-known archaeologist says it is not usual to call a place after the name of the defeated leader – King Henry; and he suggests that the word Harry is more probably a corruption of Harrow, derived by Professor Skeat from the dative case, *hearge* of the Anglo-Saxon *hearg*. It signifies a heathen temple, and there are several places called Harrow, possibly once pagan places of worship such as Harrow-on-the-Hill, and Harrowden in Bedfordshire. There is also Harrow Hill near Arundel.

So that those who require direct evidence would question the connection of Mount Harry with the battle, as much as they may question that of this cross.

Blaauw, in his standard work on the Battle of Lewes, published eighty years ago, mentions this cross as being only visible under certain conditions of light; so we may well assume that for a hundred years this cross has been much as we see it now. If this spot should be the place of meeting at the seventh centenary of the battle I do not think there will be much change in its appearance.

Of the chroniclers it seems that the most reliable are Wm. Rishanger, who was only fourteen years of age at the time of the battle; the writer of the *Chronicle of Lanercost Abbey*, whose account is given on the authority of a nobleman present at the battle; and the *Chronicle by a Monk of Lewes* (1312).

Many chroniclers state only what they had heard and evidently did not know the locality. This also applies to some modern writers, one of whom says that de Montfort's army marched along the wooded crest of the Downs!

Tradition says that this great cross was cut by the monks of the Priory of St Pancras, Lewes, to perpetuate the memory of those who fell in the Battle of Lewes, 14th May, 1264, and to invoke the prayers of all for the repose of their souls. If this is correct, whilst the cross was kept clear of weeds and showed the white chalk, it must have been a conspicuous object. Such would have been its condition until the dissolution of the Priory in 1537–8; after this, neglected and exposed to the elements, its appearance would be such as the weather-worn features now present.

Careful and prolonged searching has failed to bring to light any evidence for or against this tradition, and even archaeologists may be pardoned for accepting a tradition which can be supported by reasonable suggestive details.

In the first place it must be noted that a white cross was worn on the breasts and backs of de Montfort's men and served a two-fold object, to distinguish the combatants, when members of the same family were fighting on opposing sides, and to bestow a religious character on the cause of the Barons. On the greenway, when de Montfort's men were in sight of the Priory and Castle, a solemn scene took place. After the exhortation of Simon de Montfort, every man bowed himself to the ground and, with outstretched arms, forming a cross, exclaimed 'Grant us, O Lord, our desire with mighty victory to the honour of Thy Name.'

Thus de Montfort entered into action in the spirit of a crusader against oppression, against unjust and excessive taxation due to Papal exaction, and against foreign influence due to the Queen.

The white cross had been adopted by the English in the Crusades, whilst the French wore a red cross. The cross moline, charged upon the shield, was attributed to the Saxon Kings about this time, and the army of the Barons was chiefly Saxon, not yet welded into the one English nation.

As soon as news was brought to the Prince, at break of day, that the enemy were in sight and were rapidly advancing towards Lewes, he issued from the Castle with his mounted men, rode forward and charged the Londoners, who had run to meet him near Offham chalk pits. The fight was sharp, but short.

The following day the Mise of Lewes was signed and a truce established. After the battle, many of the Royalists escaped to Pevensey and then on to France. Some drowned crossing the Ouse and their bodies have been found, sitting dead upon their horses, sword in hand, embalmed in the chocolatey silt. Cartloads of human bones have been recovered near Offham chalkpit where Prince Edward pursued and slaughtered Montfort's supporters. As the old chronicle put it:

> 'Many fine ladies lese her lord that day,
> And many gode bodies slayn at Lewis lay.'

When Morris Marples visited the Cross, presumably in the 1940s, it was badly faded and could only be made out under favourable conditions. Although no information on it predates the nineteenth century, one can only acquiesce to local lore and accept the Southover monks as its authors. As a monument to the fallen, it has borne their memory for many years, but grass and scrub have now closed over it, and the dead have long since ceased to care.

CHAPTER ELEVEN

THE WILDER SHORES

Over all, a grand meaning fills the scene,
And sets the brain raging with prophecy,
Raging to discard real time and place,
Raging to build a better time and place.

(Kingsley Amis 1956)

For adherents of Earth Mysteries, the December 1991 issue of *Antiquity* may have particular significance, for it featured an article on the Silbury glory or halo effect 'in appropriately dense language' by Paul Devereux, former editor of the *Ley Hunter* and expert on earth lights and many other 'fringe' areas of archaeology and phenomena. Thirty years earlier such an article would have been unthinkable. *Antiquity* was then edited by Glyn Daniel who, every so often, would release a fusillade against the barbarian hordes of flying saucer cultists, pyramidiots, straight-liners and psychic mavericks who embrace 'the black comforts of unreason' in preference to the sane and scholarly approach enshrined in his pages.

Despite Daniel's reactionary stance, several of his colleagues were in a state of ferment, mainly owing to the researches of a Cambridge University engineer, Professor Alexander Thom. After calibrating the relationship of hundreds of megaliths and henges to the movements of heavenly bodies, this Scottish academic declared that the people who built Stonehenge and Avebury possessed sophisticated astronomical and mathematical knowledge, had deliberately shaped their stone circles in egg-shaped ellipses and had spaced the stones using a precise unit of measurement known thereafter as the megalithic yard.

Thom's book *Megalithic Sites in Britain* (1967) was likened to a neatly packaged parcel bomb. This was a dramatic way of saying that some archaeologists were stunned by his findings. For years they had been examining ground-plans and soil sections, and now they were told, in order properly to understand the achievements of the megalith builders, they had to fix their eyes on the stars, become astronomers and surveyors and generally dispense with the outmoded working model of prehistoric culture which had not allowed for such sophisticated achievements.

Thom's findings quickened the resurrection of Alfred Watkins, a Herefordshire brewer who formulated the 'ley' theory, proposing that straight lines link places of ancient sanctity: henges, barrows, standing stones, castles, moats and even pre-Reformation churches (if built on the sites of earlier temples) mark the routes of prehistoric trackways laid out with fine accuracy. The Neolithic inhabitants, like the giants of folklore, were landscape-shapers and skilled surveyors.

Alfred Watkins, discoverer of leys.

DODMEN AND INITIATES

Hill-figures were incorporated into Watkins' scheme. The Long Man of Wilmington depicts the prehistoric dodman, or surveyor, holding his aligning rods. The old name for the common snail was dodman – an allusion, presumably, to the cocked horns – and this likeness is repeated in the Sussex giant. He possessed something of the status of a high priest or wizard, and his magical rods were synonymous with the caduceus of Hermes and the wand of the magus.

All this precise orientation seemed to rest uncomfortably on the shoulders of a people who inhabited fairly rude settlements and died young from various painful complaints. Yet Thom's view of the megalith builders as engineers capable of erecting sensitive lunar and solar observatories threw into question many past presumptions.

Consider the legacy of folkloristic and anthropological works postulating that early man considered the earth as akin to a vast female body, the sun a male generative force, with the moon the product of the other two's conjunction. Does this accurately reflect the psychology of a folk capable of predicting lunar and solar eclipses and who, in the view of some researchers, had knowledge of such specialized areas as equinoctial precession or the axial 'wobble' of the earth that brings about the earlier occurrence of the equinoxes in each successive sidereal year.

Scarcely was it to be wondered that, in the light of Thom's findings, concepts of our barbarian forefathers, whether right or wrong, were gradually replaced by a vision of groups of initiates, mystic technocrats, looking inwards as well as outwards and subtly utilizing the 'earth-spirit' to maintain the equilibrium of a Golden Age. Such radical ideas extended to hill-figures:

> I see the Long Man [wrote Alistair Brinkley, deviating somewhat from Watkins' hypothesis] as the initiate in the symbolic door, achieving the understanding that there is for all of us to reach, if we have the courage. Earlier accounts speak of not knowing if the figure 'holds' staves, spears, rake or scythe. There are no internal features (as at Cerne Abbas) other than mounds for eyes, nose and mouth, so why does our condition let us see the lines by the hands in three dimensions? The figure is in two dimensions, and, I believe, presses the palm of his hand against the inside of a dolmen, the human being joyously on the threshold, the emergence of the developed personality.

A splendidly Jungian interpretation and, metaphorically speaking, as valid as that styling the Long Man as opening the doors of dawn or summer. However, it does carry an element of projection, of channelling occult sentiments into a past which may have possessed a wholly alien conceptual apparatus. Little history can be written without imagination to fill the gaps, but when the gaps are huge – as is the case with our knowledge of Neolithic society – there is the danger of nothing but imagination filling the vacuum.

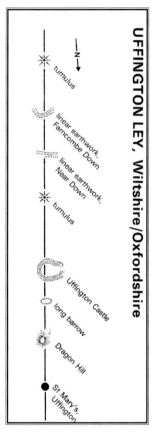

Uffington Ley (*Paul Devereux & Ian Thomson*)

THE UFFINGTON DRAGON

With the advent of Earth Mysteries came an upsurge of richly romantic speculation. The badlands of learning were opened up and the chipped and shattered busts of discredited scholars and wild men of learning were rescued from the rubble, conscientiously dusted down and remounted on their pedestals. Old theories were restyled and marketed to an audience which hungered for broader horizons, for a poetry of distant horizons and strange past epochs that official archaeologists had failed to appease.

One example was the promotion of the ideas of Harold Massingham, founder of the 'Plumage Bill Group' as well as a delightfully genteel writer on history and topography. Massingham was known for his hyper-diffusionist ideas. In *Fee, Fi, Fo, Fum* (1926), he subscribed to the daring opinion that the White Horse of Uffington was not a horse but a dragon, and coeval with Wayland's Smithy. The Norse smith-god, in his view, amounted to a Saxon version of Hephaestus, or Vulcan, the Greek god of the forge, one of whose sons, Ericthonius, became a king of Athens in serpent form. The chalk dragon, therefore, denotes the grave of a Pendragon or warrior-lord entombed in the chambered mound.

What then is the animal which is the source and inspiration of all bestiaries, ballads and bewizarded folk-lore? Obviously it is a dragon. The reader of Geoffrey of Monmouth will remember that at one time England suffered from a pest of dragons. The very air breathed the scorching breath of dragons; the tower of Vortigern could not be built at all because two dragons sat on two stones under a pool beneath the ground where the foundations were laid. The golden habergeon of Arthur (whose father was Uther Pendragon) had a dragon crest, and the great name of Merlin is so mixed up with dragons that his feats might well be called the dragonades, rather than the gasconades of the illustrious sorcerer.

To be fair, Massingham was probably only half serious in proposing this theory – indulging in mythological jugglery to bemuse or charm – but his argument was nevertheless taken up by Paul Screeton, former editor of the *Ley Hunter* and author of a fine book on North Country dragon legends. He stated in *Quicksilver Heritage* that the Horse represented the dragon and all that fabulous creature symbolizes. He questioned whether the length of figure, 365 ft, was intended to be equated with the days of the year.

Dragon – symbol of the vitalizing currents of earth energy.

Another approach invoked the aid of extra-terrestrials. Brinsley Le Poeur Trench, better known as Lord Clancarty, was an omnivorous gleaner of eclectic fragments. In one of his works on ancient civilizations, he informed us that in symbiology the White Horse stood for Mind. Acting the part of enthusiastic ombudsman between earthlings and sky-folk, he stated that the White Horse was intended to be viewed celestially and posed a series of questions to which few glib answers spring readily to mind: 'This particular white horse was pictured on White Horse Hill, and Uther Pendragon, the Paramount Sovereign, King of Kings, is said to be buried nearby. Was the white horse a sign – a symbol – to other men, Sky People? Was it a permanent landmark – a signpost – to those who came to rehabilitate the planet after the sinking of Poseid? Was the White Horse Hill area the burial ground of the Royal Line of Arthurs?'

A variant of this logic surfaced in Arthur Shuttlewood's book, *Warnings From Flying Friends*. Something of a rustic Von Daniken, he did much to publicize Warminster – a stolid Wiltshire town – as a gathering place for UFOs. He incorporated into his study research undertaken by Doug Chandy connecting various chalk horses with routes pursued by the saucers. The pattern revealed that Cherhill, Alton Barnes and Pewsey horses are aligned; the outermost figures are equidistant from the centre one. Cherhill and Pewsey horses, when joined by straight lines to the Uffington Horse, form an isosceles triangle, one side of which passes over the Broad Hinton Horse. Extend the sides of this triangle and the lines dissect such sacred places as Glastonbury Tor, Butleigh Hill and the Prescelly Mountains. Do these horses, then, mark out the channels of terrestrial magnetism which the saucers utilize for celestial locomotion? There is pathos and sublimity in such rhetorical questions. Never has so much been assumed by so many on the basis of so little.

DECIPHERING THE GIANT

This geometrical fervour can prove wearisome, for all regular shapes are bound by a consistent relationship of sorts, and if one rattles around numbers with sufficient dexterity, sooner or later the proof required will come to hand. However, the idea that ancient monuments encode messages expressed in numerical, linear or purely proportional terms has a long and venerable history. The Great Pyramid of Ghiza clearly hoards sacred wisdom enough to see scholars into the fourth millennium AD. Yet that Fort Knox of occult knowledge has its competitors in, for example, Avebury, Stonehenge and Glastonbury Abbey. John Michell, by adroit mathematics, has succeeded in equating the aforementioned monuments with the proportions of the sacred city specified in the Book of Revelation.

The Cerne Giant was subjected to this form of analysis by W.H. Black in 1872. He classified it as one of the ancient landmarks 'made by Roman surveyors in Britain, serving uses analogous to the stones, or circles of stone, and to the mound'. Black extended various lines from the Giant to various allegedly Roman sites: the Whiteleaf Cross, the mouth of the River Nene flowing into the Wash, the island of Ushant on the north-west tip of Britanny, St Catherine's Chapel, Abbotsbury, and the Norfolk coast near Happisburgh 'where an ancient Roman place of great importance formerly stood, now covered up with drifted sand, excepting the top of the round tower of Eccles which served both as a landmark and as a sea mark'.

Next Black considers the proportions of the Giant, the most important being the height, 180 ft, and the length of the club, 120 ft. Both are multiples of 60 and indicate geographical miles. The club, when applied as a radius of measurement, informs the enlightened that a cromlech at Fishguard in Pembrokeshire and another such monument, Kit's Coty in Kent, together with a vanished megalith at Constantine, Cornwall, lie 120 miles from the Giant. The latter cromlech, known as the Cornish Pebble, 'had a series of lines and points carved on the top showing, as I believe, the geometric uses of that noble and glorious stone'. Using the body as a radial measure, he extends lines to Wicklow Head and Berwick-upon-Tweed 'which town I take to be the Roman *Borcovius*' and then, halving the length of the club, he takes a measure of sixty miles to North Cerney and Havant, 'which still preserves the original Roman name *Venta*, and its British translation, Y-gwent, under the aspirated pronoun Havant' and cites the imperial itinerary as supportive evidence.

Clearly someone of Black's erudition is capable of proving anything satisfactorily to himself, but the basic concept of laboriously making a hill-figure to encode statistics more easily set down on paper lacks plausibility. His method anticipates the work of some modern speculative writers on ancient sites, although the evidence he accumulates would today result in a Bronze Age interpretation. Even at the time Black was writing, the assumption that cromlechs were constructed by Roman surveyors was mildly heretical.

A far more nebulous world than Black's (which, after all, has a relatively precise basis in geometry) is that occupied by the clairvoyant, Grace Cooke, who visited various ancient sites with the intention of uncovering their secrets. The vision she conjured in her book *The Light in Britain* (1971) does not accord with known archaeological fact. Myth and legend mingle in a kaleidoscopic mist in which such figures as Ar-Thor, Christ and the people of Atlantis join forces and combat dragons of darkness. Cones of light, spirals, serpents, gold crowns – all the symbolic evasions of specificity appear in this world of poetic abstraction. However, there are passages which achieve a sterile lyricism, such as the fragment relating to a time in 1949 when she climbed Dragon Hill with her husband:

We climbed past Dragon Hill, past the shape of the horse or dragon cut into the side of White Horse Hill, to the castle above and stood facing the great valley of the Thames with its horizon of hills. The sun was a deep gold as it set in a cloudless sky, casting

a soft amethyst light over the hills and valleys. . . . I saw a great
assembly of simply clad people filling the amphitheatre or manger
below Dragon Hill, and heard the sound of trumpets, summoning
the people to take part in some grand ceremony of sun-worship. I
saw then that twelve high priests were conducting the ritual now
taking place on Dragon Hill, and they appeared to be summoning
the great angels of the White Light . . . and around the hill itself
there seemed to be a host of lesser nature spirits, sylphs and
salamanders, gnomes and other fairy forms.

Such writing demonstrates how the potent image of the chalk horse
can act as a trigger or master key, unlocking pent-up dream worlds,
wild psychic landscapes and spiritual cravings, while retaining its
essential enigma.

PARADISE ON EARTH

Emphasis on the sacred, ubiquitous number twelve is apparent
in Grace Cooke's book. The same number finds favour with John
Michell, the father of modern Earth Mysteries, who stimulated the
Glastonbury Revival. Scholar, old Etonian, defender of traditional
measures and currency, Michell is an alluring stylist whose innate
conservatism has such deep roots that it emerges as a kind of
radicalism. His books on Stonehenge, Avebury and gematria are
classics of their kind, regularly reprinted, and he now edits the
Cerealogist, a periodical dedicated to the crop circle debate.

The essential thing to state about Michell is that he is a Platonist
– a denomination that allows a broad range, from politics to mysticism,
from ethics to mathematics, art and drama. As Alfred North Whitehead
remarked, all of Western philosophy can be regarded as a footnote to
Plato. Aside from his political formulations, Plato believed that a more
intense spiritual realm lay behind the world of appearances. Ordinary
mortals are unable to penetrate this intense spiritual reality, for they
prefer squatting in the cave of their preoccupations, observing the
shadow-play and mistaking it for the sun.

How does one crawl out of the cave? How does one gain insight
into this spiritual realm? By pondering eternal truths found
in abstract structures that transcend the sensual realm, such as
geometry, music and mathematics. Through symbolic and numerical
structures, Michell (1990) believes, one attains the realm of pure
form. By refining a tradition, by attuning oneself to a sacred pattern

and perfecting it, one creates the necessary opening to draw heaven down on earth. Whether the investigation concerns Glastonbury, Stonehenge or Avebury, a vision of the Eternal City binds it into a whole:

> As an abstract idea, paradise on earth has a universal attraction, but the question of its actual form gives rise to a multiplicity of images. It is something that everyone wants, but no one knows exactly what it is. The only profitable way of examining it, therefore, is on the level of its own abstract reality. On that level it can be imagined as universal harmony, an intensified combination of all the sounds, scents, forms and colours which delight the senses. Inherent in it is the idea of perfect relationships between every particle in God's creation – a state which already exists, whether or not we choose to perceive it. Once that fact becomes evident, its power for transformation is possible.

So paradise 'already exists' – where exactly? In the spirtual realm? Beyond the cave of gross materialism? It may be gathered that Michell is a visionary, taking forward the tradition of William Blake and waiting for mystic Albion to awake from slumber. The novelist, Peter Ackroyd, shares a similar obsession with recreating heaven on earth by alchemical union or prolonged ritual acts allied to a systematic derangement of the senses. However, Ackroyd moves frankly in the sphere of fiction whereas Michell seeks to promote a myth that transcends mere entertainment, which is perhaps why he seldom dwells on the more repugnant physical details of the sites he evokes – the messy sacrificial rituals, the skulls with bad teeth, the mutilations and decapitations. Such details are hardly the point; one judges men by their highest moments, their supreme symbolic attainments, and not by their soft, perishable cores.

Despite Michell's eloquence and a booming occult market, the end of the 1970s marked a slight dampening of ardour in the Earth Mysteries circuit. Thom's parcel bomb proved to be an implosion rather than an explosion, collapsing his own reputation when it was found that his calculations were not impeccable and his egg-shaped circles were more likely the result of casual rather than rigorous measurement. The revision of the Carbon 14 dating process rendered his stellar alignments problematic. Added to this, not a single measuring rod could be found to back up his megalithic yard.

The result was not an abandonment of astro-archaeology but a modified acceptance of standing stones as celestial markers pertaining to landscape features at certain times of the year. During the 1980s there was a toning down of megalithic speculation, a backslide into traditional modes of interpretation together with a disinclination to make stupendous statements or breakthroughs, but men like Aubrey Burl did benefit from Thom's insights and went on to extend this important area of research.

CELESTIAL MARKERS

The most dramatic leap in our celestial knowledge of barrows, henges and hill-figures is found in John North's *Stonehenge, Neolithic Man and the Cosmos* (1996). Here we will only deal with his theories pertaining to the latter. North emphasizes that too much attention has been paid to the form of the carvings rather than to their positioning with regard to the rising and setting of certain stars. Concerning the Uffington Horse, for example, he picks out two stars in the constellation of Taurus, Aldebaran and gamma Tauri, the two brightest stars in the head of the bull. These two stars would have made a near-perfect fit to the slope of the White Horse in the late fourth millenium BC; also, from the same sightline, the two stars, beta Tauri and zeta Tauri, would have made an equally exact vertical set above Dragon Hill. The marker points of the Horse were the eye and penis (conventionally interpreted as the right back leg); furthermore, there was a 'gallery' of observation points (some placed in the modern car park above the Horse) built to preserve these relationships.

Similarly exciting evidence can be drawn from aligning the Long Man to the constellation Orion *c.* 3480 BC. Viewed from the gate leading to the road, the star-drawn giant would have seemed 'to walk along the ridge' between the rising and setting of Rigel. Over five thousand years later, however, the picture has altered:

From the gate, Orion can no longer be seen striding across the horizon as he once did. One no longer has to look for Orion at an altitude of around 10 or 11°, but at about 30°. Doing so, the old effect can almost be seen not far from the foot of the figure. (Whereas Orion's right foot was formerly above the ridge, now it is out of sight below. . . . To preserve the effect of the striding giant it was necessary to move closer to the figure.

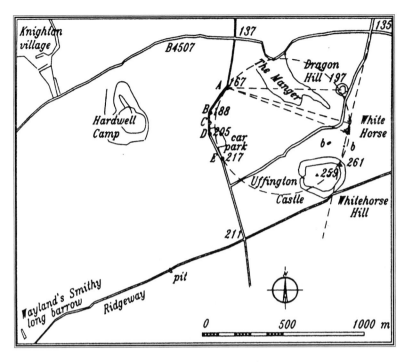

Diagram illustrating the shifting viewpoints of the prominent constellations around White Horse Hill, from J. North's *Stonehenge, Neolithic Man and the Cosmos.*

Whiteleaf and Bledlow Crosses offer further possibilities as Neolithic star markers. Here, however, North is far less definite about the viewing points: from a bay to the north of the Whiteleaf Cross – 'if it is not illusory' – the rising of Aldebaran or Betelgeuse *c.* 3500 BC; from 'the faintest suspicion of a mound of a long barrow' above the Bledlow Cross, an aligment on Rigel *c.* 3660 BC.

North's book is technical, authoritative and – he is a professor of the Exact Sciences – diagrammatically ravishing. Allowing that all well-marshalled arguments are a type of privileging – seeing something in terms of one's own specialization – the functional elegance of the thesis seems at odds with galloping horses and striding giants. Why use untidy, irregular shapes when a more surveyor-like mound or standing stone might do? The answer is that the hill-figures are zodiacal illustrations. The Uffington Horse may depict Taurus – after all, it has cattle-like characteristics – while the Long Man represents Orion, and the Cerne Giant can be lined up with the constellation of Hercules during the Roman occupation. North's tendency to date figures by what he interprets as complementary constellations can seem like an act of faith. This is in keeping with many 'great' intuitions. The detail and evidence he accrues, however, are formidable, even if they do not invariably support his hypothesis.

STINGING THE SENSES AWAKE

Living, as many of us do, artificially enclosed lives, when we are
not always aware of the passing of the seasons, it can be difficult to
accept this twinning of Neolithic society and endless star-gazing.
Technology brings insulating comforts that diminish the capacity
to feel – or retain – radical astonishment. If we strip away modern
accoutrements – electric lights, tower blocks and cars – nature
may once again be perceived as a series of startling revelations,
from spring flowers to comets, from oppressive cloudy dawns to
Thomas Hardy's 'full-starred winter sky'. In order to reinstate such
vanquished perceptions, to sting the senses awake, we look to the
arts of music and poetry:

> A shade I am remote from sombre hamlets.
> The silence of God
> I drank from the woodland well.
>
> On my forehead cold metal forms.
> Spiders look for my heart.
> There is a light that fails in my mouth.
>
> At night I found myself upon a heath,
> Thick with garbage and dust of stars.
> In the hazel copse
> Crystal angels have sounded once more.
>
> *(De Profundis)*

Trakl's lines are as keen as an Arctic wind. Such honed, heightened
sensations may be near allied to those of the barrow-builders who had
to rely wholly on their senses. Not possessing the means to filter and
control nature, they lived a skin's thickness from the frosted earth;
the wetness or dryness of the season saturated their bones. Spending
hours gazing at the night sky, noting its monthly and yearly changes,
produced mental states of an entirely different order from that of a
modern office worker or factory manager.

That the stars are integrated with archetypes of myth and legend
has been noted by psychologists and anthropologists from Jung to
Stan Gooch. The latter cited the importance in Ancient Greece of
the tale of Orion which described the hunter amorously pursuing
six sisters and their mother through a wood. Zeus, overcome with

compassion, changes them all into stars – hence the constellation Orion set beside the Pleiades. Among the Aborigines of Australia, the lustful hunter Wurruna chases after seven maidens, but seven trees spring up, magically tall, transporting the maidens to the heavens where they become the Pleiades. Among the Indians of Wyoming, there is a tale of seven maidens hunted by a bear; to escape they climb on a rock which suddenly raises itself up, pushing into the sky, forming the Pleiades.

As Gooch (1997) has pointed out, the Pleiades 'is a very tiny cluster of fourth magnitude stars, very hard to spot at all', so why this emphasis in separate cultures? Does it not indicate a deep-rooted primordial preoccupation? Human beings, whatever their environment, dream and perceive and tell stories in the same way. Early cultures must have viewed the night sky as the campfires of the distant gods. Neither were these fires static, but alive and changing with the hour. Stars rose and passed out of sight like the lives of individuals. Souls of the dead blended with the firmament, like smoke from a Hindu funeral pyre.

To the peoples of the Neolithic, death was not a reduceable or vanquishable fact. Corpses were not hidden under cover; they were displayed in open-air cemeteries where they were, quite probably, visited and spoken to by relatives and friends. Stages of bloating, decay and consumption by birds and insects were noted. Eventually the skeletons, picked clean and dissembled, were stored in mortuary houses and covered over with wood, stone and turf. Yet these hard, enduring fragments – mortal armatures – needed to be irradiated by that which is permanent, eternal. Hence the tombs were set at fixed positions, so that stars would rise and set over them, and their eternal fires reanimate the sparkless chill of physical dissolution. Stars conserved – perhaps reanimated – the energies of those who had passed on. Their shifting positions spelt out messages to priests and scryers, and in time they became personalized until each self-contained point held a power charge of myth and heroism.

DEATH ROADS

Although one might have expected North's book to receive a rapturous reception in Earth Mysteries circles, suprisingly it did not, receiving only a respectful, coolish review by Neil Mortimer in *3rd Stone* (subtitled the *Magazine for the New Antiquarian*) and a guardedly favourable response by John Michell in the *Spectator*. Is this an indication of the present state of afffairs, when astro-archaeology is losing ground to 'cognitive' or psycho-archaeology? The latter attempts to climb into the skull of early man and gape out through the sockets of his eyes. This is manifested in a renewed interest in prehistoric art, in lozenge, cup-and-ring and zig-zag markings, seeing them as the upshot of trance states, induced by drugs or magical rituals, or of shamanistic flights into the 'interworld', the threshold zone between the inner self and the palpable world – a similar reality, in fact, to that inhabited by abductees when they are whisked away and experimented upon by grey-skinned humanoids. Unfortunately this realm is impervious to rational experiment or geographical expedition. It is all mind-space, tiny and infinite at the same time, and there is therefore a deal of heated, complex discussion about what exactly goes on there.

Interest in ley-lines has lagged somewhat and been substituted by a mournful preoccupation with spirit ways and death roads. Whether this is because some Earth Mysteries writers have progressed in years and their thoughts are turning towards mortality, one forbears from speculating, but it appears to have exposed an intriguing lode of postmortal speculation:

> The . . . medieval Dutch *Doodwegen* (death roads) which run straight to cemeteries, the straight roads for conducting the bodies of Viking chieftains, and Native American straight tracks in Costa Rica, are used for similar purposes. Their 'dead straight' nature seems to have been related to the way the spirits of the dead were thought to travel. For instance . . . German *Geisterwegen* (ghost paths) which were thought to run invisibly but straight between cemeteries. Such ghost and death roads probably developed from an archaic core concept. Celtic 'fairy paths' may also relate to this and the Chinese geomantic system of 'feng shui' also claimed spirits move in straight lines.
>
> (*Ley Hunter* 127)

With this new emphasis on death roads and the neural networks, the ley line has become desacrilized. To paraphrase current thinking, the concept seems to have arisen out of a mistaken collusion between mental and physical topography in which the key figure is the shaman. After undergoing symbolic or ritual death, he enters the spirit world and flies across the landscape in a disembodied or 'astral' vehicle. In this out-of-body or near-death state, the patterns of his consciousness are replicated in terms of tunnels, lattices, zigzags, straight lines and spirals – all the motifs, in fact, one finds in Neolithic art. For example, the shaft of light that penetrates the chamber at Newgrange, Ireland, at the time of the winter solstice, is symbolic of this re-awakened state. It is a tunnel of transformation, a dawning beam of consciousness tracing a route of spiritual ascent.

In view of this, the editor of the *Ley Hunter* maintains that the 'old' ley is defunct (Sullivan 1997):

So then, what is a ley? I would say there is no such thing as a ley. As a defined thing or phenomenon in its own right, it does not exist. Watkins saw the remains of archaic spirit lines, medieval corpse ways and church road alignments. He didn't recognise what he saw and chose to weave a theory around the remaining evidence shaped by his own personal experience. The decades of wild speculation that buried his original vision have relegated ley hunting to the academic sidelines whilst all the time archaeologists, anthropologists, geographers and folklorists have been advancing our knowledge of the archaic landscape line, side-stepping the excesses of the energy line modellers and twig twitchers. It is time that the contribution of genuine ley hunters is more widely recognised. It is time to bury the ley.

To those latecomers who have only recently learned about leys, this seems a ruthless line. Out goes friendly, calm-footed Alfred Watkins from Herefordshire; in his place enters a wild-eyed, drug-stuffed shaman from Siberia – or, at least, his British counterpart. It remains to be seen whether the Asian visitant will prove of lasting value to antiquarian culture or whether he will be exchanged eventually for some new magic-man with even more amazing qualities?

Of course, such theorizing resurrects the time-honoured philosophical conundrum with which David Hume bedevilled the thinking establishment of the eighteenth century: how does one establish the existence of anything outside of one's mental impressions and sensations? What is 'out there'? If all is mindscape, topography is reduced to hallucination and archaeology a branch of psychology. Conversely, if people and objects are self-contained and discrete, why not allow for diversity and sharp distinction? If a path has been employed as a coffin-route, why draw in strands of folklore and enforce a connection with shamanistic spirit-flight? While it is true that, in dream and symbol, everything jostles, blends and metamorphoses, psychic archaeology is in danger of entombing itself in the metaphors and analogies of literary criticism.

Like Timothy Leary and Aldous Huxley, early man, then, was preoccupied with contacting the spirit world. He was a flatliner, altering his state of consciousness, so that he might 'fly' psychic airways and entopic corridors. Judging from material drawn from the Egyptians, Aborigines and Aztecs, this has more than a grain of truth in it, but correlating abstract patterns with states of mind is a fuzzy activity – after all, if one draws a circle in a state of deep depression or soaring elation, will it ultimately spell out anything but a circle? Nevertheless, if one considers the scale of certain megalithic monuments, the protracted labour of earth-shifting and stone-levering, it becomes obvious that the most effective manner by which such endurance could be maintained was by attaining a hypnotic rhythm, a mantric beat, in which time shortens, identity atrophies and one literally *becomes the act*.

To what extent drugs were used in magical ceremonies, as spiritual inducements, is another question, but Cambridge-based archaeologist, Jeremy Dronfield, has argued that cave art is an externalization of trance states induced by sensory deprivation, drumming and mind-changing substances. Taking as a prime example the passage tombs of the Boyne Valley, Ireland, at the Core Moot held at the University of London Union (1996), he drew comparisons between images produced under drugs and the mesmeric repetitions of cave carvings. Extending the field of contemporary comparisons, he showed slides of 1960s Op Art – patterns designed to disrupt or displace the visual field – and explained how flickering lights might achieve a similar effect in the confines of a dark tomb.

Orthodox archaeologists question Dronfield's findings. If one buys a cloth with a strong, bold repetitive pattern on it, they argue, one does not assume its creator is working under the influence of cocaine rather than cocoa. However, a larger question emerges that perplexes staid archaeologists, maverick archaeologists and the earth mystic fraternity alike. How do contemporary men and women relate to their distant predecessors, to those who, in a sense, shaped their world, made them who they are, yet still seem incredibly remote? Some archaeologists regard prehistory as a sacrosanct enclosure not to be cluttered with too much contemporary fashion or ideological whim. Rather the evidence should arise from analysis of the environmental context alone. Earth mystics tend to be more interactive in outlook, employing new insights in psychology, astronomy, drug research – even quantum physics – to extend the realm of speculation. Their outlook is that past wisdom is recoverable and may be used to enrich and preserve the planet – an optimism that, one hopes, is not misplaced.

Alternative magazine, edited by Muz Murray and named after Tolkien's character, announcing the mystical renaissance of the hippie era of the late 1960s. Based at World's End, Chelsea, *Gandalf's Garden* stood for 'the magical garden of our inner worlds, overgrowing into the world of manifestation'.

APPENDIX A

THE CERNE GIANT

An address made to the Commission of Enquiry concerning the
origins of the Cerne Giant, 23 March 1996.

The image of the Cerne Giant stands as antiquity's rebuke to
political correctness. Naked, angry and aroused, he wields a club
– an outdated, not particularly effective weapon even at the time of
the Iron Age to which he has been attributed. Back then a club was
something of an archaism, during a time of slings, swords and spears,
and possibly the giant was a nod to traditional masculine values, a
strong man able to fight his way through the world equipped with
nothing save his block of wood and rampant virility.

To ask – or even enlarge – on what he stands for is rather naïve. If
confronted in the street by a man in an identical posture, doubtless
one would not ask him to explain himself symbolically, but flee the
area as quickly as possible. Like the god Mars, the Giant combines
the qualities of fertility and aggression, much-needed and respected
traits back in Roman times, and not altogether sneezed at in the
present when survivalism is touted as a prudent strategy.

Who carved the figure? The Phoenicians? The Celts? The Romans?
The Saxons? Successive waves of invaders or settlers have been posited
at different times by different writers. But not every scholar or expert
has invariably assumed that the Giant dates from distant antiquity.
The poet Geoffrey Grigson suggested that the carving might have been
'the obscene jest of a ribald free-thinking eighteenth-century nobleman
making fun of the antiquaries'. However, if there existed a Dorsetshire
wing of the Hellfire Club, it has escaped the notice of contemporary
chroniclers. Furthermore, if the carving had been incorporated in a
park or artificially contrived wilderness – a scandalous centrepiece, say,
outlined by statues of naked nymphs – one would have little difficulty
in placing it squarely in the eighteenth century.

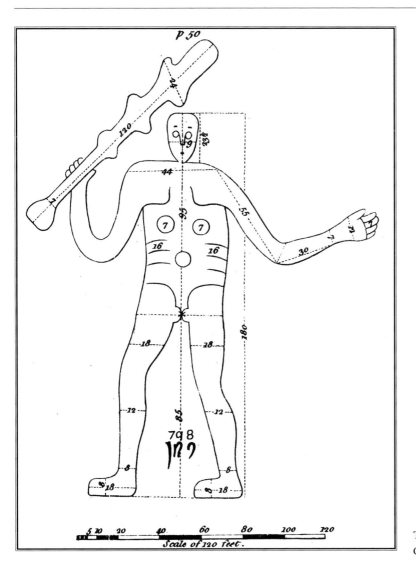

The dimensions of the Cerne Giant (Hutchins 1774).

But the Giant is very much an isolated gesture, standing alone on a sheep-cropped hillside, and the issue does not end with designing and cutting. We are dealing with the inauguration of a continuous, arduous obligation to scour and maintain the figure down through the centuries. It is this prolonged effort that makes one assume that the figure arose from the collective concerns of the community rather than impulse or whim or playful prank.

Yet a custom must start at some point. It is mere sentimentalism to assume that a new tradition could not arise in the seventeenth century or later. The problem is that the primary themes expressed by the Giant – violence, nakedness, sexual arousal – stand as blatant affronts to Christian values. Of course, in their daily lives people were frequently violent, often seen naked, and knew all about erections, but such commonplaces were not perpetualized on hillsides.

A proud physique and an enormous club had little relevance to the Age of Monasticism or the Enlightenment. Neither would the Giant relate to Cavaliers and Roundheads or the subsequent Restoration. The Age of Elegance offers no suitable niche either. Jane Austen might have admired his rude enthusiasm or primitive honesty, but would not have dwelt overmuch on the social possibilities embodied in his stance.

Unabashed Phallicism

To seek a period where the qualities expressed by the Giant belong, where he does not stand out as a gross anomaly, it is necessary to go back two thousand years and more, to a time when his primary features corresponded closely with the outlook and practices of many communities.

Let us first deal with the obvious aspect of the Giant, those qualities that Aristophanes parodied in the fifth century BC (in *The Acharnians*) as being comic and quaint: the rampant, unabashed phallicism, a concept as old as creation or, should one say, procreation?

There is a Bronze Age carving from Löfåsen, Sweden, showing a figure half-man, half-bull, wielding a mallet and, simultaneously, experiencing a turbulent erection. One imagines that this figure stands for fertility in men and cattle, and there are several hammer-wielding Celtic equivalents, like Succellos the good striker, to whom he might loosely relate. Ox-like qualities are locally reflected in the Ooser, a bull-masked man who used to caper through the streets of Dorset, demanding refreshment and kisses from the women. In Shillingstone he was called the Christmas Bull, for he appeared at the coldest, most blighted time, when the spirit of fertility and growth struggled against the hanged year.

So initially we have an animal god, erect and brandishing a mallet. Centuries later, man has established supremacy over oxen and bulls, and we are presented with the Cerne Giant, a hero freed of animal appendages but retaining the upraised weapon and phallus. No longer is he a beast but a 'tamer' of beasts: the hero-god Hercules.

This must be qualified, however. 'Hercules' is a loose rather than strict identification. The Celts were great incorporators and copiers

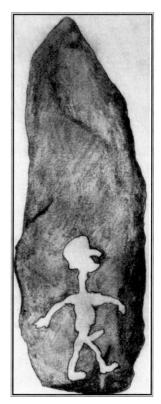

Truehoj petroglyph. It is likely that the Scandinavian rock-carvings expressed a similar religious cult, revolving around human, animal and vegetable fertility, to that which produced the Cerne Giant.

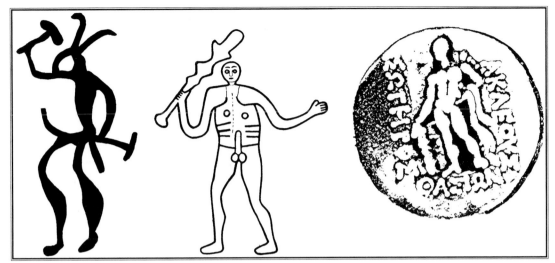

of the styles and icons of other cultures, and the figure of Hercules – a warrior-god, virile and brave – fitted unobtrusively into their pantheon. (Incorporated within their *mythos*, he might have acquired a Celtic name and additional qualities, but that is presently less significant than establishing his widespread acceptance.) Evidence for this is prominent in the third example, an imitation of the Macedonian tetradrachms of Alexander III (336–23 BC), minted by Celtic tribes in central Europe during the second century BC and later. On the obverse side, they show a head of the young Dionysius with leaves and grapes in his hair; on the reverse, the standing figure of Hercules, holding a club in his left hand and the skin of the Nemean lion over the arm of his right.

Consider the three depictions, noting stages of transition. Starting out with someone who is half-man, half-beast, erect and brandishing a mallet, we later find that he has shed his horns, evolving into a Hercules figure, discrete from the animal, yet still emphatically virile and wielding a weapon. Centuries pass and Hercules the tamer has himself been 'tamed' by civilization and imprinted on a coin. He is no longer phallically excited. Neither does he wield his club; the implement is at rest like a furnishing. In fact, the coin shows a stylized, formally posed Hercules, a civilized role model.

What we find at Cerne, however, is no dead piece of Classical statuary, but a native interpretation, a halfway house between blatant animality and restrained formality. The Giant is a hero who preserves the virile qualities of an earlier tradition. He is a mediator between

Evolution of the Hero – three stages. The Bronze Age rock-carving from Sweden (left) shows a horned or bull-man brandishing a mallet and simultaneously experiencing an erection. In this stage, man and animal are equal. The Iron Age (?) Cerne Giant (centre) marks the next stage where man has become emancipated from the natural world. The god is no longer half-animal, but a man-god, the hero-figure, Hercules, a tamer and slayer of animals; yet he still retains the earlier bull-like qualities of aggression and virility, as reflected in the upraised club and phallus. The third illustration (from a second-century BC Celtic coin) shows the finally 'civilized' Hercules, stripped of his aggressive maleness; he has become a passive piece of Classical statuary, a socially acceptable role model.

the Bronze Age and the Classical period, not necessarily in strict chronological time – for icons and beliefs, especially in the 'folk' tradition, overlap and thrive contemporaneously – but in terms of how civilization was developing. A hero-god, if you like, reflecting the concerns of warriors and cattle rearers.

Seasonal Magic-Making

When trying to reach back into a period in which many gods and spirits were of local origin – assigned to individual springs, hilltops and tribes – it may be misleading to draw extensively on Classical and continental comparisons and forget that the Giant should be seen as something special to Cerne Abbas and Dorsetshire. Whatever deity he recalls – Hercules, a sun-god, a Celtic warrior holding a cloak-shield – it is subsidiary to his role as Cerne's local Dagda or 'Daddy' whose overpowering presence was preserved down through the centuries. He was the Great Village Elder, occupying the hill below the maypole enclosure, the place where the *duende*, or earth pulse of the village, beat clearest and loudest.

The significance of drawing a figure is different from that of erecting a building; the resultant outline is not meant to entrap or enclose a congregation. A hill-figure has a function closer to myth, drama and seasonal narrative. One draws it on the earth like stage scenery and, despite its considerable size and avowed age, it may be wrong to see the Giant in terms of the monumental figure he has become – but more as a talismanic gesture, a piece of seasonal magic-making, intended to urge men and crops around the bend of the Celtic year.

Proximity, of course, does not always denote intrinsic relationship. A bank may be situated next to a church though their outlooks and aims are different. Similarly the (alleged) placement of the maypole in the Iron Age earthwork called the Trendle, immediately above the Giant, might be a coincidence, but because there is a unity of meaning – both deputize for the life-urge and fertility – many writers have been inclined to look on the two as at least complementary if not contemporaneous.

Lateness of Record

Much has been made of the comparative lateness of record. In particular, Jo Bettey found no mention of the Giant previous to Francis Wise's letter of 1742 (that statement is now amended, the parish accounts of 1694 having come to light, referring to a bill of three shillings for repairing the Giant). Even so, the Cerne Giant was acknowledged before the Long Man of Wilmington, Sussex, the earliest known sketch being that of Sir William Burrell in 1776 (until 1993, that is, when the discovery of a drawing of 1710 by Thomas Rowley, surveyor of the Chatsworth estate, established a deeper antiquity). Yet the Long Man must have been scoured and maintained down through the centuries; traces of Roman brick were mixed up in the subsoil beneath the figure. Even in the far more populous town of Plymouth, where the giant figures of Gogmagog or 'Gogmagog and Corineus' (whom John Leland, incidentally, omitted to mention in his *Itinerary*, though they had been recut in 1486) were regularly maintained by the town council, the records are scant; some brief references in an old audit and receivers book are all that is left of two huge carved figures that guarded the Hoe for centuries.

The evidence of eloquent omission – absence of documentation equalling non-existence – places a heavy responsibility on the shoulders of a small literate segment. It is akin to arguing what is not recorded by clerks or antiquaries has no role in historic time, an argument that coils around and, ultimately, strangulates itself. For the absence of record also applies to the core event – the actual cutting of the figure – so one could argue with equal strength that, if such an extraordinary, learned, satiric spoof as the Giant had been coordinated during the Middle Ages, or in the middle of the seventeenth century, when people were becoming increasingly antiquity-conscious, some memory or explanation might have been expected to survive.

Revolution in Perception

It is easy to forget that a revolution in perception is often required before things are *properly seen* or grasped as possessing intrinsic value. Educated Europeans did not bother overmuch about mountains, lakes and long country walks until thinkers like Rousseau awakened Europe to the beauties of nature, and then, decades later in England, we have Wordsworth, Coleridge, De Quincey and a host of minor poets flocking to the Lake District, observing and praising each waterfall, crag, tarn and precipice.

Similarly John Aubrey had not recognized Avebury until he visited it in 1649, comparing it to a place where giants had 'fought with huge stones against the gods'. The monument was regarded as a haphazard structure for another century. It awaited the Revd William Stukeley, in a flash of perception, to conceive it as a patterned unity – and afterwards, in subsequent decades, antiquaries followed suit, combing the British landscape, finding new henges and arrangements of stone, until almost every high outcrop was seen as a Druidical altar or rude temple to Thor or Odin. In their enthusiasm, antiquaries began to discover patterns where none existed (many believe that this is exactly what Tom Lethbridge did when he uncovered the missing Sawston giant) but at least the clay had been washed from their eyes.

Antiquaries were never fired by hill-figures in quite the same way as they were by henges and burial mounds, presumably because the former were not considered proper 'monuments' – neither did they hoard the promise of uncovering gold or silver artefacts. Thus, while many stone monuments were surveyed and their associated folklore recorded, the same consideration was not applied to hill-figures, save the Uffington Horse which, because of its visual prominence, has always been thought an important landmark. Even the solid red figure of the Horse of Tysoe, praised by Michael Drayton in his poem *Poly-Olbion*, was neglected and allowed to grass over and fade from sight.

It must be borne in mind that hill-figures are very much a now-you-see-me-now-you-don't type of artefact. A lapse of scouring for a couple of decades, to which may be added the work of sheep's hooves and men's footprints, and a once-splendid figure is no more than a faint outline. If we see the Giant as among the prehistoric wonders of Britain – a startling, overpowering presence – it is only because decades of historians, archaeologists, scholars, plus the guardianship of the National Trust, have given us the spectacles.

'Works of this sort,' Dr Maton wrote of the Giant in 1796, 'especially when contiguous to encampments, were the amusement merely of idle people, and cut with as little meaning as shepherd boys stripping turf off the Wiltshire plains.' Despite its tone of dismissal, it is interesting that Dr Maton alludes to such a custom, as if it were a recognized diversion to strip away turf and doodle on the landscape. What designs did these shepherd boys trace out in the ground? Horses? Dragons? Sheep? Men? Buxom ladies?

This is a diversion about which little is known and, contrary to Dr Maton's views, it can no longer be disparaged as having 'little meaning', for the Giant survives as an image redolent with meaning, concerning warrior-heroes, fertility, aggression, the tenacious adherence of rural communities to a totem, a Father-Protector. He has handed us back a portion of the past that would otherwise have grassed over and been lost forever.

APPENDIX B

HILL-FIGURES AFTER 1700

This section catalogues the more recent hill-figures, the cuttings of which are historically recorded. They present no particular headache for historians and researchers, being part and parcel of the whims of squires, schoolteachers, students, stewards, farmers and businessmen, and the product of bright afternoons with compasses, spades, squared paper, megaphones and marking flags. They are charming follies which, as the years go by, will no doubt acquire a portion of the veneration accorded to their ancient predecessors.

WHITE HORSE OF STRICHEN/WHITE STAG OF STRICHEN (ABERDEENSHIRE)

On the south-west side of Mormond Hill, near the village of Strichen, Aberdeenshire, is a white horse, 162 ft long, thought to be the work of one of the members of the Fraser family who were former lairds of Strichen. One of the Frasers, reputed to be an eccentric, entertained Boswell and Johnson in 1773 (see *Journal of a Tour in the Hebrides*). He has been held responsible for the Horse and was said to have died suddenly of frustration because he could not make the legs natural-looking. If this was true, he must have been a man of great integrity; other artists seemed to have no qualms about inventing equine grotesques for permanent public display. The Strichen Horse is far from chalk country. Native quartz was used to block in the shape, and the eyeball is a crystalline dome 18 in high.

On the other side of Mormond Hill, facing south-east, there is a Stag, 240 ft long, covering almost an acre of ground and filled in with limestone and quartz. This was cut by Mr Gardner, an architect, in 1870.

Mormond Horse, Aberdeen.

Mormond Stag, Aberdeen.

WHIPSNADE LION (BEDFORDSHIRE)

A colossus among hill-figures lying on the western face of Dunstable Downs just below the Zoo Park, the Lion is 483 ft long and held together by a tensile concrete edging. It was designed by R.B. Brook-Greaves and cut in 1935. Although there is something rather lumpen and literal about this beast, it effectively advertises the zoo and can be seen for miles around.

The Public Relations Officer of Whipsnade Zoo provided the following information, February 1986. 'The Lion covers a fairly large area – approximately 6,525 square metres. The outline is ⅜ mile . . . and during the war it had to be covered with bracken as it was a conspicuous landmark for enemy aircraft, but nowadays it is lit up with 750 40-watt bulbs and can be seen for many miles around. Members of the public can sponsor the Lion to light it for £5 per night.'

One of the best viewing places is Ivinghoe Beacon. The Dunstable Gliding Club are always swooping above it and getting the most dramatic impression of all.

INKPEN HORSE (BERKSHIRE)

Another vanished steed allegedly cut in 1868 by Mr Wright, the owner of Ham Spray House, below the escarpment of Inkpen Beacon. His handiwork appeared on the Ordnance Survey Map of 1877. The outline was not professionally blocked out, and the Horse soon became overgrown.

OSMINGTON HORSE (DORSET)

The Osmington Horse, situated near the village of that name, lies nearly four miles north-west of Weymouth and is said to have been made to commemorate the visits of George III and his brother, the Duke of Gloucester, to the seaside resort. It is a massive animal, covering nearly an acre of ground, and supporting a hatted rider – allegedly the Prince Regent. The carving exudes a kind of cumbersome stateliness, against which the Uffington Horse, composed of flying loops and impressionistic whirls, appears whippet-lean and thoroughly untameable.

Oddly enough, Llewelyn Powys, musing on the horse in his *Somerset and Dorset Essays*, surrendered himself to a mild attack of the rhetorical horrors and described this well-mannered beast in an entirely unfamiliar way. 'I have seen,' he wrote, 'the chalk figure in the spring-time as ghostly pale as that terrifying white horse in the Apocalypse ridden by one whose garments had been *dipped in blood* and whose name was unknown to any but himself.'

By now George III's association with Weymouth is a guidebook cliché. He first visited the town in 1789 accompanied by his queen and their official entourage. His intention was to recuperate after a bout of illness, and from that period stemmed his affection for the watering place. The feeling was wholly reciprocated by the Weymouth citizens, who erected a magnificent memorial to the King and provided musical accompaniment to his bathing activities – playing the national anthem whenever the sovereign entered the water. The bathing women of Weymouth had 'God Save the King' embroidered on their belts.

Despite all this well-attested anecdote, the origin of the Osmington Horse poses a problem. Who actually cut the figure? Was it a group of engineers stationed at Weymouth at the time when the threat of Napoleon's invasion brooded menacingly on the horizon? Or was it the work of a single soldier, as Plenderleath recorded? Or does it, as Thomas Hardy stated in *The Trumpet Major*, commemorate the Battle of Trafalgar? The cutting of the Horse is described in Chapter 37. John Loveday, a trumpet-major in the war against Buonaparte, takes Anne Garland for a walk.

The Osmington Horse, Dorset.

He pointed to a distant hillside which, hitherto green, had within the last few days begun to show scratches of white on its face. 'Up there,' he said.

'I see little figures of men moving about. What are they doing?'

'Cutting out a huge picture of the king on horseback in the earth of the hill. The king's head is to be as big as our mill-pond and his body as big as this garden; he and the horse will cover more than an acre.'

The two set off towards the Horse. At one point the trumpet-major is ragged by a group of urchins who taunt him for being deficient in amorousness. 'Why don't he clipse her to his side, like a man?' they exclaim. He beats them with a switch and continues the walk.

When they reached the hill they found forty navvies at work removing the dark sod so as to lay bare the chalk beneath. The equestrian figure that their shovels were forming was scarcely intelligible to John and Anne now they were close, and after pacing from the horse's head down his breast to his hoof, back by way of the king's bridle-arm, past the bridge of his nose, and into his cocked hat, Anne said she had had enough of it.

The usual explanation is that the Horse was probably extant in 1807, the figure of the King being added later, to commemorate his visits. The Horse does not point towards Weymouth but appears to be stepping away from the town. It has been suggested that this represents the wishes of George's sophisticated courtiers, who, tiring of the babble of tradesmen and the soft croakings of asthmatics, desired the monarch to return to the more bracing social life of the capital.

WOOLBURY HORSE (HAMPSHIRE)

This horse is cut on the southern rampart of Woolbury Camp, two miles east of Stockbridge. It is fairly small – around 30 ft long – and lies outside Stockbridge Down which is owned by the National Trust. I could find out very little information about the horse beyond Morris Marple's description, so I wrote to the historian, Rosalind Hill, who provided me with this lively local account of the nag.

Our beast isn't prehistoric, but a kind of eighteenth-century memorial, inspired, I expect, by contemporary antiquarianism. I'm afraid I can't pin-point the date. Local tradition says that an unfortunate traveller was set upon and killed at the point where the south-east corner of the Stockbridge Down impinges upon the Stockbridge–Winchester road. This place has always been known as 'Robbers' Roost' (quite rightly; I had my car broken into in the National Trust car park there a few years ago). The traveller died at once, and a cross of flints pressed into the turf marks the place where he fell. The horse was wounded, but galloped up the drove road to Woolbury, where it expired.

The horse's shape is picked out in chalk and flints on the south side of the ramparts of Woolbury. Unfortunately it isn't on National Trust land but belongs to the neighbouring farmer, so we have difficulty in getting it scoured. It is a naturalistic horse (not a dragon) in a standing position, facing right . . .

Morris Marples saw the Horse as 'a very crude little animal, angular and shapeless', with twelve flints stuck into the ground to form the tail, but also mentioned that a reference to the creature appeared in *Notes and Queries* (November 1859), which established the age of the animal as being at least 130.

The Buffs' regimental badge, Canterbury.

BUFFS BADGE (KENT)

This dragon was cut in 1922 by CSM Oliver Mason of the Buffs Regiment in Military Road, Canterbury. It was 51 ft long and has now grassed over.

WYE CROWN (KENT)

Wye Crown.

Outside Wye village, Kent, above the old chalk-pit near Cold Harbour Farm, there is a chalk crown, about 180 ft wide at the base and about 180 ft high, the trench outlining it being some 13 ft wide. The work was organized by T.J. Young, lecturer in agriculture and later Vice-principal of Wye College, after an initial suggestion had been made by Principal Hall. It was cut in 1902 by an ingenious method, wherein a paper model of a crown, copied from a silver florin, was stuck on the viewing lens of the theodolite, and the flagholders, mainly students, were signalled into position until the shape was satisfactory. The rough plan was then triangulated and laid down to scale on paper. For digging, the college was divided into six gangs who worked at the Crown for four days; a perpetual stream of barrows and sledges was kept up, using the old chalk-pit as a suitable dumping-ground. Some complaints arose over the 'severity of the cutting through layers of flint', but those in charge of the gang were 'seldom called upon to use their native eloquence upon would-be defaulters'. On Coronation night, in 1902, the crown was lit up by 1500 fairy lamps creating a magnificent effect; similar celebrations took place in 1935 on the occasion of George V's Silver Jubilee. The Crown is a conspicuous landmark, standing on a shoulder of the North Downs, and can be seen from such distant points as Rye and Tenterden. (Information taken from *Agricola Club Journal*, Vol. 1, no. 3, Michaelmas 1902.)

Since writing the above, I have received a great deal of additional material on the Crown from Mr J.D. Sykes, the former Estates Bursar. He sent me Dr Glasscock's article (1965) which enlarged on several points. There is a fine description of the 5 November celebrations:

> The burning of Fawkes is nowadays preceded by an unregimented army of torch bearers which, at peak, stretches from the College to Coldharbour Farm. This march begins immediately after dinner, the paraffin-soaked torches being lighted near to the main entrance. By the time the Crown has been reached, its shape is already scintillating with the yellow flames from hundreds of paraffin wicks. Just above is soon seen the red orb of the bonfire with its satellite rockets and coloured lights.

And of the precautions taken during the Second World War:

> Not only could enemy navigators have checked a course to daytime targets further inland, but the emblem would have acted as a badge marking the headquarters of the most easterly division of South Eastern Army Command. Thus, for nearly five years, the Crown wore a battledress of brushwood. The excellence of the disguise supported the view that a master of camouflage was employed for the tailoring and there is little doubt that he belonged to one of the first units of military intelligence to be housed at Withersdane.

Mr Sykes also added that 'in late June 1977, on the occasion of the retirement of the then Principal of Wye College, Dr Harry S. Darling, a farewell notice was created in huge letters using (presumably) paraquat spray. The notice read "Goodbye Harry" and was easily visible from Ashford, some 4 to 5 miles away'.

The Crown was illuminated for the Queen's Silver Jubilee in 1977 and the last cleaning took place in June 1982 on the eightieth anniversary of its original creation.

LITLINGTON HORSE (SUSSEX)

This beast was cut in 1925 by a descendant of an earlier turf artist (another horse formerly occupied the site: Queen Victoria's Coronation, 1838, was the occasion of its appearance). The animal is 90 ft long and lies on Hindover Hill, near Litlington village. A legend states that it is a monument to a girl who was killed when her horse bolted downhill and threw her. J. Pagden writes of the original horse that his father, J. Pagden of Frog Firle, together with his brothers, did the work in a single day.

Litlington Horse, Sussex.

ALTON BARNES (WILTSHIRE)

The Horse at Alton Barnes was cut eight years after the Marlborough creature by Mr Robert Pile, a tenant of the Manor Farm, Alton Barnes. He selected the southern slope of a hill known as 'Old Adam' and employed a journeyman painter, one John Thorne, to carry out the design. Thorne agreed to complete the work for £20 and quickly sketched the outline of the turf. Although he had been paid to excavate the Horse himself and fill the cavity with chalk, he decided upon the dishonest but wholly unstrenuous method of sub-contracting someone else – John Harvey of Stanton St Bernard – to do the digging and turf-stripping. As John Harvey set about his task and the outline of the Horse became plainly visible, John Thorne decided it was time to make himself invisible, and this he did, taking the £20 payment with him.

Although one cannot applaud John Thorne for his less than scrupulous attitude towards the duties he had undertaken, he has enlivened the annals of turf-cutting by bringing to this eccentric art a low, Bohemian shiftiness, pleasantly at variance with the solid trustworthiness of the squires and local worthies so often encountered in the histories of these figures. Poor Thorne was eventually hanged – one hopes not for this miniscule crime – and Pile was left to complete the Horse himself. 'The good ended happily and the bad unhappily,' as Miss Prism put it in *The Importance of Being Earnest*.

The Alton Barnes Horse faces right and resembles the Cherhill Horse, except it is somewhat larger, being 166 ft high and 160 ft long. This contrasts with the Revd E.H.M. Sladen's statistics, which made it 180 ft high and 165 ft long; he measured the horse in 1868, when he was the incumbent of Alton Barnes. Since then it has been scoured many times, by Scouts, Guides and local organizations, and was concealed during the Second World War. Its appearance is distinctive, with its docked tail and trotting stance. E.V. Lucas, poet and essayist of the 1920s described it having 'a swan-like neck and a penetrating eye' as if he had a score to settle with an aristocratic Englishwoman.

BROAD HINTON HORSE (WILTSHIRE)

This creature is cut on the slope of Hackpen Hill and lies adjoining the Marlborough road. In Plenderleath's time (1885) it was in an admirable state of preservation:

> This figure may be seen upon the downs east of Winterbourne Bassett, on the right hand side of the road leading from Wootton Basset to Marlborough, and just within the boundary of Broad Hinton. It was cut out by Henry Eatwell, parish clerk of the last-named village, in the year 1835, and measures ninety feet square,

the extreme length and extreme height being equal. It appears in fair proportion when viewed from the Devizes road, and is not unlike the Marlborough Horse, but differenced from it by the possession of two ears, whereas the former shows only one. The tail, however, with its very short upstanding dock, more resembles the Cherhill and Alton Horses.

BROAD TOWN HORSE (WILTSHIRE)

Plenderleath stated that the chalk horse cut at Broad Town, near Wootton Basset, was the work of William Simmonds, the then occupier of Littleton Farm. The animal was carved in 1864 and measured 86 ft long by 61 ft tall. However, these were not intended to be its final proportions, and Simmonds informed the Revd Mr Plenderleath that he proposed 'to enlarge it by degrees'. At each scouring its dimensions would swell a little until it assumed a really impressive aspect. However, Mr Simmonds did not keep his farm long enough to try out his theory.

In 1919 the Curator of the Imperial War Museum told a local newspaper that, as a schoolboy in 1863, he had actually visited the Horse and spent a day scouring it in the company of a friend. He added that an elderly relative of his had informed him that it had been there for at least fifty years. If this account is accurate, Mr Simmonds would merely have been a renovator rather than an innovator.

The Horse is cut on the left of the Wootton Basset–Marlborough road, about half a mile north-east of Broad Town, and occupies a steep 45° slope which enables it to be seen to fine effect from the Swindon–Bristol railway line. It is a conspicuous landmark for some twenty miles around.

BULFORD KIWI (WILTSHIRE)

The huge image of a kiwi, 420 ft long, was cut by New Zealand troops stationed at Sling Camp at the end of the First World War. I wrote to the Garrison Adjutant, Colonel P.W. Herring OBE, and he promptly replied with a photograph and an article by Major W.J.A. Withers from which I quote the following:

Towards the end of 1918 the occupants of Sling Barracks became very unsettled. They were all New Zealanders and had seen much active service on the Western Front. Casualties had been terribly high and these survivors wanted to get home p.d.q. There was no air trooping in those days and what ships were available were required in the main for tasks of higher priority. The results were predictable and, following a serious fracas in Sling Bks, Major Metcalfe proposed to his CO, Lt. Colonel A.G. Mackenzie, that it might be a far better idea to occupy the men with digging out the country's Kiwi emblem on the side of Beacon Hill, than to order endless, repetitive and soul-destroying 'spit and polish' parades and training programmes. These were, after all, battle-seasoned men, signed on for the war's duration and desiring, now that it was all over, to get back home.

The Colonel agreed and sent the Major to see their senior NZ General Officer, General George Richardson. The General thought the idea had great merit and arranged for the Major to go up to London to the War Office to meet with a party of British senior officers. The party was made up of four; three quickly agreed that it was a first-class idea, the fourth did not and took considerable persuasion ('I think he was a county and Wiltshire Regiment man' said the Major with a chuckle). After much ado he was given permission to get it organised.

The man he chose to do the drawings was Sergeant Major P.C. Blenkarne, a Drawing Instructor with the NZ Education Corps, who frankly admitted that he had not the faintest idea of the actual size, shape or proportions of a Kiwi, never having seen one before! After much chasing around they finished up, late one evening, trying to arouse the night caretaker at a locked and shuttered British Natural History Museum. It took all their persuasion, plus their written authority, for him to let them in and it was only after much searching that they eventually found a publication which provided the information they required (I have given Colonel Herring a copy of that sketch, made by the originator, given to me by the Major).

Percy Blenkarne, later to become a very successful Auckland merchant, together with a certain Victor Lowe complete with theodolite, pegged out the Kiwi shape on the hill. It was then just a matter of some very hard and heavy physical work to excavate the turf and top soil thus exposing the natural chalk beneath. This task was done, in the main, by the NZ Canterbury Engineers and the final dimensions proved to be:– Length: 420 feet. Beak: 150 feet. NZ letters: 65 feet high, the whole covering an area of some 1½ acres. The KIWI Polish Co. Pty Ltd. did, over many years, contribute the maintenance costs to keep the figure weed free and as a fitting tribute to New Zealand and its peoples. Costs escalated however and about 1967 the Company had to withdraw. Since that time various units have taken on the task, with the latest major renovation being done by 249 Signal Squadron.

The massive Bulford Kiwi with the 249 Signals Squadron standing in formation.

The 1981 restoration of the Kiwi, which had become almost entirely obscured by weeds, was masterminded by Colonel Danny Fisher, Commander 249 Signals Squadron of NATO. It took a team of 160 officers and other ranks working twelve hours a day three days to clear the vegetation and dig out the outline to a depth of 12 in. They excavated about 100 tons of chalk for resurfacing the figure. They estimated that about 20 tons of chalk applied twice a year will be necessary to keep the Kiwi in perfect condition.

CHERHILL HORSE (WILTSHIRE)

Although the white horse of Cherhill lies in proximity to an Iron Age camp, it has no claims to antiquity, being cut near the London road by Dr Christopher Alsop in 1780. The slope is steep, around 45°, and plunges dramatically from the ramparts of Oldbury Castle. Stukeley, examining the site in 1724, wrote: 'The precipice is altogether inaccessible, falling down in narrow cavities or ribs, as it were the great roots of a tree, and with an odd and tremendous aspect.' It is not really quite so awesome as this, but Stukeley was writing at a period when Gothic exaggeration was rife: every hill was a mountain, and all slopes were grim precipices.

To return to Dr Alsop, the author of the Horse, he used the following procedure. First he marked out the outline with small sticks bearing white flags. He then took a position between the Downs and Calne about 200 yd from the top of Labour-in-Vain Hill. After establishing his vantage point, he shouted directions through a megaphone, directing his labour force to shift and replant the stakes until a credibly horsey pattern was recognizable. When the perfect likeness was achieved, the turf was then pared, exposing the solid white horse.

An ingenious feature of the Cherhill Horse was the inner circle of its eye, which was filled with glass bottles supplied by Farmer Angell of Studley. None of these remains. (The solemn acquisitive fervour of the English tourist accounts for their

Cherhill White Horse.

disappearance.) They must have been extremely effective in sunlight, making the eye flash like diamonds and providing the landscape with a genuine winking hill-figure.

The scouring of the Horse was formerly undertaken by the lord of the manor. A windlass was erected on top of the hill, immediately above the Horse, and small, chalk-filled trucks were slid down, their contents being spread evenly over the figure. However, this nineteenth-century method had disadvantages. When it rained, the fresh-laid chalk would form a copious white stream which would torrent down the legs, over the hooves and produce fantastic sticklike extensions – making it appear as if it were mounted on 300 ft stilts.

In 1876 a truck broke away from its anchorage and hurtled down the hill with impressive velocity, nearly killing a workman engaged in scouring. Fortunately he moved in time, and the truck buried itself in the base of the hill.

During the Second World War the Cherhill Horse was camouflaged. Afterwards it was restored with an experimental mixture of chalk and cement which proved unsatisfactory.

DEVIZES HORSE (WILTSHIRE)

This was cut at Whitsuntide in 1845 by the local shoemakers and was called 'the Snobs' Horse'. It lay on the slopes of Roundway Hill below Oliver's Camp but has now vanished.

FOVANT BADGES (WILTSHIRE)

At the outbreak of the First World War, there arose a need for land to accommodate and train the New Army. The government acquired thousands of acres which included part of the village of Fovant, Wiltshire, midway between Salisbury and Shaftesbury, on the A30 London–Exeter road. Local farming land was converted into a military town equipped with hospitals, recreation rooms, rifle ranges, metalled roads, a cinema and single-track railway. Vast numbers of troops from Britain and the Commonwealth lived for a period here before passing on to the Western Front. Quite a number – particularly the Australian troops – died of injuries in Wiltshire, as the silent war graves in Fovant churchyard testify. Others made a vital contribution to village life, leaving keepsakes in human form, and many elderly villagers tell stories of the soldiers and their impact on civilian routine.

Badge of the Wiltshire Regiment.

The most spectacular evidence of the soldiers' presence is the badges cut on the chalk downs facing the village, many representing regiments that are no longer extant, and all of them maintained by the Fovant Badges Society which organizes an annual Drumhead Service on the afternoon of the first Sunday in July.

The first badge to be cut was that of the London Rifle Brigade in 1916. There is a surviving working routine sheet recording that, 'Working parties will muster at 0500 hours'. Apparently the soldiers' attitude to this form of activity was thoroughly enthusiastic, and after the first badge was finished, others followed suit. The sector was a danger zone, where rifle ranges were constantly occupied, so the work had to be done fast, in the early morning; afterwards the men would toboggan downhill on their shovels. Many of these glittering, intricate badges – perhaps the ultimate in detailed fidelity – became overgrown, but in June 1949 the Fovant Home Guard Old Comrades Association started restoration. They were cleaned and weeded, and a new badge – that of the Wiltshire Regiment worn by the Fovant Home Guard during the war – was added. The Australian Expeditionary Force badge was also repaired. The map of the Continent, on the Downs at Compton Chamberlayne, was also cleaned and a flagpole mounted in the centre.

Today the figures are maintained by a special trust fund known as the Fovant Badges Society, and a booklet is available chronicling their full history. Here is a list of the regiments represented:

The Royal Wiltshire Regiment
YMCA
6th Battalion, London Regiment (Rifles)
7th City of London Battalion
Devonshire Regiment
Post Office Rifles
London Rifle Brigade
Royal Warwickshire Regiment
Australian Map
Australian Imperial Force
The Royal Wiltshire Yeomanry
Royal Corps of Signals

Something of the flavour of camp life at Fovant is captured in the recollections of a member of the Fovant Badges Society who was a child during the First World War:

The most interesting thing to a boy of some four or five summers was the railway, and I remember often seeing the train as it crossed the road. We entered the camp area at Sutton and it was like a town of green corrugated iron huts with verandahs in front of many of them. Strangely I cannot remember having the badges pointed out to me, though I have a vague idea that one had a red cross on it, made I think of broken tiles or brickbats. . . . I also remember seeing German

Fovant Badges.

prisoners of war in the yard in front of my grandfather's house. They were dressed in dull grey with flat hats and what seems to me now to be a kind of gum-boot. I knew them because I was used to seeing them near Blandford working in the fields or picking rabbit food in the hedges. I presume they kept rabbits as a help to their rations. They also made little animals out of some bright metal or perhaps tinfoil which were brought to school and sold for a penny or so.

The writer goes on to speak of the wayward Australian troops, who, angered by the slowness of demobilization, took to the 'bush' and went off to live in the woods around Fovant. On one occasion a group of soldiers carried a barrel of beer down beside the main road and stopped every passer-by, inviting them to have a drink with them or have the beer poured over their heads. Another time, a bunch of Aussies attempted to fish in the lake at Compton, and the local landowner, Squire Penruddocke, asked them what they were doing trespassing on his property. The soldiers asked him how he had acquired the land, whereupon he replied that his ancestors had fought for it. One of the Aussies then took off his coat and offered to fight him for it also, but the Squire wisely declined the challenge.

LAVERSTOCK PANDA (WILTSHIRE)

In 1969, when everyone waited with baited breath to hear whether London Zoo's panda, Chi-Chi, and Moscow Zoo's panda, An-An, were going to become romantically involved, students from the University College of North Wales cut this on the hillside by Laverstock on the Exeter Road. Its dimensions were listed in *The Times* as 55 ft by 40 ft. When last seen by the author (April 1984), it looked grubby and forlorn.

MARLBOROUGH HORSE (WILTSHIRE)

On Granham Hill, near the village of Preschute, there is the form of a smallish horse, about 60 ft long and facing left. It is a queerly shaped quadruped with a certain wistful appeal, but lacking the authority and distinction of its Cherhill counterpart.

The animal was cut in 1804 by schoolboys, already acquainted with the art of desk-carving, who attended an academy in Marlborough run by Mr Gresley. The designer of the Horse was Master William Canning, son of Mr Thomas Canning of the Manor House, Ogbourne St George. He marked out the figure with wooden pegs, after which the boys set to work, skimming off the turf and filling up the vacant space with chalk broken to the size of a couple of fists.

The scouring became an honoured tradition of the school and was broken only by the death of Mr Gresley in 1830. This heralded a period of neglect until the year 1873 when Captain Reed of Marlborough, an ex-pupil of Mr Gresley's academy, decided to take up the spade and restore the horse.

> Ah, then we'll cry, thank God, my lads,
> The Kennett's running still,
> And see, the old White Horse still pads
> Up there on Granham Hill.

This verse from the Marlborough School Song indicates that the Horse endeared itself to generations of pupils, who, locked among decaying Latin textbooks in stultifying classrooms, envied the galloping spaces occupied by their equine mascot.

Marlborough Horse, Wiltshire.

PEWSEY NEW HORSE (WILTSHIRE)

A white horse was cut on Pewsey Hill about 1785 by Robert Pile, a farmer of Alton Barnes. This may have been the same Robert Pile who was so artfully deceived by Jack the Painter, alias John Thorne, or it may have been his son, for thirty years separates the cuttings. Tradition maintained that the horse carried a rider.

Digging the Pewsey New Horse, 1937.

George Marples of Sway, a noted authority on hill-figures, was responsible for the creation of the new Pewsey Horse. The year was 1937, and all over the country people were suggesting suitable activities to commemorate the Coronation of George VI. George Marples had the idea of restoring the old Pewsey Horse cut by Pile. He submitted three designs, including one of a jumping horse carrying a rider (in deference to the tradition of the original Pewsey figure), but the most conventional of these, an elegant trotting horse, was selected.

Under the supervision of Mr Marples, the local fire brigade pegged out the Horse, which measured 65 ft long and 45 ft high. The date 1937 was added to ensure that there would be no confusion as to its age and purpose.

At the time of his death, George Marples had amassed an impressive amount of information on the subject of hill-figures. The task of bringing all this together in a book was undertaken by his son, Morris Marples, who in 1949 published an authoritative account to which most subsequent books and articles are heavily indebted.

ROCKLEY HORSE (WILTSHIRE)

The Rockley Horse lay north-west of Marlborough, 200 yd south of the Marlborough–Wootton Basset road, on the slope known as Rockley Down. The Horse is depicted moving at speed. When the field was ploughed, its outline was highlighted and an aerial photograph taken. It is no longer visible today.

Mr H.C. Brentnall (1948) contributed a note entitled 'Albus Equus Redivivus' describing how, during the course of ploughing up Rockley Down, the turning of sods revealed the form of a white horse. The figure had been filled with loose chalk rubble which the plough had shifted, 'so that there is now to be seen a sort of transfer of the original . . . a furrow's width to the left.' Its dimensions as judged by Mr D.W. Free were: nose to tail-end, 126 ft; barrel, 30 ft; forelegs, 36 ft; hindlegs, 39 ft. It faced to the left like most others of its kind.

Shepherds on the farm remarked they had made out the figure of the Horse during the dry season, but no record of its cutting exists, and although it is probably early nineteenth century in origin, it has been connected (rather implausibly) with the Battle of Barbury, AD 556. It may have been a whim of the owners of Rockley Manor and it is thought that the files of a local paper may hold the secret, but the *Marlborough Times* did not come out until 1859.

Despite a proposal to preserve it, the figure has now been lost.

KILBURN WHITE HORSE (YORKSHIRE)

The village of Kilburn, Yorkshire, is doubly famous – for a horse and a mouse. The latter is the motif of the late Robert Thompson (nicknamed 'the Mouseman') who developed a business in handmade oak furniture.

The White Horse of Kilburn (314 ft long and 278 ft high) is carved on the side of Hambleton Hills and is visible for twenty miles. Twelve people, it is claimed, can picnic on the animal's grass eye. Thomas Taylor, a native of Kilburn, who developed a highly successful grocery business in London, had the animal cut in 1857. It is thought that he had seen the Uffington Horse during the course of his travels and decided that he would enhance the aspect of his home town with a similar landmark. The job was done by thirty men supervised by the village schoolmaster, and 6 tons of lime were used for whitewashing. Taylor paid the cost of scouring during his

Kilburn White Horse, North Yorkshire.

lifetime, and the burden was afterwards undertaken by public subscription aided by the Ecclesiastical Commissioners, upon whose land the figure was carved. The upkeep of the Kilburn Horse is aided by the Kilburn Feast, held in the second week of July, which among its several attractions features a lady mayoress (a man in civic drag) who runs rustically amok extorting kisses from females.

AEROPLANE AT DOVER

In Northfall Meadows, Dover, an aeroplane was cut in 1909 to celebrate the first cross-Channel flight by Blériot. It is not very big, not much over 10 ft wide, comprising granite sections pressed into the subsoil, with a central plaque presented by the Aero Club.

BLACK HORSE OF BUSH HOWE

The majority of hill-figures are genuine artefacts, carved by human hands, but there is another class of figure which is more of an appearance or a fleeting impression. Its existence is a matter of faith or intuitive perception. The most mysterious of these spectral hill-figures is the Black Horse of Bush Howe, ('Busha' in local dialect), set high up on the Howgill Fells in the Pennines north of Sedbergh. It is said by some to represent a native Celtic deity – a later folk tradition suggests that it was used as a landmark by smugglers at Morecombe Bay, some twenty miles to the east. Little is known about this figure, measuring 427 ft long by 361 ft high and made up entirely of black shale. Writing of it, Guy Ragland Phillips said, 'Clouds and their shadows often fall on these hills. When they lift, they reveal for a moment a strange shape high on the flanks of Bush Howe: the dark outline of a huge black stallion like the horses painted by ancient man in French and Spanish caves. It dominates the entire valley.'

Black Horse of Bush Howe as interpreted by artist Craig Chapman.

Phillips (1986) has suggested that the horse preserves the vestiges of a 'dobbie' cult, the latter being a shape-shifting spirit of river-crossings, holed stones and possibly embodying an echo of 'dobbin', the classic title of a faithful equine retainer. The elusiveness of the Black Horse recalls apparitions like the Brocken Spectre of the Harz Mountains (caused by the sun's rays projecting and magnifying shadows of observers upon clouds) and there are many who refuse to recognize its existence. It is not marked on Ordnance Survey maps and guidebooks tend to overlook it.

AFTERWORD

A few years ago, I was exploring the area around the White Horse of Uffington with my partner. We passed the towering terraces overlooking the Vale that a glacier had carved thousands of years ago and Dragon Hill with its chalk scar and distinctive flat summit that, some claim, was artificially levelled. After admiring the view, we left to take a closer look at the hill-figure. By the time we'd reached the leg of the White Horse, it was so hot that sheep were seeking shelter in the trenches of the figure. Going up over the carving, we joined the Ridgway and headed for the Neolithic chamber tomb of Wayland's Smithy – a vast green longship of a sepulchre with massive upright sarsens guarding the entrance. Wayland was the smithy of the Norse gods and his resting place was solemn and monumental.

It had started off bright, but now the day was darkening. The sky shadowed over and people began to move away. Abruptly the rain started coming down heavily, in thick, battering drops, and the chalk path on which we were walking transformed itself into a mass of puddles and then a yellowish swirling stream that we found ourselves paddling through. The next instant there was a ragged flash of lightning. Thor, I sensed, had made one of his rare appearances to send a shiver down the spines of the tourists. The thunder god was out, lobbing his flaming spear alternating with freezing rushes of rain and gloomy infusions of shadow as more clouds passed over.

I had visited the region several times before. With its openness of gold and green uplands broken by barrow, earthwork and coppice, what 'magic' it possessed seemed of the kind that would cleave to one's disposition, but now I had observed other forces working through the geology and climate – forces that could abruptly turn and twist. I thought about what it had been like in prehistoric times when protection against storm was non-existent compared to today's central heating and coal fires. If faced with onslaughts of such rage and intensity, I would have found it natural to pay homage to the god of thunder and plead and bargain for clemency or assistance against my enemies.

The way we confidently frame our convictions is the result of a mass of information that defines the world in contemporary terms. The Uffington Horse, Wayland's Smithy and the Ridgway are atavistic shrines that trigger the wonder and strangeness of long-gone eras: the huge glacial terraces, the long green body of the burial mound and the amazing skeletal apparition of a horse, trailing streaks of chalk and galloping motionlessly through the valley of time.

MYTH OF ALBION

In a sense, so far as the Uffington Horse is concerned, people's wishes and preconceptions have been verified. Light-dating the soil has established its origin in the Late Bronze Age (c. 800–1200 BC), an astounding, humbling revelation that such a magnificent, friable artefact had been kept groomed 'like the first plume of the snow' by the devotion of waves of tribesmen and local folk for nearly three thousand years. Here was antiquity indeed. Here was care and reverence for something generations and lifetimes long.

Yet sometimes we treasure overmuch the concept of a bewitching and unfathomable distant past, a world so apart from ours that we cannot imagine the daily details of it. Because it was long before the world became a conurbation engirdled in a cloak of carbon dioxide, we often see it in terms of a Golden Age. What we do not know has become more important than what we do know. Furthermore, we prefer to solve a historical problem in a special, satisfying way. The idea of King Arthur as a Roman cavalry officer has never properly caught on because it is a diminution of the magnificence with which men like Mallory and Tennyson have imbued the concept. We don't want to let go of Excalibur, the Grail, Camelot and the banner of Pendragon that easily. Such attitudes affect our reading of history and the manner in which we project upon it, making us interpret arresting survivals like hill figures to bolster myths of Albion, notable battles and our Saxon heritage.

It is an established methodology, tracing back from still-thriving or forgotten country customs and attempting to explain what figures like the Uffington Horse signified to those who made them. But it is also a dubious, problematic approach, assuming 'meaning' back then was static and definitive rather than a process that was changing and adjusting as most things do. Naturally I cannot exempt myself. This present volume has plenty of folklore that is on the speculative, incautious side. I remember once writing a book on dragonlore and becoming more entangled as the project advanced. From ideas put forward by various authorities, I had the impression the world was a vast cultural happy family joined by cross-relating artefacts and mythic motifs. Every civilization shared the dragon – that was the thesis of Sir Grafton Elliott Smith in his absorbing *The Evolution of the Dragon* (1918). The mythic monster gained amazing elasticity as it was stretched to take in cloud-dragons, elephant-dragons, fish-dragons, sea serpents, fire snakes, lions and crocodiles. A version of the monster could be picked out in every continent, and its diffusion could be traced by way of the exploratory voyages conducted by the legendary 'Children of the Sun' who originated in Ancient Egypt. In his estimate, the dragon stood for violence, evil, fertility, rainfall, thunder, the moon goddess, uniting ceremonies and beliefs around the world that were in other ways disparate. Finally and enthrallingly the rare beast expressed itself in the search for the secret of immortality:

> If we seek for the deep motives which have prompted men in all ages so persistently to search for the elixir of life, for some means of averting the dangers to which their existence is exposed, it will be found in the instinct of self-preservation, which is the fundamental factor in the behaviour of all living beings...

Despite its desperate ingenuity and assertiveness, *The Evolution of the Dragon* was not *that* wrong-headed because many of the similarities Elliott Smith cited were undeniable. How could that be so if his thesis was fundamentally wrong? Was it because men and women everywhere, sharing the same mental and physiological construction, dream the same dreams and develop similar stories and customs? Was that more likely than a single culture delivering 'civilisation' to each part of the world in turn?

Carl Gustav Jung attributed the parallels and comparisons uncovered by men like Elliott Smith to the buried 'archetypes' or forms locked in the unconscious mind. The latter he likened to deep river courses through which thoughts, dreams and behavioural tendencies are predisposed to flow. In special circumstances, when these are reawakened, the outcome might prove explosive for a people or nation. In the destructive context, he cited the Norse god Odin as relating to the warlike, genocidal nature of the Nazi regime who were re-enacting the ecstasy of bloodlust that pulsed through the veins of their Teuton forefathers.

Even if we discard Jung and the notion of a psychic inheritance, there is left the bedrock similarity of human experience. Hence, while culture in general is obviously beholden to diffusionism – for highly isolated tribes, such as the Aborigines or Kalahari Bushmen, do not develop into civilisations – sensory experiences are common to all races: night and day; birth, copulation and death; the sun and stars; rain, snow, wind and ice; animals, insects and plants – things that cultivate and shape basic responses and finally influence agriculture, building, work patterns and story-making, so that far-apart peoples end up by having a good deal in common.

Full acceptance of a single 'family of man', while an upstanding political goal, can draw people into believing things that appear to specialists as flaky or downright fallacious: for instance, ascribing an unidentified settlement to the survivors of Atlantis, deducing the early achievement of space-flight from obscure stone carvings, creating breathtaking cultural linkages on the basis of the proportions of a buildings or the manner in which they are sited in relation to a star system. In the arena of 'Earth Mysteries', a celebrated 'apostle of unreason' was the likeable, teetotal and industrious chemist and photographer, Alfred Watkins, who uncovered patterns of straight lines linking sites of ancient sanctity and significance all over Britain. Had he uncovered a mystic language, reviving the myth of Albion, the English Jerusalem of which William Blake was a prophet? Certainly he *did* create a renewed enthusiasm for landscape and archaeology among his original wave of followers and subsequent generations – his work was revived by John Michell in the 1970s – and it is remarkable how many of them, once their obsession with straight lines had worn off, became effective field researchers and, in some cases, professional archaeologists.

Likewise Robert Graves' erudite analysis of poetic inspiration, *The White Goddess*, is not looked upon as dependable history, but thousands prefer his version to those of his critics. Why is this? Is it because Graves' ideas relate to men's wishes and desires as humans beings, their need to venerate or abase themselves before a powerful, mysterious, bewitchingly seductive goddess figure rather than, say, a contemporary politician of crumpled demeanour? Experts may say, 'No, you've got it wrong there!' but perversely the wrongness of poets like Graves is often more appreciated than an expert's rightness. And, of course, although Graves might not be technically an expert, he was a much-venerated practitioner of poetry and believed that, through his entranced dialogues with the Muse, he was able to drink from a sacred, inspirational well that others could not. While less accurate therefore, his books may be 'truer' in that special sense than those of his detractors. This is because they strike chords that yearn to be strummed and re-awakened like the Pied Piper's tune that drew rats and children after him. This may be termed 'psychological truth' or the truth to which the human mind *responds at the time* as opposed to the facts, both of which, it should be noted, can be manipulated. *The White Goddess* traces the cultural strand of a single gripping idea and enters a seductive labyrinth of scholarship and symbolism. Likewise Elliot Smith's notion of a universal megalithic culture transmitted through the seafaring 'Children of the Sun' – a title coined by his fellow diffusionist, William Perry – took him on a lengthy intellectual voyage and Margaret Murray's provocative view of the witch cult stirred others to produce better-balanced works on the subject. Such eccentric studies, provided they are not held up as oracles, may prove effective starting-points, avoiding the complication of polyglot works that are less penetrable. The sheer, contradictory wealth of material that goes into the making of any broad thesis may prove overwhelming.

Hence there are two contrasting approaches: the pan-cultural that seeks to explain by seeking out commonality and likeness and the distinction-driven that makes things stand more apart. Both in a sense rebound off each other. In reaction against the broad approach of Sir James Frazer and other interpreters of ritual and custom, hordes of books and papers have appeared that snap the chain of association that identified a Babylonian Baal-fire as being akin to a Celtic Bel-fire and the incinerations of Carthage finding their counterpart in the Wicker Man. These corrective works are admirable and put straight the record. But they do not invariably acknowledge that as sentient beings we redefine and recreate the past *inside ourselves* in a manner that is 'outside time' as measured by clocks and watches. Anyone today who places stag antlers on his head and starts dancing is seen as 'reviving' an old custom. We do not look upon him as the genuine article, possibly believing that, were such an outfit donned by a caveman in the Palaeolithic, it was more likely an attempt to help achieve the body of the animal through miming its pursuit, but this could be an example of academic solemnity with regard to our forefathers. In the Palaeolithic they very likely danced and fooled around with skins, skulls and bits of bone in much the same way that medical students do today. Are they doing the same thing? Not exactly, but the humour is almost identical. And surely there is a profound link between a young woman smoothing face cream over her cheeks and a dairymaid, centuries back, applying the dews of the first morning of May to the same part. Part of folk history is the rediscovery of old truths in new clothes and, though some of our oldest, most venerated festivals are rather more new-fangled or self-consciously put together than many would have us believe, that does not disqualify the indestructible potency of their symbolism. The existential anchor of the agricultural year continues to pervade these festivals bearing the elemental truth of death, springtime renewal and summer ripeness. And it would be rash to dismiss some folklore evidence, like the wondrous anecdote of Charlotte Elizabeth (p.66) in Ireland recalling the Midsummer Fire Festival and the appearance of the ghostly horse standing for 'all cattle'. That ceremony might have sprung from nowhere, been altered and varied down the years, and yet the substance and significance of it reaches back into thousands of years of rearing and herding animals. What I am emphasising is that, whatever variants it may have undergone, the basic meaning was active and those who participated grasped it *personally*.

Something is going on here which is as amusing as it is confusing. While the discipline of history is concerned with dates or the chronicling of appearances at specific times, the language of symbolism is timeless. For instance, if yesterday a friendly greengrocer held an orange pippin before a girl, urging her to take a bite, that would be a recent event and yet, in a sense, a replay of the Devil's role in the Garden of Eden that brought about the fall of man. Hence folk ceremonies, whether of short or long lineage, are carriers of more knowledge and significance than it is a reasonable for an ordinary man or woman to bear, and that is why some performers may not articulate their experience, though they're deriving an age-old pleasure from it.

It is possibly a dubious truism that the dancer knows more about the dance than the astute professor who writes a book on it, and the soldier, who has been many times in the thick of battle, knows more about fighting than the military historian. We are talking about *being there* rather than interpretation by others. If Jack-in-the-Green feels springtime bounding through his veins and dances accordingly, it is little use reminding him that he is actually a mechanic from Bayswater. Besides, what is the real thing? Did it ever exist? This debate has an equivalency, incidentally, in matters of language when the deconstructionist, the late Jacques Derrida, pointed out controversially that we are not in control of the words we use. We do not speak language; language speaks us. Similarly music and folk customs operate through us and pull our strings according to their momentum which is naturally subject to exterior influence. What takes place at an emotional level finally governs the facts we present. 'I suspect the truth is that the Celts are still here,' Alan Garner observed of his native Lancashire, 'and have always been here. In a way, before they arrived. What this land has the ability to do is not to be invaded, but to assume and consume and take unto itself and make its own.'

Writing about the people of the distant past is only possible by assuming they were like us, but maybe living in sparser conditions (unless royal or rich) and dominated by a politico-religious structure involving sterner justice than that of a present-day Western democracy. The problem is that they are dead. Our world did not exist when they were alive. To them we are unthinkable, and yet we still judge them from the standpoint of common humanity going about their daily tasks. Whether lighting a fire, shooting an arrow or skinning a deer, what they did, we assume, was done in the same deft, procedural way in which a mechanic tightens a nut on an engine or a farmer escorts his sheep into a dip. Occasionally we privilege their acts, overshadowing them with gods, kings and emperors, as if they encountered such beings in their daily lives which usually they did not. To say these people worshipped such a god is no more significant than saying, 'Every Sunday Mrs Riley attended the local Catholic church.' In fact, it is very much a question of speaking for them without securing permission or ratification. The nearest, we suppose, to what might be an enlightened impression is history presented both as personal and impersonal, like Jorges Luis Borge writing about the death of an anonymous Saxon at the time Britain was changing over to Christianity:

In a stable that stands almost within the shadow of the new stone church, a man with gray eyes and a gray beard, sprawled amidst the odor of the animals, humbly seeks his death as though he were seeking sleep... Outside there are plowed fields, and a ditch clogged with dried leaves, and perhaps some faint tracks of a wolf upon the black clay at the edge of the forest. The man sleeps and dreams, forgotten...but, in his boyhood, the man has seen the face of Woden, the divine horror and exultation, the cumbrous wooden idol overladen with Roman coins and unwieldy vestments, the sacrifice of horses, dogs and prisoners. The man will die before dawn, and along with him will also perish, never to return, the last direct, eyewitness images of the pagan rites.

Admirable prose as it is, it cannot be anything like the real thing simply because Borges invests the Saxon with historical perspectives that did not then exist but were to be conceived by academics and writers centuries afterwards. It is language designed to make vivid a specific historical moment to an informed reader. When customs are flourishing they are taken for granted. Only when they are in decline does enthusiasm take the guise of erudition and scholarship. The Owl of Minerva flies in the Dusk, as Heidegger observed, or vital knowledge arrives just before a catastrophe engulfs it. Hence intellectual revivals of old gods tend to take place after the body of the sacred being has been laid to rest. The Cult of Pan reared up in the Late Victorian and Early Edwardian era simply because the woodland habitat of that god was under threat in England and all over the world forests were being cut and razed for building ground and other developments.

THE EVOLUTION AND ORCHESTRATION OF HORSEPLAY

How does the preceding disquisition reflect upon hill-figures? In his riveting historical overview *The Rise and Fall of Merry England*, Ronald Hutton makes plain how traditional customs suffered under the Reformation and Civil War. This is attested by John Aubrey who noted how the rites of his youth, such as midsummer bonfires, were discontinued: 'the civil wars coming on have put all these rites or customs quite out of fashion.' In particular, he singles out how the decorating the salt-well at Droitwich on the patron saint's festival was prohibited; the well promptly dried up. When the ceremony was allowed the following year, the water sprung up again.

Another so-called ancient rite was thought to be Morris dancing until the historian, Barbara Lowe, pointed out how the craze first appeared c.1450 in the courts throughout Western Europe and was afterwards copied and taken up by the masses. Likewise anyone who experiences the Padstow 'Obby Oss', with its thundering Breton drum and capering, devil-faced beast, assumes here's something dark and ancient beyond written record:

Throughout ancient Europe the symbol of the horse goddess was part of a pagan solar cult; the sun was perceived as being carried across the sky in a chariot pulled by a team of horses. In the archaic May Day celebrations at Padstow, Cornwall, the Obby Oss dances at dawn, and this may give a clue to the significance of the 112-metre-long Uffington Horse, which actually appears to run from east to west, as if galloping out of the dawn.

(*Twilight of the Celtic Gods*: David Clarke & Andy Roberts)

Yet the historian of folklore, Dr E.C. Cawte, looked into this carefully and found out that hobby-horses throughout most of the sixteenth century appeared as components in pageants, standing in for a horse and rider. 'It is only toward the end of that period,' he wrote, 'that there are records of a single hobby-horse with a morris team.' An example of the latter is found in Robert Plot's account (1686) of the Abbots Bromley Horn Dance that refers to 'the Hobby-horse dance, from a person that carried the image of a horse between his legs, made of thin boards, and in his hand a bow and arrow, which passing though a hole in the bow...he made a snapping noise as he drew it to and fro, keeping in time with the Musick; with this man danced 6 others, carrying on their shoulders a reindeers' heads, 3 of them painted white, and 3 red...' Apparently the hooded, masked horses appeared around the beginning of the nineteenth century: 'There is evidence neither for a hooded animal much before that date, nor for an association between hooded animal and the morris dance, nor that this type of construction was ever called a hobby-horse before [the twentieth] century...'

This is drawing a finer boundary of definition between horse-types than is usual in most reference works and Cawte does not deny that a broader prospect exists, acknowledging 'records of animal disguise in every century since the thirteenth, in either Great Britain or France.'

Later, after their revival and reinstatement, country customs were gentrified by the Victorians who took exception to some of the ruder games and coarser pastimes.

In the past revisionist articles on this topic had appeared, but until Hutton's study there was no great rolling thesis to dislodge the blithe, incautious tendency to ascribe any careless dressing up in animal trappings back to the famous shamanic figure in the *Les Trois Frères* or any plump, antiquated carving of a female as being a representative of the Great Mother. Part of the fun of folklore studies was the creation of astounding, free-ranging connections on the evidence of similarity of name along with a practical attribute like a sword or girdle supported by a legendary or mythic motif. Hence St Michael could be transformed into a solar figure with ease and every figure who wielded a club was a brother to Hercules.

The abandoning of old customs, together with the espousal and creation of new ones, in response to unfolding political and social pressures, may account for how little is known about the older hill-figures. For it is fairly clear that carvings formerly promoted as ancient are beginning to be thought of as Medieval or Early Modern constructions. Though there is need for more detailed investigation, it is now believed that the Long Man of Wilmington – hitherto regarded as the most mysterious and haunting of British hill-figures – was an Early Modern construction (c.1545), created around the time of the Counter-Reformation when the Roman Catholic faith was seeking to restore papal supremacy. But it could just as well relate to the accession of Elizabeth I (1559) and the pageantry and giant-making associated with the promulgation of the noble legend of Albion, popularised by Geoffrey of Monmouth's *Historia*. For her coronation, Gogmagog and Corineus were set up in Temple Bar to extend warm wishes to the Queen en route to the abbey. Former London giants, like Hercules and Sampson, were either replaced or renamed after these doughty combatants who also flaunted their might on Plymouth Hoe. They were adopting a fully British identity, anticipating the giant of the Gogmagog Hills, later recorded by John Layer, and similar patriotic incentives. Eventually, during the Regency and Victorian periods, the legend of Albion was eclipsed by the celebration of all things Saxon and, naturally, the White Horse of Uffington and the Westbury Horse were enlisted in this resurgence of historic fervour.

A MYTHICAL UNITY

Since the development of OSL, the study of hill-figures has been whittled down to a 'waiting for the dating game', an issue only to be taken forward by the application of the technique. It is merely a question of time, money and organisation. Nevertheless, over the past decade, some publications have appeared that extend and modify our knowledge.

A notable contribution to hill-figure studies was the paper *The Scouring of the White Horse* by Brian Edwards, published in *The*

Wiltshire Archaeological and Natural History Magazine in 2005. This was exceptionally enlightening because it did not confine itself to the age of the horse, but rather concentrated on the social history of the creature, in particular the craze for all things Saxon that was reflected in the lusty scouring celebrations that accompanied the revival of the Scouring Revels of 1838 and that the fact that there was a small cult around George III and his charger 'Whistlejacket'. Edwards also pointed out that not only was the emphasis accorded to their Saxon heritage but to the fact of their whiteness. In the Victorian age,

> Hill figures and scouring no longer represented their celebrated origin, but a long-standing feudal relationship born of the 'free' Christian English, the white horse coming to represent a mythical unity between England, monarchy, church, and all classes of people, passed down with continuity through the ages from a Saxon Christian beginning. The Anglo-Saxon ancestry projected on to the hill horse, complete with Alfred the Great, liberty, law, defence, constitution, and chivalry born of heroic Christianity, was firmly rooted at the heart of the national identity.

Yet another welcome contribution was an update of the booklet published by Kenneth Carrdus and Graham Miller in 1965 entitled *The Search for Britain's Unique Lost Hill-Figure*, referring to the Red Horse of Tysoe. This is a gripping account of the investigation by two men for the missing Saxon horse of Tysoe. It tells of the difficulty in tracking down the Red Horse, the cuttings, references, dimensions and sketches and the curious walk-on of S.G. Wildman of *Black Horseman* fame. The site was narrowed down to Old Lodge Hill but the figure did not prove traceable until Mr Miller used colour filters on his camera that, on being processed, revealed an 'extremely pale horse-shaped crop mark...in the pastures of the Hangings on the steep hill above Old Lodge Farm.' The small book is a local history classic and it is good to see it updated and available.

Rodney Castleden, a distinguished scholar who had already written two classic studies on the Long Man and Cerne Giant, brought out a fresh, accessible book *Ancient British Hill Figures* (2000) that not only ably summarised his past researches but presented new material on these figures and lesser-known ones like the Plumpton Cross. In addition, he looked deeper into the histories of the forgotten hill-figures, notably the Shotover Giant, usually thought of as the work of high-spirited Oxford undergraduates, that he located on the north slope of Thorn Hill, east of Oxford, noting close by a spring, earthwork and ochre pits, further enforcing the site as a scene of ancient industry, perhaps ritual as well as industrial. The evidence 'incomplete as it is, suggests that an ancient hill-figure, possibly of the same general type as the Cerne Giant, existed on Shotover Hill as late as the seventeenth century…'

ANATOMY OF THE LONG MAN

More significantly, three years later, Rodney accompanied Martin Bell and Christopher Butler in their exploratory investigation of the Long Man. This time serious attention was paid to the red brick or 'Roman' pavement that was said to originally surround the figure. After vindicating its physical presence (which had often been questioned) he considered the evidence and probable dating:

> The orange-red brick fragments found in the 2003 excavation at the foot of the Long Man were given a mean thermo-luminescence date of AD 1545. At the same time, I was independently mapping the incidence of the orange-red brick fragments I found weathering out at the surface all over the figure. Over the period 1990–2004, I found twenty small fragments (1–4 cm), all within half a metre of the outline, which strongly implied that that they came from a disintegrated brick outline. I coincidentally submitted for TL dating, to the same lab at the same time, a sample of the orange-red brick fabric found at the surface close to the outline of the Long Man at hip level. This was given a date of AD 1630+/-90. Ed Rhodes, who undertook the dating at the Research Laboratory for Archaeology and the History of Art at Oxford, commented that the later date was probably only apparent, produced by the sample having been exposed at the ground surface. By implication the fragments that I had found on or close to the modern outline had all formed part of the brick outline constructed in the mid-sixteenth century.

But he did not think the exploration thorough enough, for it did not pay sufficient attention to the large trench that was cut to accommodate the red brick surround. In one of the excavated trenches he retrieved a flint flake, a Neolithic scraper, to which his fellow archaeologists showed scant regard, giving the impression that a contradictory detail might throw into disarray the model that was suggesting itself. Rodney acknowledges how the 'orange-red bricks add something very significant to the archaeology of the site, extending its archaeologically proven history back to around AD 1545' while questioning the disappearance of the rest of the brick and raising awkward points like the ghostly outline of the left leg indicated by a hint of darker turf. Was that part of the old trench preceding the brick-surround? If so, it is possible the restorers had gone slightly off course or were trying to 'improve' the shape of the figure. What of the allegedly vanished features of the Long Man – eyes, plume and teeth of the rake? If these formerly belonged to the figure, an original sample from the infilling soil would be of tremendous value in settling the dating issue.

> Another important question is whether the 1545 orange-red brick outline marked the creation of the Long Man, or a re-creation. Conceivably the 1545 bricking could have been an attempt, just like the 1873-4 bricking, to rescue a deteriorating image in the grass that was in danger of disappearing. In that case, the Long Man could have been cut or marked out with bricks 100 years or more before 1550. It may be argued that no evidence has been found for an older outline, but then again the amount of brick surviving from the 1545 bricking is negligible, so one could expect to find no brick fragments whatever surviving from an earlier bricking.

The last surviving British hill-figure that remains undated is the Cerne Giant, the most barbaric and primitive-looking of the older chalk figures, with his dual weapons of creation and destruction permanently upraised. Exuberant and triumphantly phallic, he would seem to have no truck with the Catholic or Protestant churches, though parish money was involved in his maintenance. If he stands for the heathen god Heil, who was banished by St Augustine, it would be akin to the monastery or church patronising or preserving a gigantic gargoyle or demon. He is outrageous-seeming in any Christian political context, and yet this *is* a world of eccentricities and exceptions. Is he then an authentic Celtic carving or might he instead be fitted into the Medieval or Early Modern wave of legendary patriotism that spurred the creation of Gogmagog on Plymouth Hoe, the London Giants and the vanished outline on the Gogmagog Hills of Cambridgeshire? Or was he, as Joe Bettey suggested, a cartoon of Oliver Cromwell? There's little point at this crucial stage adding further speculative embellishment, only to wait for investigators to apply OSL dating and then try to establish a credible context for his coming into being.

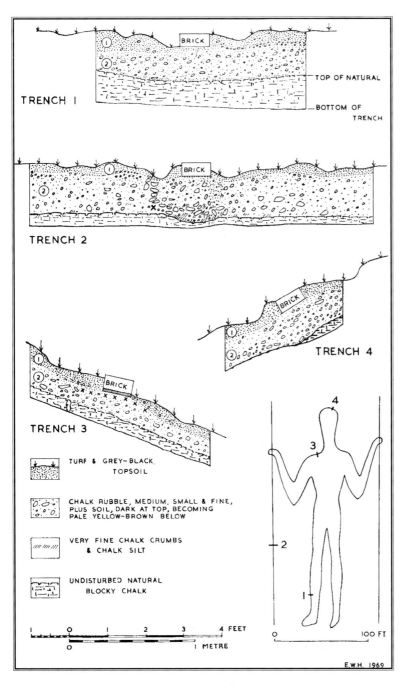

TRENCH 1

TOP OF NATURAL

BOTTOM OF TRENCH

TRENCH 2

TRENCH 4

TRENCH 3

TURF & GREY–BLACK. TOPSOIL

CHALK RUBBLE, MEDIUM, SMALL & FINE, PLUS SOIL, DARK AT TOP, BECOMING PALE YELLOW–BROWN BELOW

VERY FINE CHALK CRUMBS & CHALK SILT

UNDISTURBED NATURAL BLOCKY CHALK

4 FEET

1 METRE

100 FT.

E.W.H. 1969

E.W. Holden's 1969 diagram of the Long Man showing cross-sections though the cuts in the trenches Interestingly, Holden noted evidence of a hollow under the 1873 brick outline in Trench 4, adding 'The hollow and the silt may, very doubtfully, be considered as representing some traces of an earlier channel.' (*Sussex Archaeological Society*).

SELECT BIBLIOGRAPHY

Amis, Kingsley (1956) 'Against Romanticism', in *Collected Poems 1944–79* (Hutchinson)

Anon. (1764) 'Description of a Gigantic Figure', *Gentleman's Magazine* 34, 335–7

Anon. (1997) 'Lines on the Landscape: Spirit Ways and Death Roads' (a collection of reports from Germany, Holland, Siberia and England) *Ley Hunter* 127, 8–11

Anon. (1979) *The Fovant Badges Society* (reprint)

Anon. (1997) 'The Snob's Horse Spotted', *3rd Stone* 27, 7

Baker, Revd A. (1855) 'On the Ancient Crosses incised on the Chiltern Hills', *Records of Bucks*, 1, 219–24

Beckett, Arthur (1909) *The Spirit of the Downs* (Methuen)

Bergarmar, Kate (1968) *Discovering Hill Figures* (Shire Publications)

Berlin, Isaiah (1953) *The Hedgehog and the Fox* (Weidenfeld & Nicolson)

Bettey, J.H. (1981) 'The Cerne Abbas Giant: The Documentary Evidence', *Antiquity* 55, 118–21

Black, W.H. (1872) 'The Giant at Cerne', *Journal of British Archaeological Association* 38, 234–7

Blight, J.T. (1858 & 1872) *Ancient Crosses and other Antiquities in the East of Cornwall* (Simkin Marshall & Co.)

Bradbury, Ray (1959) *The Day it Rained Forever* (Penguin)

Bray, Warwick and Trump, David (1970) *A Dictionary of Archaeology* (Allen Lane)

Brentall, H.C. (1948) 'Albus Equus Redivivus', *Wiltshire Archaeological Magazine* 52, 396

Brinkley, Alistair (*c.* 1980) quote from the *Ley Hunter*

Brown, Martin (1996) The Long Man of Wilmington and the Cerne Giant: some points of comparison (typescript)

Brown, Theo (1970) *Trojans in the West Country* (Toucan Folklore Series)

Burl, Aubrey (1987) *The Stonehenge People* (Dent), quotation pp. 218–19

Camden, William (1772) *Britannia*, Richard Gough's edition

Castleden, Rodney (1983) *The Wilmington Giant: Quest for a Lost Myth* (Turnstone Press)

—— (1996) *The Cerne Giant* (Dorset Publishing Company)

Chesterton, G.K. (1911) 'Ballad of the White Horse' from *Collected Poems* (Wordsworth)

Clark, W.A. (1997) 'Dowsing Gogmagog', *3rd Stone* 27, 8–10

Coates, Richard (1978) 'The Linguistic Status of the Wandlebury Giants', *Folklore* 89, 75–8

Colt Hoare, Richard (1812) *Ancient History of Wiltshire*

Cooke, Grace & Ivan (1971) *The Light in Britain* (White Eagle Trust)

Cooper, G.M. (1851) 'Wilmington Priory and Church', *Sussex Archaeological Collections* 4, 37–63

Delorme, Mary (1985) *Curious Wiltshire* (Ex Libris)

Dewar, H.S.L. (1968) *The Giant of Cerne Abbas* (Toucan West Country Folklore Series No. 1)

Dugdale, Sir William (1656) *Antiquities of Warwickshire* (Dugdale Society Publications)

Elizabeth, Charlotte (1847) *Personal Recollections*, cited in the Revd Hislop's (1929) *The Two Babylons: Papal worship proved to be the worship of Nimrod* (Partridge and Co.)

Ellis Davidson, H.R. (1969) *Scandinavian Mythology* (Hamlyn)

Farrant, John (1993) 'The Long Man of Wilmington, East Sussex: the Documentary Evidence Reviewed', *Sussex Archaeological Collections* 131, 129–38

Geoffrey of Monmouth (*c*. 1140) *History of the Kings of Britain* (Everyman Series)

Gibbons, A.O. (1962) *Cerne Abbas: Notes and Speculations on a Dorset Village* (Longmans [Dorchester] Ltd), quotation p. 11

Glasscock, H.H. (1965) 'Wye Crown', *Agricola Club Journal* 6, No. 2, 29–31

Gooch, Stan (1997) 'Cities of Dreams: the ancient wisdom of Neanderthal', *Ley Hunter* 126, 32–4

Grigson, Geoffrey (1966) *The Shell Country Alphabet* (Michael Joseph)

Grinsell, Leslie (1939) *White Horse Hill and Surrounding Country* (St Catherine's Press)

—— (1980) 'The Cerne Abbas Giant: 1764–1980', *Antiquity* 54, 29–33

Hawkes, Christopher (1965) 'The Long Man: A Clue', *Antiquity* 39, 27–30

Hayes, Andrew (1993) *Archaeology of the British Isles* (Batsford)

Heathcote, C. (1980) The Red Horse(s) of Tysoe: Geophysical Report (typescript)

Heron Allen, E. (1939) 'The Long Man of Wilmington and its Roman Origin', *Sussex County Magazine* 13, 655–60

Hill, Rosalind (1986) Letter to P. Newman on Woolbury Horse

Holden, E.W. (1971) 'Some Notes on the Long Man of Wilmington', *Sussex Archaeological Collections* 13, 655–60

Housman, A.E. (1956) 'A Shropshire Lad, XXXI', *Complete Poems* (Penguin)

Hughes, Thomas (1857) *The Scouring of the White Horse* (reprint 1992: Macmillan)

Hutchins, John (1861) *History of Dorset* (Third Edition)

Jones, P.E. (1957) 'Gog and Magog', *Transactions of the Guildhall Historical Association* 2, 136–41

Laing, Lloyd & Jennifer (1980) *The Origins of Britain* (Routledge & Kegan Paul)

Lawrence, D.H. (1930) *Apocalypse*

Legg, Rodney (1971) *Cerne's God of the Celts* (Milborne Port)

Lethbridge, T.C. (1957) *Gogmagog: the Buried Gods* (Routledge & Kegan Paul)

Lipscombe, G. (1847) *History and Antiquities of the County of Buckinghamshire* (Vol. 2)

Marples, Morris (1949) *White Horses and other Hill Figures* (Country Life)

Massingham, H. J. (1926) *Fee Fi Fo Fum* (Chapman and Hall)

Maton, W.G. (1794 & 1796) *Observations relative chiefly to Nat. Hist. Picturesque scenery and antiquities of the Western Counties of England* (2 volumes: Salisbury)

Meyrick, O. (1964) 'An Elusive White Horse on Rockley Down', *Wiltshire Archaeological Magazine* 59, 183–4

Michell, John (1990) *New Light on the Ancient Mystery of Glastonbury* (Gothic Image)

Miles, David and Palmer, Simon (1996) 'White Horse Hill', *Current Archaeology* 142

Miller, W.G. and Carrdus, K.A. (1965) *The Red Horse of Tysoe* (privately printed)

Muir, Edwin (1965) 'The Horses', from *Collected Poems* (Faber)

North, John (1996) *Stonehenge, Neolithic Man and the Cosmos* (HarperCollins)

Payne, E.J. (1896) 'Whitecliff Cross', *Records of Bucks* 7, 559–67

Pennick, Nigel (1973) *Geomancy* (Cokaygne)

Petrie, Sir Flinders (1926) *The Hill Figures of England* (Royal Anthropological Institute)

Philalethes Rusticus (Revd W. Asplin) (1739) *The Impertinence and Imposture of Modern Antiquarians Displayed*

Philips, Guy Ragland (1976) 'The Black Horse of Busha', *Ley Hunter* 72

Piggott, Stuart (1931) 'The Uffington White Horse', *Antiquity* 5(17)

—— (1932) 'The name of the Giant at Cerne', *Antiquity* 6, 214–16

—— (1938) 'The Hercules Myth – Beginnings and Ends', *Antiquity* 12, 323–31

—— (1950) *William Stukeley* (Clarendon)

Pitts, Michael (1985) *Footprints Through Avebury* (Stones Print)

Plenderleath, Revd W.C. (1885) *The White Horses of the West of England with Notices of some other Turf-Monuments* (London: Alfred Russell Smith; Calne: Alfred Heath)

Pococke, Richard (1889) *Travels through England (1747–60)* (Camden Society, 42 & 44 Vol. 2)

Powys, Llewelyn (1957) *Somerset and Dorset Essays* (Macdonald)

Rawe, Donald (1971) *Padstow Obby Oss and May Day Festivities* (Lodenek Press)

Ricketts, Michael (1986) Letter to P. Newman on Whipsnade Lion

Roberts, Anthony (1978) *Sowers of Thunder* (Hutchinson)

Ross, Anne (1967) *Pagan Celtic Britain* (Routledge & Kegan Paul)

St Croix, W. de (1881) 'The Wilmington Giant', *Sussex Archaeological Collections* 26, 97–112

Scott, Lindsay W. (1937) 'The Chiltern White Crosses', *Antiquity* 41, 100–4

—— (1954) 'Excavation of Neolithic Long Barrow on Whiteleaf Hill, Bucks.', *Proceedings of the Prehistoric Society* 20, 212–30

Screeton, Paul (1974) *Quicksilver Heritage* (Thorsons)

—— (1974) *The Mystic Leys: their ancient legacy of wisdom* (Thorsons)

Sidgwick, J.B. (1939) 'The Mystery of the Long Man', *Sussex Country Magazine* 13, 408–20

Spence, Lewis (1928) *The Mysteries of Britain* (Aquarian Press edition 1970)

Stanley, J.S. (1968) The Red Horse of Tysoe – Resistivity Survey of Probable Site (typescript)

Stukeley, William (1764) Paper read to Society of Antiquaries, 16 February (Minutes Book of Society of Antiquaries, 9, 233 (15 March))

Sullivan, Danny (1997) 'Ley Lines: dead and buried – a reappraisal of the straight line enigma', *3rd Stone* 27, 13–17

Sutcliff, Rosemary (1977) *Sun Horse, Moon Horse* (Bodley Head), quotation p. 99

Sydenham, John (1842) *Baal Durotrigensis: a dissertation on the antient colossal figure at Cerne, Dorsetshire* (W. Pickering)

Thompson, E.W. (1977) *General Pitt-Rivers: Evolution of Archaeology in the Nineteenth Century* (Moonraker Press), quotation p. 72

Udal, J.S. (1922) *Dorsetshire Folklore* (2nd edition 1970 by Toucan Press, Guernsey)

Underwood, Guy (1965) *The Pattern of the Past* (Museum Press)

Warne, C. (1872) *Ancient Dorset* (Bournemouth)

Warwickshire Sites and Monuments Record, No. WA 2065, *Possible Site of Hill Figure at The Hangings*

Warwickshire Sites and Monuments Record, No. WA 2066, *Site of Hill Figure at Sun Rising Covert*

Watkins, Alfred (1925) *The Old Straight Track* (Methuen)

Whipp, Christine (1996) The Cerne and Wilmington Giants (typescript)

Wilson, Colin (1993) *Strange Life of I.D. Ouspensky* (Aquarian/Thorsons)

Wise, Revd Francis (1738) *A Letter to Dr. Mead concerning some Antiquities in Berkshire*

—— (1742) *Further Observations upon the White Horse and other Antiquities in Berkshire*

Wise, Julia (1993) 'A Survey of the Prehistoric and Later Earthworks on Whiteleaf Hill, Princes Risborough, Buckinghamshire', *Records of Bucks* 33, 108–13

Withers, Major W.J.A. (*c.* 1984) 'Haere Mai, Haere Mai-Pakehas' (typed article on Bulford Kiwi)

Woolner, Diana (1967) 'New Light on the White Horse', *Folklore* 78, 90–111

Wrench, Margaret Stanley (1958) poem published in the *Countryman*

Young, T.J. (1902) 'The Crown and the College', *Agricola Club Journal* 1, No. 3, 4–5

INDEX